Early American Diplomacy
in the Near and Far East

ADST-DACOR DIPLOMATS AND DIPLOMACY SERIES

Since 1776, extraordinary men and women have represented the United States abroad under widely varying circumstances. What they did and how and why they did it remain little known to their compatriots. In 1995, the Association for Diplomatic Studies and Training (ADST) and DACOR, an organization of foreign affairs professionals, created the Diplomats and Diplomacy book series to increase public knowledge and appreciation of the professionalism of American diplomats and their involvement in world history. Hermann Eilts's *Early American Diplomacy in the Near and Far East,* the 50th volume in the series, provides deeply researched historical, diplomatic, and personal perspectives on the challenges faced by U.S. envoy Edmund Q. Roberts in his pursuit of treaty ties in the age of sail.

OTHER TITLES IN THE SERIES

Gordon Brown, *Toussaint's Clause: The Founding Fathers and the Haitian Revolution*
Charles T. Cross, *Born a Foreigner: A Memoir of the American Presence in Asia*
Stephen H. Grant, *Peter Strickland: New London Shipmaster, Boston Merchant, First Consul to Senegal*
Parker T. Hart, *Saudi Arabia and the United States: Birth of a Security Partnership*
Dennis Kux, *The United States and Pakistan, 1947–2000: Disenchanted Allies*
Jane C. Loeffler, *The Architecture of Diplomacy: Building America's Embassies*
Terry McNamara, *Escape with Honor: My Last Hours in Vietnam*
William B. Milam, *Bangladesh and Pakistan: Flirting with Failure in South Asia*
Robert H. Miller, *Vietnam and Beyond: A Diplomat's Cold War Education*
William Michael Morgan, *Pacific Gibraltar: U.S.-Japanese Rivalry over the Annexation of Hawai'i 1885–1898*
David D. Newsom, *Witness to a Changing World*
Richard B. Parker, *Uncle Sam in Barbary: A Diplomatic History*
Nicholas Platt, *China Boys: How U.S. Relations with the PRC Began and Grew*
Howard B. Schaffer, *Ellsworth Bunker: Global Troubleshooter, Vietnam Hawk*
Ulrich Straus, *The Anguish of Surrender: Japanese POWs of World War II*
Nancy Bernkopf Tucker, Ed., *China Confidential: American Diplomats and Sino-American Relations, 1945–1996*

Early American Diplomacy in the Near and Far East

The Diplomatic and Personal History of Edmund Q. Roberts (1784–1836)

Hermann Frederick Eilts

ADST-DACOR Diplomats and Diplomacy Series

NEW ACADEMIA PUBLISHING

Washington, DC

New Academia Publishing, 2012

The opinions and characterizations in this book are those of the author and do not necessarily represent official positions of the United States Government, the Association for Diplomatic Studies and Training, or DACOR.

Printed in the United States of America

Library of Congress Control Number: 2012951213
ISBN 978-0-9860216-5-7 hardcover (alk. paper)

To Helen

Who has lived in and with Arabia
—and the seemingly unending quest for Edmund Roberts—
as long as I have—my profound thanks.

Contents

Acknowledgments

My research on Edmund Roberts's Arabian and Southeast Asian activities have benefited materially from the help, advice, and encouragement of many archival institutions and the people associated with them. I am grateful for the courteous and efficient assistance accorded me over the years by the staffs of the Library of Congress and the National Archives, both located in Washington, DC; the Peabody Museum of Salem and the Essex Institute in Massachusetts; the New Hampshire Historical Society of Concord, New Hampshire; the Baker Library of Dartmouth College in Hanover, New Hampshire; the Maryland Historical Society in Baltimore; the Portsmouth Public Library in New Hampshire; the Registry of Probate of Rockingham County in Exeter, New Hampshire; the Massachusetts Historical Society in Boston; and Boston University's Mugar Memorial Library. The individuals who helped are too numerous to list, but each of them has in one way or another contributed to this study. Their enthusiasm was infectious; their patience, Job-like; their responses to my requests, expertly professional; and their counsel, when sought, invaluable.

Joseph Copley, former curator of the Portsmouth Athenaeum of New Hampshire, deserves special mention. He not only made available his curator's file on Roberts, but he guided me to other sources on the man, including the invaluable records of George A. Nelson. My colleagues at Boston University, Professor Richard Candee, chairman of Special Collections at the Portsmouth Athenaeum, and former ambassador Stephen R. Lyne, who has had long academic and direct experience with Vietnam, also provided significant help. I am likewise indebted to Michael Albin of the Library of

Congress, a former diplomatic colleague, for providing me with a reproduction of a pertinent issue of the *Daily National Intelligencer*, a newspaper published in Washington, DC, from 1813 to 1867.

I also want to thank two graduate assistants, Michael Harris and Lisa Ferrari, for their effective work in tracking down a number of obscure references relating to the Roberts family and to French spoliation claims issues. Their findings helped fill out this study. Carole Chandler, my administrative assistant, has my profound gratitude: She not only typed the initial draft and innumerable revisions of this study but also effectively shepherded it from its initiation into its final stages. Indisputably, she has had more than her fill of Edmund Roberts, but she tolerated him with grace and exemplary patience.

Finally, let it be emphasized that any errors, shortcomings, or misinterpretations are solely my own.

Hermann Frederick Eilts
7/24/90

Introduction

From the inception of the republic to the Civil War, a particular set of circumstances drove early U.S. diplomacy.

First, consistent with President George Washington's farewell precept of "no entangling alliances," the United States eschewed political involvement—at least nominally—in the affairs of foreign states. Instead, it focused on furthering legitimate American commerce abroad. Legitimacy was interpreted in favor of American merchants, shipmasters, and supercargoes (officers in charge of cargo) and their desires, of course. Foreigners who frustrated such purposes, or appeared to do so, were by definition suspect.

There were exceptions to this American golden rule, mainly in Latin America after the enunciation of the Monroe Doctrine in 1823 and, separately, in the form of an inexorable, underlying American compulsion toward continental expansion in North America. These, however, could somehow always be subsumed in a self-righteous public and official avowal of U.S. disinterest in the affairs of Europe and an abnegation of any national desire for extracontinental territorial expansion, except perhaps for Cuba.

Beginning in the 1830s, facilitating American Protestant missionary activities abroad became an added U.S. policy objective. Reluctantly undertaken, particularly by the navy, the task was forced on the State Department by the effective lobbying activities of Protestant missionary boards in this country. American missionaries abroad often invoked treaty provisos, where such existed, guaranteeing legitimate pursuit of American commerce or most-favored-nation arrangements, whichever best suited their particular situation.

Far-fetched though American missionaries' treaty interpretations might sometimes be, few officials in Washington were prepared to challenge them. Missionaries could usually muster some congressional support, even if it was uninformed. Nor did American missionaries hesitate to demand consular support, and even on occasion U.S. naval support, for their activities abroad. Resident American missionaries were often as assertive—at times more so—as visiting American ship captains could be. It is surprising that they so frequently had the influence they did in Washington, especially since their proselytizing successes abroad were almost universally nil. The nation still prided itself on its self-proclaimed Christian purposes.

Second, even as the U.S. government grandly proclaimed disinterest in the political affairs of foreign states, it was not loath to use its navy in the pursuit and protection of its commercial objectives. Nascent "gunboat diplomacy" was often a feature of U.S. diplomatic efforts, and the country's naval officers frequently acted as surrogate diplomats in negotiating arrangements with foreign governments. Having the support of ships' guns at their backs tended to facilitate getting what they wanted, but it did not always lead to enduring success.

Third, again in order to demonstrate political noninvolvement in foreign affairs, incipient U.S. diplomacy was conducted for many years on the cheap. The nation's diplomatic representatives, whether resident or itinerant, were customarily given the lowest feasible diplomatic ranks. Invariably, too, they were underfunded in terms of personal salaries, staffs, representation expenses, contingent expenses for expected presents to foreign leaders, and so on.

In the eyes of Congress, diplomacy might be a requisite adjunct of independence, but it was nevertheless held in low esteem. Successive administrations had to reckon with the likelihood of consistently inadequate financial appropriations to achieve the nation's foreign policy objectives. Prying money for effective diplomacy from Congress was not an easy task, and most administrations were unwilling to invest much effort in unloosening congressional purse strings for diplomatic needs.

Fourth, in contrast to their modern-day successors who receive instructions from their home offices daily, early American diplomats and consuls had to perform their duties largely on their own. Communications, long dependent entirely on sailing vessels, were excruciatingly slow. It might take six months or more, for example, for a message from the State Department to reach its itinerant diplomatic representative or its consuls in Southeast Asia, and dispatches to Washington took just as long. The occasional instructions they did receive were usually general in nature and represented parameters within which they had to work. Thus, much depended on the judgment and the skill of these representatives. Whatever they did, they had to reckon with the likelihood of some criticism from home.

Europe and Latin America, including the West Indies, were the geographic areas of prime concern to the fledgling United States. To be sure, American merchantmen and whalers visited countries east of the Cape of Good Hope and in the Pacific long before the United States evinced official interest there. The U.S. flag, in the symbolic form of treaties and consulates abroad, tended to follow American trade rather than the other way around, as British tradition asserted.

In pursuit of mercantile objectives, American consuls and commercial agents for years outnumbered diplomats. Generally speaking, they were merchant consuls appointed by the State Department, but they retained their associations with commercial principals at home. Their loyalties were understandably divided between private and official responsibilities. Since private trade secured their livelihoods, small wonder that their consular duties often took second place and were sometimes used to further personal and company interests. The system was organically flawed and lent itself to abuse (which eventually spelled its demise). Unless they were naval officers, itinerant and temporary U.S. diplomats were usually also drawn from this merchant strata.

Edmund Q. Roberts, the subject of this study, labored in this diplomatic milieu. A merchant from Portsmouth, New Hampshire, who once had been reasonably prosperous but had fallen on hard times, he used family connections to obtain a consulship in British Guiana (now the independent nation of Guyana), which he never took up, and then, years later, a roving diplomatic assignment as commissioner and subsequently as a special agent.

In his diplomatic capacity, he was tasked with ascertaining the terms on which American merchantmen might be received in various Indian Ocean and Southeast Asian polities and, if possible, negotiating commercial treaties with those states. An earlier private venture to Zanzibar (which had been marginal from a commercial point of view) and his subsequent efforts in Washington to promote a treaty with the ruler of Muscat and Oman (who also had suzerainty over much of East Africa) were contingent factors in his designation. Even more so was the support of a New Hampshire senator, Levi Woodbury, who, fortuitously for Roberts, became secretary of the navy at exactly the right time.

Roberts pioneered U.S. diplomatic dialogue—as opposed to consular relationships—with a limited number of states in the Indian Ocean and Southeast Asia. He succeeded in negotiating the first U.S. commercial treaties with the ruler of Muscat and Oman and with the king of Siam (Thailand), although he was unable to conclude a treaty with Cochin China, as Vietnam was then called. After having exchanged treaty ratification documents with both Muscat and Siam, Roberts died of dysentery in Macao and was buried there. Hence, his contemplated attempt to open Japan never materialized, and it would be left to Commodore Matthew Perry to do so twenty years later.

This study is not intended as a biography of Edmund Roberts. Rather, its purpose is to disinter his memory and to illuminate selective aspects of his life—mainly, but not exclusively, his venture into American diplomacy "East of Suez" (the Asia-Pacific region). As a businessman, he can hardly be judged a success; as a widower and father of eight young daughters, his constant absences, whatever their justification, were regrettable; as a temporary U.S. diplomat, however, he deserves praise.

His experiences in Southeast Asia, in particular, were instructive. The State Department gained valuable procedural and protocol lessons from Roberts's reports, which it used in good stead with later U.S. diplomatic missions to Indian Ocean states and the Far East. The federal government discovered that, while the nation might preen itself on being a democracy, one that disdainfully rejected royal and imperial procedures and practices, its representatives had to conform to at least some of the traditional customs of the East in dealing with those distant and culturally different lands. Those practices, no matter how unpalatable and expensive , were essential to success. Perry's arrival in Japan, for example, combined costly pomp and circumstance with a threat of force.

Moreover, Roberts's experiences in Cochin China and Siam demonstrated the formidable linguistic difficulties confronting U.S. diplomats charged with negotiating treaties with Asia-Pacific countries. Problems of translation were omnipresent and serious. The texts of treaties rendered in multiple languages by foreign translators might understandably be obscure or ambiguous in some instances, yet diverse language recensions—i.e., critical revisions—to resolve ambiguities introduced uncertainty about which text would prevail in the event of disagreement. Future problems seemed assured.

Finally, the concept of time, so important to Americans then as well as now, had a totally different meaning for Asians, as Roberts and his successors would regularly discover. Asians would not be hurried.

Roberts's diplomatic efforts, limited though they were, set the stage for future U.S. diplomacy in Southeast Asia and the Pacific Ocean region. They revealed, sometimes graphically, what American diplomats in the East could expect to encounter. His American diplomatic successors, though they might not know it, benefited from his experiences and from the State Department's growing understanding of what effective American diplomacy in the East required. Gradually, clearer diplomatic and procedural instructions came to be written.

Not only did Americans need to learn the stylistic requirements of effective diplomacy in these distant regions; equally important, they needed to gain a more detailed geographical knowledge of these as yet poorly known areas. Roberts and his colleagues, not to mention those elements of the U.S. government that sponsored his two missions, suffered from the prevailing limited American geographical knowledge of regions beyond the Cape of Good Hope. For navigational and anchorage data, U.S. government officials, naval officers, and American shipmasters in the early 1800s relied on several English collections of maps and portolan (navigation) charts, first published in 1784 and periodically reissued with additions into the 1830s. Most widely known were *East-India Pilot* and its companion text, *Oriental Navigator*; and *The India Director, or, Directions for Sailing to and from the East Indies, China, Japan, Australia, and the Interjacent Ports of Africa and South America,* by James Horsburgh. Both publications were prepared by employees of the British East India Company. Initially based on the explorations of Jean Baptiste Nicolas Denis d'Après de Mannevillette, an indefatigable French maritime cartographer of the eighteenth century, these periodically published editions distilled evolving Western geographical knowledge of those remote areas. Nevertheless, useful though their revised charts were for general purposes, particularly for rudimentary harbor and pilotage information, they were sadly imprecise on provincial and political delineations.

This was especially true with respect to present-day Vietnam, where early European cartographers regularly failed to distinguish between Annam (now central Vietnam) and Cochin China (southern Vietnam). Instead, they applied the latter term indiscriminately to both the southern and central regions of that country. The Portuguese had first dubbed these regions of Southeast Asia as Cochin China in contradistinction to the seventeenth-century Portuguese foothold of Cochin on the Malabar coast of the Indian subcontinent. Subsequent European mappers unquestioningly adopted this all-embracing nomenclature.

Although Europeans used the appellation "Cochin China," the indigenous populations of these regions generally did not. Rather, Cochin China and its neighboring area of Annam to the north were loosely and collectively designated locally as Annam, after the dominant Annamese-speaking population. (Horsburgh claimed that the Chinese called Cochin China "Onam.") Within this broad area, there were at various times as many as twenty-two provincial subdivisions, extending in the early nineteenth century from the southernmost point on the Gulf of Siam, at approximately latitude $9°N$, as far northward as latitude $17°N$, where Tonkin commenced. The northernmost limits were extended as far as latitude $19°N$, and even slightly beyond, in Emperor Gia Long's period (1802–1820), as he subdued and incorporated contiguous parts of Tonkin in his directly administered domains. Areas in the far north and south were entrusted to often fractious, semiautonomous, royally appointed viceroys.

The collective area designated as Annam or Cochin China had its own subdivisions. A map that John Walker prepared for the East India Company on the basis of a detailed report from English envoy John Crawfurd, listed the provinces from north to south: Kamboja (literally Cambodia, but including at the time the fortified city of Saigon), Bin-thuon (Binh Thuong), Nha-trang, Phu Yen, Qui-nhon, Quang-ai, Quang-nan, and Hué. Other European travelers recorded somewhat different prefectural designations, including the term "Lower Cochin China" for the southernmost parts of the country. Some referred to "Cochin China Proper" when writing of present-day central Vietnam, or Annam. Generally speaking, however, both Europeans and Americans used the term "Cochin China" for this entire area. Its people were generically designated Annamese or Cochin Chinese, regardless of ethnic or linguistic differences.

Edmund Roberts employed this imprecise nomenclature, as had his English predecessors such as Crawfurd and the British traveler John Barrow, who in 1806 visited parts of Annam—which he specifically called "Cochinchina." In his posthumously published memoir of his first visit to the spacious trivillage anchorage of Shundai (Xuan-dai, according to Horsburgh), Vung-chao and Vung Lam in Phu Yen Province, Roberts referred to the area as "Cochin-China." In the same vein, he described Turan Bay (now Da Nang Bay), farther to the north, as "on the northern coast of Cochin-China." The USS *Peacock*'s surgeon, W. S. W. Ruschenberger, who represented Roberts in meetings with various Vietnamese officials in Turan (Da Nang) when the American envoy was seriously ill in 1836, entitled his description of that part of his life "Sketches in Cochin-China" in his memoir. In fact, of course, Roberts and his colleagues were in Annam during their two visits to Vietnam, not in "Cochin China." The commander of the USS *Peacock* had Horsburgh's charts aboard and relied heavily on them. So did Roberts.

The failure of early nineteenth-century European and U.S. visitors to distinguish clearly between Cochin China and Annam may well be surprising to a generation of Americans who painfully learned the provincial separations of that heterogeneous country during the Vietnam War in the 1960s and 1970s. But geographical designations alter over time, and we need to be tolerant of what may seem to be the geographical lapses, inaccuracies, and inconsistencies of an earlier period.

Because Roberts is the subject of this book, I have adopted his nomenclature. Thus, with apologies to modern Vietnam specialists, I use "Cochin China" and "Annam" interchangeably in those parts of this chronicle that relate to Roberts's two visits to present-day Vietnam. Similarly, the terms "Cochin Chinese" and "Annamese" refer to the peoples of these regions. Roberts and his American and European contemporaries would have understood these designations as essentially synonymous. The Wade-Giles romanization system was used for place names in Roberts's period; I've added the modern Pinyin designation parenthetically after the first mention of locations rendered in Wade-Giles.

1

Antecedents and Early Years

The Definitive Treaty of Peace signed in Paris in 1783 acknowledged the independence of the United States from Great Britain after seven years of war. With the lifting of the protracted British naval blockade of the Atlantic states, it also spawned an extraordinary burst of American maritime activity that was global in scope. Mercantile entrepreneurship and vision, coupled with severely depressed economic conditions in most ports on the eastern coast, spurred the process.

As part of this maritime eruption, American commerce with the Far East and the adjacent Indian Ocean area began in 1784, when the ship *Empress of China* sailed from New York to the Whampoa (Huangpu District) anchorage of Canton (Guangzhou) in China. Thereafter, starting with a trickle of vessels to Canton, commerce expanded dramatically in ship numbers, aggregate tonnage, and diverse and multiple destinations. American shipmasters explored trade prospects not only in Canton but also in ports of the Indian Ocean littoral: Port Louis in Île de France (Mauritius), Calcutta, Bombay, Batavia (Jakarta, in Indonesia), and other East Indian harbors.

Few Asian markets had any substantial demand for American or European products except for ginseng, firearms, powder, and shot, although coarse cotton cloth and sundry manufactures gradually came to be included in outbound cargoes. Hence, for many years, American shipmasters and supercargoes had to purchase Asian products with specie, mainly in the form of Spanish milled silver dollars minted in Mexico and Latin America. Recurrent specie shortages constrained their purchasing ability, however, emphasizing the need to develop greater demand for American products to facilitate barter arrangements.

Since for many years local demand remained restricted, the markets of established Asian ports of call were often saturated with American-brought goods, causing depressed local prices for those imports. Conversely, the competition of American shipmasters and supercargoes for the locally produced commodities of native markets created shortages and thus price escalation. Moreover, indigenous merchants or local officials withheld local products from markets, accentuating normal economic demand-and-supply phenomena.

Enterprising shipmasters inevitably sought other locales in the vast Indian Ocean region that were relatively untapped. With this proliferation of destinations, American shipmasters and supercargoes complained that the indigenous officials in these various destinations exacted inequitable levies. Predictably, the Americans desired the lowest possible port and entry charges to maximize the profit of their ventures. Instead, as itinerant foreigners, they regularly found themselves hostage to port officials and local merchants whose aim was to maximize their own profits in their commercial interactions with these external visitors.

Local laws in all the Asian ports were patently slanted against foreign traders, whether Portuguese, British, French, Dutch, or American. Moreover, in many cases the precise nature of local laws concerning foreign trade in a particular locale was unknown and often difficult to ascertain. Apart from areas under direct British, French, or Dutch control, rarely were port regulations or customs schedules available in written form. Even when these laws were known, indigenous officials interpreted them erratically and— hardly surprisingly—to their advantage.

Seeking help from their government, many American merchants, shipmasters, and supercargoes argued that treaty relations between the United States and Asian polities was the only feasible way to protect American external commerce from venal local officials. Periodic U.S. naval visits to these remote areas were likewise frequently proposed. The term "gunboat diplomacy" had yet to been coined, but American traders could point out that occasional naval demonstrations by the British, French, and Dutch had seemingly had a salutary effect in curbing the rapacity of local officials.[1]

The federal government, while not blind to the need to protect American commerce—a lesson learned during the long and often humiliating Barbary Wars in North Africa—was slow to respond. Until well into the 1800s, U.S. naval assets were few, and they were of necessity concentrated in the Atlantic Ocean and the Mediterranean Sea. Problems in Europe and the Mediterranean basin had priority. Relations with the so-called Barbary states had intermittently preoccupied the fledgling United States from 1784 into the 1820s. Although the independent sultan of Morocco had initiated talks that led to a generally satisfactory treaty with the United States in 1787, the rulers of Algiers, Tunis, and Tripoli, nominally tributaries of the Ottoman sultan-caliph but actually despots answerable to no one, regularly used their fleets to menace American (and other) merchant ships in the western Mediterranean and to capture and enslave American seamen.

After more than two decades of appeasing these North African rulers through, among other things, payment of tribute and ransom for the release of enslaved seamen, the United States had expanded its naval capability enough to enable it, either forcibly or through the threat of force, to conclude treaties with these entities. These agreements, even if sometimes violated, generally freed American commerce and seamen from the depredations of the Barbary pirates.[2]

Furthermore, the United States concluded a treaty of commerce and negotiation with the Ottoman Empire in 1830, but for almost two decades after that, American commerce in the area stagnated. The long delay was engendered in part by the Greek war of independence against Turkey, which broke out in 1821 and generated strong anti-Turk pressures in the United States.[3] Although the treaties with the Barbary states and the Ottoman Empire were of value to American shipmasters sailing in the Mediterranean, their countrymen engaged in the Indian Ocean and Far Eastern trade continued to have to fend largely for themselves.

Much of the credit for persuading the federal government in Washington, DC, to pursue formal negotiations aimed at concluding commercial treaties with various Asian polities goes to Edmund Quincy Roberts Jr., of Portsmouth, New Hampshire. In contrast to most other American merchants, his initial interest centered on East Africa. An energetic, able, imaginative individual, personable in manner, imposing in appearance, sometimes given to bending facts to achieve his purposes, and not above bluster when he deemed it appropriate, Roberts virtually single-handedly promoted, negotiated, and followed through final ratifications the first U.S. treaties with the kingdom of Siam and with the sultanate of Muscat and Oman. He failed in an attempt to conclude a similar treaty with Cochin China.[4]

Family Antecedents

Born on June 29, 1784, in Portsmouth, Edmund Quincy Roberts Jr. was the only son of Edmund Quincy Roberts, a successful, retired mariner, and Sarah Griffith Roberts. His mother was reputed to be one of the most beautiful women in America. A daughter, also named Sarah, had been born to the couple four years before Edmund's birth.

Data on the origins of the Roberts family are sketchy. It is believed that Samuel, the father of the elder Roberts and a joiner by trade, left England in the 1760s and, accompanied by his wife and three children, settled in Somersworth, New Hampshire, where he may have been engaged in shipbuilding on the Piscataqua River. He apparently prospered, since he was able to acquire a twenty-five acre farm, livestock, and other goods, all of which he conveyed in 1787 to his eldest son, Edmund. Samuel Roberts and his wife both died in 1794.[5]

The senior Edmund Roberts, like his younger brother, Josiah (later known as Joshua), is believed to have served at some point as a commissioned officer in the English Royal Navy and to have attained the rank of lieutenant. Because of his reputed service in the Royal Navy, he was addressed in Portsmouth as "Captain." From 1772 to 1787, the year of his death, Edmund Roberts was listed on the Portsmouth tax lists.[6]

In 1779, the New Hampshire state authorities commissioned him as first lieutenant to serve under Captain Titus Salter aboard the colony's twenty-gun ship of war *Hampden*. The vessel was to be deployed as part of a larger New England land and marine force organized to destroy a protective fort then being built by the British on the Penobscot River.[7] There, at Bagaduce (now Castine) in the province of Maine, the British planned to resettle American Loyalists who were not well-received elsewhere in the erstwhile colonies.

The *Hampden* had only shortly before returned from a daring but unsuccessful privateering voyage off the coast of England. Badly damaged, she had managed to limp to her home port to undergo repairs. Although the expedition on which she would now embark was largely a Massachusetts effort, some fifty Portsmouth merchants strongly urged that New Hampshire participate in the enterprise. They persuaded the New Hampshire authorities to deploy the refitted *Hampden* to join the expedition.

From the outset, the undertaking was ill conceived and ineptly executed. Not surprisingly, it suffered an inglorious end. An English fleet, sent from New York, destroyed—without a fight— all but one of the forty-three ships and transports of the combined New England forces. The *Hampden* alone survived, but only by surrendering.[8]

History is silent on the role of the senior Edmund Roberts in this military and naval fiasco. Most of the soldiers and sailors of the continental forces managed to avoid capture by escaping overland, and the elder Roberts may have been among them. In any event, although the American naval commander, Commodore Dudley Saltonstall of Massachusetts, suffered disgrace for the defeat, Lt. Edmund Roberts was spared such obloquy. The debacle was essentially a failure of planning and command and, in Portsmouth at least, it could always be blamed on Bostonian incompetence.

Modestly well-to-do for the times, Edmund Roberts Sr., in addition to the property in Somersworth conveyed to him by his father, was able to acquire, with what was termed "lawful money" (indicating some degree of financial liquidity), various pieces of property in and around Portsmouth. He died in 1787 at the age of forty-two, leaving his widow, his seven-year old daughter, and his three-year old son. Because he died intestate, his widow, Sarah, had to appeal to the New Hampshire probate court for inheritance rights; the court appointed her administratrix of her deceased husband's estate.[9] A court-ordered inventory showed several parcels of property in Portsmouth and Somerset, furniture, silver, silver plate, a silver watch, and, appropriately for her late husband's lifetime profession, a mariner's quadrant. The total value of such movable assets was assessed at just over £1,225.[10]

It took time for foreign and domestic creditors to make claims against the estate. By 1790, foreign claims amounting to £630 and domestic claims totaling £445 had been submitted to the New Hampshire probate court.[11] On November 1, 1790, three years after her husband's death, the court awarded Sarah one-third of the estate, including two pieces of property.[12] The remainder was distributed among creditors.

Growing Up

Two years after her husband's death, while the estate was still being probated, Sarah remarried. Her second husband was Captain Moses Woodward, a Portsmouth shipmaster and general importer. The marriage was hardly a happy one. Woodward, who already had a daughter from a previous marriage, claimed child support for Edmund Jr. for a year after the senior Roberts's death and before the boy was seven years of age.[13] The boy's adolescent years were spent in the atmosphere of his mother's tension-filled second marriage; his mother was doting, but his stepfather showed no affection, was sometimes hostile, and often was away at sea.

Little is known about Roberts's elementary education, but it is believed that he attended the local Portsmouth school for basic instruction in reading, writing, and numbers. As his father before him, young Roberts at an early age showed an inclination for a naval career. At the age of thirteen, through the intercession of Captain John McClintock, a former Revolutionary War naval officer and prominent Portsmouth shipowner and master, he was offered a midshipman's warrant in the incipient U.S. Navy. His mother expressed strong objections and elicited a promise from him to never leave her as long as she was alive. Instead, therefore, Edmund entered the counting house of Edward Parry, an old family friend and merchant of Portsmouth, to train for a mercantile career.[14] Until destroyed by fire in 1802, Parry's place of business was located on the old Portsmouth pier, then the hub of the port's thriving mercantile life. Under Parry's guidance, Roberts learned commercial accounting and the intricacies of maritime commerce.

Three years after beginning his mercantile training, in 1801, Roberts's mother died at the age of forty-three. She was interred beside her late husband in the family plot in Portsmouth at South Cemetery (previously known as Proprietors Burying Ground). Rather than remain with his stepfather, who had shown scant interest in the boy and who would remarry later that same year, young Edmund went to Argentina to live with his bachelor uncle, Captain Joshua (Josiah) Roberts, a one-time lieutenant in the Royal Navy who was then associated with a British firm in Buenos Aires. There he continued his training under the tutelage of his uncle. His stepfather, Woodward, was drowned at sea in 1802, bequeathing nothing to either of his two stepchildren.[15] In fact, Roberts's sister, Sarah, sought for some years after their mother's death to obtain a court judgment requiring her stepfather to return a parcel of land that she alleged had belonged to their father, but which Moses Woodward (and subsequently his heirs) insisted belonged to him. Her efforts were unsuccessful.

Although few details of Roberts's early years have survived, he seems to have sailed as supercargo on one or another of his uncle's ships. Just where is uncertain, although a later friend, who presumably heard it from Roberts, suggested that he sailed to unspecified ports east of the Cape of Good Hope.[16] Bombay is thought to have been one of them. Family drama was added to these nebulous reports of early voyages when his sister later related, allegedly on Roberts's authority, that he and his shipmates had sometimes been reduced to eating rats when supplies gave out.[17] Such experiences were not unknown on long voyages, but were also often the stuff of old seafarers' tall yarns.

On the death of his uncle a few years later, Edmund, as sole heir, assumed charge of his late relative's mercantile interests. He went first to London and conducted business activities from there. In the British capital, he lived at what he described as a "very genteel" boarding house in Surrey Street on the Strand, but he complained that the food was too sparse. Generally, however, he spent his time at the New England Coffee House at 41 Threadneedle

Street, near the Royal Exchange, or at the London Coffee House at Ludgate Hill, near St. Paul's Cathedral. Such establishments were where merchants gathered to transact business arrangements in an age before telephones.

From London, Roberts frequently wrote to his sister, Sarah, while she was boarding with the Parrys. Whatever his business interests may have been, he was also something of a social dandy and recounted to Sarah his diverse social activities in London. In one letter, he observed that he had dined at a noted eating house at St. Giles for six pence. Indicative of the clientele, the ladder by which customers climbed to the second-floor dining room was removed after they had ascended so that no one could leave without paying, and cutlery was chained to the tables so that customers could not make off with knives, forks, or spoons. Roberts also sent his sister some fancy dresses bought in London.[18] On a brief visit to Paris, he had a small wax bas-relief made of himself, one of the few contemporary depictions of the man. A passport, issued to Roberts on March 22, 1806, by the American consulate in London, still survives.

Return to Portsmouth

Roberts's letters to Sarah suggest that he yearned to return to the social life of Portsmouth. In 1808, at the age of twenty-four, he did so. After a whirlwind courtship, he married Catherine Whipple Langdon, the youngest daughter of the respected Judge Woodbury Langdon, on September 10, 1808.[19] The Langdons enjoyed considerable prominence in New Hampshire. John Langdon, the bride's uncle, had been governor of the state. The Roberts family and the Langdons had long been neighbors, and Edmund and Catherine had known each other since childhood.[20] The marriage was generally a happy one, but life would often be trying for Roberts's wife.

In the early years after his return to Portsmouth, Roberts cut a considerable swath in that city's society. He and his family, elegant in dress and appearance, lived graciously in a house on Mill Street, where they entertained handsomely. They quickly engaged a family pew at St. John's Episcopal Church, and were soon regarded as respected pillars of the community. From 1818 to 1825, Roberts was a proprietor of the prestigious Portsmouth Athenaeum and a donor to its library. The Roberts family steadily grew as Catherine gave birth every year or so to another child. Between 1810 and 1828, eleven children were born, nine daughters and two sons. Of this number, eight survived to adulthood.[21] Sadly, three—two sons, each named Edmund, and a daughter—died shortly after birth.

Initially, Roberts's business enterprises too seemed to fare well. In 1807 and 1808, he bought at least seven pieces of property in and around Portsmouth, and later, in 1817, he sold three such pieces at a profit. One was sold to Daniel Webster, acting as trustee for a minor female ward. He invested heavily in ships; between 1808 and 1819, he owned or had a partial interest in no fewer than ten trading vessels. Among his shipping ventures, he purchased a share in the Portsmouth-based privateer *Mars*, which received a letter of marque and reprisal to prey on English ships during the War of 1812.[22]

The times were full of risks for American shipping. From 1794 onward, Britain and France were at war with each other. In May 1806, a British Order in Council declared the European coast from the mouth of the Elbe River to Brest, in France, to be in a state of blockade, and enacted other trade restrictions aimed at impeding American trade with France. Six months later, by the Berlin Decree of November 1806, the French emperor, Napoleon, retaliated and placed the British Isles under nominal blockade. In December 1807, a second Napoleonic decree, issued at Milan, further aggravated the shipping problems of neutral countries. After the second decree, any neutral vessel that submitted to British search was declared to be subject to French seizure. Thus, American merchantmen dealing with either of the belligerents, even if their ships were searched involuntarily and under protest, risked condemnation proceedings by the other warring power.

To make matters worse, in December 1807 President Thomas Jefferson prevailed on Congress to embargo, by legislation, the export of almost all American goods, by land or by sea. Not until March 1809 was this self-defeating and highly contentious legislation repealed and replaced by the U.S. Non-Intercourse Act, which permitted American commerce with all but Britain and France.[23] Denouncing this legislation, in March 1810 Napoleon issued the

Rambouillet Decree, which declared that all American ships entering French ports would be seized, as well as those U.S. ships still in ports if they had entered the port after May 1809.

Tensions grew, especially between the United States and Britain. Britain's harsh trade restrictions, its forcible induction of American seamen into the Royal Navy, and its military support of American Indians resisting the expansion of the U.S. frontier, among other issues, led the United States to declare war. The War of 1812 lasted until 1815. During that period, many American shipowners turned to potentially lucrative privateering, but American trading vessels were in jeopardy of British seizure. These circumstances adversely affected Roberts, as they did other American merchants. Yet some of the losses Roberts began to sustain stemmed from his own poor business judgment.

Business Losses

From 1807 onward, Roberts began to lose his shipping assets. His ship *Victory*, with Caleb Hopkins as shipmaster, was seized by French port authorities when it arrived in 1807 in Cherbourg, on the grounds that the shipmaster had allowed the vessel to be searched by a British cruiser. She was one of the first American vessels confiscated under the Milan decree. Although Captain Hopkins protested the French action, it was to no avail. When apprised of the seizure, Roberts, on the advice of a New York merchant colleague, formally abandoned ownership of the vessel and her cargo to the Columbian Insurance Company, claiming a total loss.[24] This, however, the insurance company was not prepared to accept under the terms of the policy, and Roberts would eventually have to make his claim a part of the so-called French and Spanish spoliation claims, claims that would take the U.S. government many years to resolve.

Another of his ships, the *Bedford*, was seized by the British in the waning days of the War of 1812. There would be no spoliation claims against the British. To the British, she was an enemy vessel, subject to capture and legitimate prize condemnation. Two other vessels, the brigs *Norfolk* and *Florida*, were lost at sea in 1817 and 1819, respectively. Still another of his ships, the brig *Rolla*, was in such derelict condition that she had to be broken up in 1817. Two years earlier, her master, W. M. Shackford, who had sailed from Havana to New Orleans for cargo as Roberts had ordered, had pointedly written to Roberts that of the over seventy American vessels in harbor or at the bar of the Mississippi, most were better vessels than *Rolla* and would doubtless be preferred by local shippers.[25] Roberts showed no interest in improving the ship's condition, and he probably lacked the means to do so.

For want of funds to meet unpaid obligations, Roberts's remaining vessels were sold one by one: the ship *Roberts* was sold as early as 1813; the brig *Minerva*, in 1815; the brig *Abolina*, in 1818; the ship *Islington,* the largest of his vessels, in 1818; and the ship *Frederick,* in 1823. Roberts conveyed the *Abolina* to Charles W. Cutter, a Portsmouth bondsman, in 1818 as surety for certain bond obligations that Roberts lacked the liquidity to pay. The vessel, as Cutter soon discovered, earned nothing and was eventually attached by a host of private creditors.[26] Although some Portsmouth merchants made considerable profits by investing in privateers, Roberts's shareholding in *Mars* failed to return even his original investment.[27]

Apart from these shipping losses, Roberts suffered setbacks from placing inordinate trust in some of his in-laws and friends, with whom he imprudently cosigned loans that they had secured. When they were unable to discharge their obligations, he became liable for all or part of their debts. Among such debtors were two brothers-in-law, Henry and John Langdon, a Captain Robert Harris, and a neighbor, Robert Ham, all of Portsmouth.[28] Roberts also incurred some personal obligations, including to Captain Hopkins of the seized ship *Victory,* which he persistently delayed paying because he was strapped for funds.

What is known of Roberts's nonshipping trading interests suggests they were diverse, and many seemed to founder. In 1808, for example, a Dutchman to whom Roberts had sold sugar defaulted on his payments.[29] In 1814, Roberts invested in cocoa in the belief that substantial cocoa sales could be effected in New York City, only to learn that there had been no offer whatsoever for that commodity.[30] Roberts was not heavily engaged in the coffee business, but there is a record of a small shipment of Haitian coffee that he imported in late October 1818.[31] In 1817, he was required to sell most of his property holdings, although he did purchase one piece of property in 1820. In his realtor capacity, he succeeded in selling, in early 1822, a "brick house" in New York for a Boston client for what was at the time the princely sum of $11,000.[32] With a commission of 2-1/2 percent, this earned him $500.

These were at best sporadic ventures, which hardly represented reliable sources of income. As his shipping assets steadily eroded, and as his family expenses grew with more children, Roberts found himself increasingly traveling in the United States in search of mercantile opportunities. He was frequently in New York and Philadelphia.

Encouraged by the news that the federal authorities intended to press spoliation claims against the French and Spanish governments for seizures of American ships, Roberts presented to the Congress his claim for slightly over $7,300 for the French seizure of his ship, *Victory*, representing his estimate of the combined value of the vessel ($4,000) and her cargo ($2,000), together with interest charges. It would be years, however, before the spoliation claims were settled and claimants received any reimbursements.

Not until 1831 was a treaty signed with the Bourbon monarchical government of France; under that agreement, the Bourbon government agreed to liquidate all American claims against France by paying the U.S. government, over a six-year period, the sum of 25 million French francs, the equivalent of $4.6 million, at 4 percent interest. By the time final payments were made, they amounted to $5 million. The U.S. government undertook to distribute these monies to legitimate claimants. All previous claimants were required to verify before federal commissioners the continuing validity of their claims. Roberts did so, but because of French legislative dilatoriness in appropriating the requisite funds and the resultant tensions between the two governments, five years passed before the promised French payments to the U.S. government commenced. Only then did the U.S. Treasury begin indemnity installment disbursements to certified claimants. By that time, Roberts was on his final voyage.[33]

In 1823, through the intercession of well-placed friends in the administration of President James Monroe, Roberts was offered the position of American consul in Demerara, British Guiana. A consular commission was issued to him. For family reasons, he did not take up the post. For a number of years thereafter, however, biennial State Department personnel registers wrongly listed him as consul in British Guiana.

First Voyage to Zanzibar

Increasingly anxious about his declining fortunes and determined to try to redress them, Roberts recalled earlier reports he had heard of the promising, yet relatively untapped, East African trade. Zanzibar, the island entrepôt of East African commerce, he concluded, might offer prospects of mercantile profit. The island, and much of the East African littoral, nominally belonged to Sayyid Sa'id bin Sultan Al Bu Sa'id, also ruler of Muscat and Oman. The extent of that potentate's practical control over these African domains was uncertain.

Although British and French vessels had occasionally touched at Zanzibar early in the century and continued to put into that port, the first known American vessel to do so was the Salem (Massachusetts) brig *Laurel,* captained by Jonathan Lovett, in July 1825. Finding trade prospects on the South American coast poor, Lovett had sailed his vessel around the Cape of Good Hope to Mauritius and on to Zanzibar, where he loaded a cargo of elephant tusks and a variety of other local products. A year later, four Salem vessels came to Zanzibar. The nascent Zanzibar trade was an extension of American commerce with Majunga (Mahajanga), in Madagascar, which had begun as early as 1819.[34] Such information as Roberts was able to garner suggested that Zanzibar had not yet attracted widespread American attention (but he failed to appreciate that there might have been good reasons for this seeming indifference).

Accordingly, Roberts decided to charter the New Bedford brig *Mary Ann* and to sail aboard her with a cargo of American goods for the East African market. Through fourteen separate share subscriptions, his own remaining capital, and a personal import agency management agreement with the New York firm of Fish and Grinnell, Roberts was able to scrape together the means for the venture.[35] As a condition of the venture, Roberts had to place himself under bond, with sureties, to be back in the United States by March 15, 1829, to redeem shareholders' notes amounting to $8,000.[36]

The charter party for *Mary Ann* cost $650 per month, but with ancillary expenses, anticipated monthly expenditures were estimated to be between $900 and $1,000. Cottons, Nankins (blue and white porcelain), shirtings (fabric for shirts), sugar, powder, lead, some muskets, wine, and sundry looking glasses, bought from various Philadelphia and New York firms, were loaded in New York harbor as outbound cargo.[37] The shareholders authorized Roberts, who was designated supercargo, to decide the port or ports of call to which *Mary Ann* should proceed. Purchases at foreign ports were also left to his discretion.

Departing New York harbor on June 10, the *Mary Ann* arrived at Zanzibar on October 8, 1827, after an uneventful ninety-day sail. She was one of seven American vessels, mainly out of Salem, that visited Zanzibar that year. The island, Roberts found, was administered by one of Sayyid Sa'id's governors. The sayyid, then engaged in a military effort to recapture Mombasa (in Kenya) on the East African coast from insurgent Mazrui tribesmen, had as yet not visited the island. There were reports, however, that he planned to do so once Fort Jesus, Mombasa's redoubtable citadel, was taken. Roberts, although welcomed by the sayyid's officials, soon found himself confronted by a welter of locally wrought frustrations, which threatened to make the long voyage ruinous for him and his shareholders. His experience was similar to that of other American shipmasters who had visited the island entrepôt.

All local contracts, he discovered, had to be negotiated through the ruler's agents. Foreign shipmasters and supercargoes were at their mercy. The sayyid's governor claimed the right to preempt any part of the cargo that he wished, and he did so. Payment for goods delivered, despite frequent promises, was constantly delayed, requiring the vessel to remain in port for much longer than Roberts had expected. In addition to a 7-1/2 percent import duty, a $100 anchorage fee had to be paid. Moreover, the customhouse *banyan* (trader), an Indian expatriate customs farmer, demanded more than $800 as a commission for one Bin Ahmady, a native of Quiloa (in Mozambique) whom Roberts had never met and with whom he had done no personal business. Zanzibari merchants had on their own bought gum copal from Bin Ahmady to sell to Roberts and, disingenuously and with the Indian customs farmer's collusion, they now sought to shift commission and Zanzibar customs charges to him.

Gum copal and gum Arabic, promised in exchange for American goods, were long delayed as the ruler's agents sought to pressure Roberts into taking instead inferior hides and dry dates as substitutes. Should he refuse to do so, he was blandly informed, he could leave for Mozambique or elsewhere. This was patently impossible without incurring serious loss, and Roberts's Zanzibari interlocutors knew it. All appeals to indigenous officials for equity redress fell upon deaf ears. Even the local English interpreter, Khamis bin Osman, upon whom Roberts depended heavily, joined in the charade. A cabal existed, made up of Zanzibari officials and merchants alike, determined to exploit the visiting American supercargo as much as possible.

Talks with Sayyid Sa'id

Fortunately for Roberts, Fort Jesus fell in the second week of January, and Sayyid Sa'id arrived in Zanzibar a week later. By then, the *Mary Ann* had already been in port more than three months. Roberts determined that he would petition the ruler directly for relief; he prevailed upon E. D. Gunilac, a French commission agent who had befriended him in Zanzibar, to write to Sayyid Sa'id on his behalf,.

Roberts learned other interesting news from the Frenchman. Sometime earlier in Muscat, he was told, Sayyid Sa'id had broached to Gunilac the desirability of concluding a commercial treaty with the United States to encourage more American trading vessels to visit the sayyid's ports.[38] If the ruler was serious, his interest offered promising possibilities beyond Roberts's immediate commercial problems. Roberts decided to pursue the opportunity.

In a long, carefully prepared letter to Sayyid Sa'id, which went through a number of drafts, Roberts recounted his litany of complaints against the ruler's local officials and sought redress. Introducing himself as an American merchant, and presumptuously claiming to be a consul of the United States, he implied that his journey to Zanzibar had official U.S. government sanction. Taking his cue from the tone of Gunilac's letter of recommendation, a copy of which had been given to him, Roberts lauded Sayyid Sa'id's well-known reputation for justice. He contended that British and French vessels touching at Zanzibar received better treatment, and urged that American masters and supercargoes be similarly favored.

Moreover, mindful of the ruler's extensive personal involvement in the commerce of his far-flung realm, Roberts emphasized the advantages that Sayyid Sa'id would derive through a formal commercial relationship with the United States. In contrast to England and France, he asserted, the United States had no territorial ambitions abroad and was concerned solely with commerce. Should he be entrusted with carrying dispatches to the government of the United States, stipulating the terms on which American merchantmen would be received in the ports of the ruler's domains, Roberts promised that the next season would see a U.S. ship of war visit Muscat with an envoy aboard authorized to negotiate such a commercial treaty.[39]

Sayyid Sa'id was one of the most important entrepreneurs of his realm, and his interest was readily piqued.[40] Whatever he may have said earlier to Gunilac, however, he had little detailed knowledge of the United States. Only a handful of American vessels had visited Muscat, his principal seat of residence, during his twenty-year reign. Roberts's proposal, if taken at face value, offered possibilities to further not only Sayyid Sa'id's commercial but also, perhaps, certain of his political objectives. The British, through the English East India Company and their governor at Mauritius, dominated the Indian Ocean littoral. Although it was doubtful that the United States, notwithstanding Roberts's boast of its power, could effectively counter English pressure, American help might nevertheless be of use to him in other parts of East Africa.

After ordering Roberts's grievances to be at least partially redressed, Sayyid Sa'id granted Roberts a number of audiences. According to Roberts's account of these interviews, which is the only record extant, Sayyid Sa'id now took the initiative and expressed a desire to place relations with the United States on a firm footing by entering into a commercial treaty. As a corollary to Roberts's arguments, the ruler stressed that American traders would likewise benefit from such an arrangement.

Yet, despite the sayyid's avowed interest in American trade, Roberts claimed that the ruler was initially reluctant to accord American shipmasters the same privileges allowed their English

counterparts. Roberts attributed this to the impact of English sub-
sidy payments to Sayyid Sa'id for assistance in suppressing the
slave trade. In this, he was factually wrong, although the ruler may
have left such an impression with Roberts. (The sayyid had indeed
signed a treaty with Britain in1822 to cooperate in curbing the slave
trade, the so-called Moresby Treaty, but he received no compensatory English subsidies.[41]) More likely, Arab bargaining techniques
and princely concern over the potential negative English reaction
to a treaty with Americans accounted for any reluctance the ruler
initially showed. Nor can it be excluded that Roberts was simply
seeking to tout his own persuasive skills. After further talks, Roberts recounted, he convinced Sayyid Sa'id to agree that American
shipmasters and supercargoes should enjoy most-favored-nation
privileges.[42]

Having agreed in principle to these arrangements, the ruler
wanted to send one of his vessels to the United States to directly
probe the extent of trade prospects with the United States. Omani
navigators knew the Indian and the China seas, but had not ven-
tured into the Atlantic Ocean. Lacking a suitable navigator to make
the long trip across the Atlantic Ocean, the sayyid asked Roberts to
undertake that function at a handsome price. Hardly enamored of
the idea, Roberts was able to decline gracefully when the Omani
vessel intended for the mission had not arrived at Zanzibar by the
time Roberts's business was finally concluded. Fortunately, Sayyid
Sa'id did not insist, and Roberts proceeded to Bombay as he had
originally planned.[43]

After a brief call at Bombay, the *Mary Ann,* with Roberts aboard,
returned to New York in the last week of November 1828, well within
the stipulated time period. His shareholders could be reimbursed,
although profits were disappointingly marginal. In Roberts's account to Fish and Grinnell Company, aloes, gum copal, dates, and
other sundries brought back were valued at $5,822.76.[44] Some of
these items were sold to merchants in Philadelphia, Charlestown,
and Baltimore. Roberts's overall expenses were $1,577.52, and his
commission—2-1/2 percent of total sales—came to $145.57, hardly
a mighty return for a fourteen-month voyage.

2

Preparation for Roberts's First Mission

Immediately after completing his private business arrangements, Roberts sought the assistance of the Honorable Levi Woodbury, then a senator from New Hampshire and a relative through marriage, in bringing the desirability of a commercial treaty with the ruler of Oman to the attention of the appropriate U.S. authorities.[1] With the experiences of American shipmasters and supercargoes trading in the Indian Ocean area in mind, he emphasized the need to provide adequate protection for American commerce abroad. This, he contended, could best be achieved by regular visits of U.S. warships—preferably annually—to the principal ports of East Africa, the Persian Gulf, and Mocha (in Yemen) and other Red Sea harbors. Such a show of the flag, he confidently predicted, would have a positive effect on the inhabitants of those parts. Only then would they discard their current impression that the United States was weak and feeble and that its commerce could be exploited with impunity.[2]

Woodbury reacted with cautious interest. Although willing to lend support to such a project, he noted the prevailing ignorance in the United States of Sayyid Sa'id's government and domains. Further information was needed if the federal authorities were to be interested in any such design. For example, did Sayyid Sa'id consider Muscat or some other city to be his principal seat of residence? How far into the interior (of Oman and East Africa) did the ruler's territories extend? How large was his "navigation" (i.e., his fleet)? What type of government prevailed in his realm?[3]

Roberts could provide only sketchy answers to these queries, but he sought to be as forthcoming as possible. Muscat, he replied, was still Sayyid Sa'id's principal city of residence. The Omani state possessed a substantial, well-manned fleet, and its form of government might best be described as "despotism." Sayyid Sa'id, he now confided to Woodbury, had expressly asked his assistance in obtaining weapons and ammunition for use in driving the Portuguese out of Mozambique.[4]

In advancing this view, Roberts showed no knowledge of a commercial agreement that Sayyid Sa'id had concluded a few years earlier, in 1826, with the Portuguese governor general of Mozambique. Nor did he seem to suspect that the wily ruler might have in mind using such war materiel for further punitive action against the fractious Mazrui of Mombasa. The sayyid feared the English might have continuing designs on that African port and would seek to exploit Mazrui insurgency for their own purposes. The ruler could hardly forget the behavior of the English naval captain, William Owen, who, in response to Mazrui requests, had in 1824 provisionally declared a British protectorate over Mombasa and had threatened to do likewise over Pemba Island, which made up part of the Zanzibar archipelago. Although the British authorities in London and India disavowed Owen's action when they learned of it, princely uneasiness over putative English designs lingered. The British flag, the sayyid was painfully aware, had flown over Fort Jesus for two years before it was lowered.[5] Only then could Omani suzerainty, such as it was, be reasserted.

Although Roberts's answers lacked detail, Woodbury professed to be satisfied. He circulated Roberts's letter to mercantile colleagues in the Senate, who reportedly expressed interest. Woodbury was in fact sufficiently encouraged, after discussing the matter with unidentified federal officials, to predict that an official "agent" might soon be sent to Muscat to conclude a commercial treaty with its ruler, and that one or two ships of the U.S. naval squadron in the Pacific might be ordered home by that route to show the flag at Sayyid Sa'id's ports.[6]

Seeking to expedite the project, Roberts urged Woodbury to try to arrange that the "agent" be in Muscat no later than "September next" (1829), since Sayyid Sa'id would shortly thereafter be traveling elsewhere in his domains. Any U.S. frigate sent to Muscat, he urged, should be of the "very first class" in order to impress the ruler and his subjects. Such a display of force should be balanced by appropriate presents for the ruler.[7]

Despite Woodbury's optimism, the anticipated mission did not materialize as quickly as its proponents had hoped. More pressing developments at home and abroad preoccupied the administration of President Andrew Jackson. However important New England and other shipping interests might consider the need to formalize commercial arrangements in the Indian Ocean, Sayyid Sa'id's domains were remote and only dimly understood. They hardly promised quantum commercial gains. Over three years elapsed before the treaty mission was actively pursued.

Roberts's Private Affairs

Even as Roberts continued to press the need for a mission to East Africa, he was faced with the stark, immediate necessity of earning a living. His wife and growing family in Portsmouth were dependent on him for support, and the Zanzibar voyage had netted him scant recompense. No one could be sure when, if at all, a new treaty mission would be sent, or, if one was sent, whether Roberts would be entrusted with the task.

Regardless of his enthusiasm for the mission, he had to find sources of income. The New York firm of Fish and Grinnell, for which he had made purchases in Zanzibar, agreed to retain him as a commission agent. Fish and Grinnell extended limited credit facilities to Roberts for potentially profitable ventures that he might explore in the United States.

After briefly visiting Portsmouth and New York, Roberts determined to proceed to New Orleans. In that city, he entered into contractual arrangements with one Ephraim Ware to import palmetto palms from Cuba and to ship them, through Fish and Grinnell, to Boston, where they would be used to weave chair seats.[8] Tanned deerskins from Louisiana also would be sent to New York for use in shoe and coat manufacturing.

Perhaps he lacked business acumen, or perhaps fortune simply failed to smile upon him, but Roberts's commercial ventures proved disappointing. The rain ruined much of the palmetto that Ware had sent as deck cargo. Worms infested the deerskins.[9] Despite Ware's continued expression of faith in palmetto, it was clear that he knew little about the product; it was also clear that Roberts knew even less. Having advanced some funds to Ware, Roberts found his contract partner unable to repay. In July 1830, Ware, then in prison in New Orleans for defaulting on debts, wrote to Roberts acknowledging that both the palmetto and the deerskin undertakings had failed. Returning various bills of exchange drawn on Fish and Grinnell, Ware forlornly promised to repay Roberts whenever he was able to do so.[10] There is no indication that he ever redeemed these obligations.

From New Orleans, Roberts went to Cincinnati, Ohio, with the intention of engaging in pork speculation. A local pork dealer offered him the opportunity to invest in hogs, but Roberts, heeding cautionary messages from Fish and Grinnell, decided against doing so.[11] He did decide, however, to speculate in lard. With credit facilities again advanced by Fish and Grinnell, he ordered a quantity of Cincinnati lard to be shipped and sold in New Orleans.[12] Unfortunately for him, the price of lard in Cincinnati rose before the purchase, and by the time the product reached its New Orleans destination, it had to be sold there at a loss. Advising Roberts of this, Fish and Grinnell observed that he owed them slightly over $100 as an "unfortunate result of the operation," but generously offered to cancel the debt or to allow him to pay whenever he could do so. Fish and Grinnell also made it clear that they would not extend to Roberts further credit facilities for another lard venture. Recalling an interest he had apparently frequently expressed in the "East Indies," they urged him to pursue this idea. Doing so, they opined, "would be more likely to result to your advantage."[13]

As Roberts lamented his business failures in epistolary exchanges with his long-suffering wife, Catherine, in Portsmouth, her account of the family's pecuniary distress deepened his anxiety. In March 1830, she wrote, "I am in want of many articles for the family." She needed cotton for shirting and clothes, and she said she would have to ask her husband's "friends" for more money. She owed payments to their few servants and to various creditors.[14] Two months later, she wrote that she had been required to draw on

Fish and Grinnell for $40 to make ends meet. She had economized in every way possible, she assured her husband, but debts had to be paid, food costs were increasing, and the children's wardrobes had to be bought. Added to these problems, she still grieved over the death of their second son shortly after his birth.[15]

The strain of incessantly poor health, constant financial worries, and personal grief was too much for her. Catherine Roberts died in November 1830, while her husband was still traveling between New Orleans, Cincinnati, and New York.[16] Roberts's oldest daughter, also named Catherine, was then barely twenty years of age when her distraught but continually absent father asked her to look after her sisters. She would be assisted by the family maid, Polly. And, Roberts dejectedly wrote, he would not be able to be home for the upcoming Christmas holidays.[17] It was a sad holiday season for the Roberts family.

Concurrent Treaty Promotion Efforts with Southeast Asian States

Even as Roberts sought to promote a treaty with Sayyid Sa'id, a fellow American was urging the U.S. government to conclude commercial treaties with various Southeast Asian states. John Shillaber, a New York merchant, had settled in Dutch-held Batavia as early as 1823. After American shipmasters and supercargoes visiting Batavia had asked President John Quincy Adams to appoint a consul there, Shillaber was designated the port's "agent for commerce and seamen" for the United States.[18] This was tantamount to a consular function, and he received his formal consular commission in April 1824. Shillaber became increasingly knowledgeable not only of the East Indies but also—through information gleaned from others—of the littoral states of the southeastern Indian Ocean. He likewise acquired general information on Japan, that rigidly closed, almost mythically elusive island empire that fascinated so many major trading nations.

On December 10, 1830, Shillaber submitted to the State Department a proposal that a U.S. diplomatic mission be sent to Siam and Cochin China to negotiate commercial treaties. An attached estimate of likely costs of that mission, including ship charters, interpreters, presents, and so on, totaled $21,500, a substantial sum. Shillaber initially suggested a separate diplomatic mission to open

Japan. He provided protocol details about how letters to the rulers of all of these states should be addressed.[19]

Six months later, Shillaber followed up on his recommendation. Noting the encouraging reply from the State Department to his earlier communication on measures that might be taken to promote American trade with the East Indies, he had concluded that it would be desirable for the same diplomatic mission to proceed to Japan after first visiting Siam and Cochin China. The mission—and Shillaber obviously hoped to be designated for this task—should be instructed to negotiate with the government of the empire of Japan for free access by American vessels to Japanese ports for purposes of commerce. Several foreign governments, he reported, had recently sent missions to Japan to propose trade negotiations.

Extensive, even if secondhand, observations on the governments of Cochin China and Siam were included in his dispatch. Since the U.S. government might not deem it expedient to send a "national" vessel (i.e., a U.S. warship) with the mission, Shillaber suggested that an American merchant ship be chartered at Batavia for that purpose. A considerable number of such vessels visited that port, and one could easily be engaged. The vessel should not exceed thirteen feet in draft if she was to cross the bar at the mouth of the Menam River (now the Chao Phraya) and proceed upriver to Bangkok.[20] Shillaber was aware that the Dutch already had a factory at Deshima (Dejima, in Japanese) Island, in Nagasaki harbor, and had doubtless heard of Russian and British attempts to obtain trade privileges in Japan.[21]

In late December 1831, Shillaber informed Secretary of State Martin Van Buren that he intended to return to Batavia and would resume his consular duties there. Stressing that he had been in Batavia for nine years, and that he knew the Southeast Asian area well, he reiterated the advantages that could accrue to the United States if commercial treaties were concluded with Siam and Cochin China. And, repeating the theme of American merchants engaged in trade in remote regions of the world, he now also proposed that a U.S. warship be assigned to cruise in the area.[22]

The *Friendship* Incident

Like Roberts's recommendations, Shillaber's had been gestating among federal authorities for some time. They might have done so even longer had not a requirement suddenly developed for a punitive naval expedition to the East Indies. The Salem ship *Friendship*, captained by Charles M. Endicott, had in January 1831 been attacked by Malay pirates while loading pepper at Quallah Battou (also known as Kuala Batu), on the western coast of Sumatra. (The Malays later contended that members of the ship's crew had cheated them, thus provoking the attack.[23]) Three crewmen had been killed and others wounded. The ship was in Malay hands until she was retaken by Endicott, with the help of men from three American vessels loading at nearby Muckie. More than $40,000 worth of specie, provisions, and opium were reportedly taken from the *Friendship* by the pirates.[24]

Such banditry was widespread in Southeast Asian coastal and archipelegic waters. An outraged President Jackson saw the incident as brutal depredation on American shipping and vowed reprisal, unless restitution was made. Temperamentally, Jackson was not concerned with the niceties of investigating claims and counterclaims; he desired prompt punitive action, or as prompt as remote distances would allow. His attitude was consistent with the prevailing sentiments of the American merchant and seafaring communities.[25]

To this end, the U.S. frigate *Potomac*, designated to relieve the USS *Guerriere* on the northern coast of South America in the Pacific, was ordered to proceed to Quallah Battou en route to her station to demand satisfaction for the outrage. If such was not forthcoming, Commodore John Downes was authorized to take appropriate punitive action against the natives of the town.[26]

Considering the dangers of seafaring, Woodbury, who had become secretary of the navy in May 1831, also designated the U.S. sloop of war *Peacock* (under Master Commandant David Geisinger), joined by the U.S. schooner *Boxer* (under Lt. Commander William Shields), to follow up on the punitive mission in the event the *Potomac* was lost at sea. Concurrently, the *Peacock* was to convey a special U.S. diplomatic mission to certain Asian states to negotiate commercial treaties,[27] but only after first transporting Francis

Baylies, a newly appointed American chargé d'affaires to the Argentine Republic, and his family to his post.

Baylies was under urgent instructions to demand compensation for Argentinean seizure of American fishing vessels off the Falkland Islands and to assert American rights to fish in waters adjacent to those islands. His mission, which was ultimately unsuccessful, had higher priority than that of Roberts.

The *Peacock,* like the *Boxer,* was nominally assigned to the U.S. Navy's Brazil squadron. During the two vessels' detached service in the Indian Ocean, they would constitute an independent task force under Geisinger's command, although Geisinger was not authorized to fly a commodore's pennant. An incipient U.S. Navy East India squadron, as it would come to be designated in 1842, was in the making.

Roberts's Designation

Although Shillaber had expected to be entrusted with the diplomatic mission to negotiate treaties in the Far East—and was in many ways better qualified for it than Roberts, especially in experience and knowledge of Southeast Asia—Woodbury's influence with the president and the secretary of state prevailed, and Roberts received the coveted designation.

Roberts's papers provide scant indication of his political leanings. Although he was not active in politics, as a New Hampshire businessman related by marriage to the Langdons, Roberts most likely tended to be National Republican in outlook. The National Republicans were the heirs of the earlier Federalists. The Monroe administration's offer of a consulship in British Guiana, although primarily commercially motivated, suggests that Roberts was considered politically acceptable by that group. Like some other New Englanders with Federalist backgrounds who subsequently became Jacksonian Democrats, Roberts seems to have made that transition. Levi Woodbury's strong influence on him was doubtless a factor in this conversion. So was President Jackson's willingness to send him on a roving diplomatic assignment. First and foremost a spoilsman, Jackson would hardly have named Roberts had there been any doubt about his partisan loyalty.

When informing Secretary of State Edward Livingston in December 1831 of the president's decision to send a punitive naval force to Sumatra, Woodbury had commended Roberts to his cabinet colleague. Six weeks later, in late January 1832, Livingston formally informed Roberts that he would be tasked with the mission.[28]

On January 26, 1832, President Jackson commissioned Roberts as a "special agent" of the United States to negotiate commercial treaties abroad. This was a somewhat nebulous rank in the traditional diplomatic hierarchy, which carried with it neither ambassadorial nor ministerial distinction, and reflected the somewhat low status intended for the mission. It was also one that various administrations had used, much to the annoyance of some members of the Senate, to avoid having to obtain advance "advice and consent" from the Senate for temporary diplomatic appointments, especially in instances where secret negotiations were envisioned. In addition, Roberts was sent "passports," or letters of credence, and "full-powers" documents authorizing him to explore commercial opportunities with Muscat, Siam, Cochin China, and Japan, and, if feasible, to sign commercial treaties with these states.

The letter of credence and full powers for Muscat were addressed to "His Highness, Syed Syed Bin Soultan, the Imaum of Muscat and his Government." There was initial uncertainty in the State Department on the appropriate titles of the rulers of the other three states. Two weeks later, in mid-February, Roberts received similar credentials documents addressed to the kings of Cochin China and Siam. Space was left in the documents to enable Roberts to insert the correct protocol titles of these potentates, once they had been ascertained. One set of presidentially signed but otherwise blank passport and full-powers documents was also provided, presumably for Japan, which Roberts could fill in and use as circumstances required. Any treaties that Roberts might conclude, he was advised, should be submitted to the president "for ratification by and with the advice of the Senate."[29]

Roberts was enjoined to strict secrecy lest ill-wishers, such as the British, French, or Dutch, learn of his mission and seek to subvert it. He shared such suspicions. He was asked to come to Washington for appropriate instructions. He would be paid an annual salary of $1,500. To conceal Roberts's purpose, Secretary Livingston asked his cabinet colleague Woodbury to provide some "simple employment" for Roberts aboard ship.[30] Woodbury arranged with Captain Geisinger to do so. Roberts, he instructed, was to be rated as "captain's clerk." He was "to do duty as such, but...[was] to be treated as a gentleman having the confidence of the Government and entrusted with important duties in India, Arabia and Africa."[31] These were surely confusing instructions for an American naval commander accustomed to rigorous rank distinctions between officers and crew.

On his arrival in Washington in late January, Roberts met with President Jackson and conferred almost daily with Secretary Livingston.[32] His formal instructions from Livingston, dated January 27, 1832, charged him with examining "the means of extending the commerce of the United States by commercial arrangements with the powers whose dominions border on those [Indian Ocean] seas." On the *Peacock*'s rosters, he was told, he would be carried as "captain's clerk" in order to conceal his true purposes. Roberts was informed that Captain Geisinger had been apprised of Roberts's mission, but no one else aboard was to be told unless Roberts believed that doing so would facilitate his mission. While the titular role of clerk doubtless offended Roberts's sense of self-importance, he wanted the assignment and did not demur.

Initial planning called for the *Peacock* to proceed first to Rio de Janeiro, where chargé Baylies and his family would disembark and whence they would proceed to Buenos Aires. Thereafter, the vessel was to sail around Cape Horn into the Pacific Ocean, with Cochin China as its first destination. In Cochin China, Roberts was to inspect the products of that country and ascertain Cochin Chinese military and maritime strength. He should inquire of the "king" whether American ships and products would be admitted to his ports. The Cochin Chinese should be assured that, unlike British, French, and Dutch practices in the East Indies, the United States as a matter of principle never established "forts" (i.e., factories) abroad. The president of the United States, he was to stress, was powerful and possessed many ships.

After Cochin China, a similar probe should be made for Siam and, almost as an afterthought, for "the powers of Arabia on the Red Sea." Muscat was not specifically mentioned, but Roberts had discretionary authority to go there, even though that port is not on the Red Sea—he had already been given credentials for that polity. Since the early 1800s, a substantial number of American vessels had traded at the Yemeni port of Mocha, on the Red Sea, and there had been repeated urgings that a commercial agreement be reached with Yemen's imamate. This accounted for the inclusion of Red Sea states in Roberts's instructions.

Before Roberts left, he pressed for higher emoluments. His compensation was changed to $6 per day, or $2,190 per year, along with "necessary personal expenses." He was given an advance of $1,000 and $500 for presents to be dispensed during the mission.[33] One-third of his salary would be paid by the navy; the remainder would come from the secretary of state's contingency fund for "foreign intercourse." Even with the increase, his pay was less than that of an American chargé d'affaires.

Acknowledging receipt of his official instructions, Roberts assured Secretary Livingston that, to the extent practical, he would not disclose the object of his mission. Recalling that he had been promised copies of Shillaber's reports, Roberts indicated that he was anxious to peruse them. He also sought official letters of introduction to the American consuls in Batavia, Manila, and Canton, and a State Department circular letter was in due course sent to those officials asking them to provide all appropriate assistance. Manila, Roberts suggested, might be the best place to engage the interpreters that would be needed in his travels, and he sought an additional $500 in specie to pay them.[34]

Roberts also made preliminary arrangements to purchase various presents for the rulers and officials with whom he expected to negotiate. Some, such as firearms, were ordered through the War Department; nonmilitary items were ordered through New York vendors. If the goods were not ready by the time he left, they would be transported to Canton by a merchant vessel. The expectation was that they would be on hand by the time treaty negotiations began.

Notwithstanding his new diplomatic status, Roberts understandably remained concerned about his private affairs. Shortly before leaving the United States, he authorized Fish and Grinnell Company to pursue his spoliation claim in his absence. At that time, he also had a $4,000 balance with that company, which his children could draw upon as necessary.[35]

Departure

With Roberts aboard, the *Peacock* sailed on February 7, 1832, from Boston, her home port, to New York, where Baylies and his family boarded the vessel. Captain Geisinger turned over his cabin to them. Roberts, in accordance with efforts to conceal his diplomatic mission, initially slept in a hammock on the gun deck. One month later, on March 8, 1832, the vessel sailed from New York for Rio de Janeiro, arriving on May 4 after a fifty-six day sail.

The *Peacock* was supposed to rendezvous with the *Boxer* there, but Geisinger learned that all Brazil squadron vessels, the *Boxer* included, had been ordered south by the squadron commodore as a show of force to impress the Argentine government. Hence, the *Peacock* proceeded to Montevideo, where Baylies and his family disembarked. When in two week's time the *Boxer* had not returned to station, Geisinger sailed for eastern waters. Instructions were left for the *Boxer* to rendezvous with the *Peacock* off the coast of Sumatra. From Buenos Aires onward, Roberts shared the captain's cabin with Geisinger.[36] By then, his "captain's clerk" cover no longer fooled anyone aboard ship. It was a charade that could not be long maintained, especially not by Roberts, who was keenly conscious of his status as a gentleman and as a newly designated American diplomat.

While waiting off Montevideo, Roberts received modifications to his instructions. New "original" credentials, made out in a form that the State Department had learned was likely to be more acceptable to Asian potentates, were sent to him along with a few of the presents that had been ordered. He was enjoined to "husband" the presents as much as possible. The *Peacock* would sail by way of the Cape of Good Hope rather than around Cape Horn, as had initially been planned. The revised sailing plan, it was wrongly assumed by the State Department, would probably bring Roberts first to the Arabian states. Clearly, the State Department's liaison with the Navy Department left much to be desired.

As far as Muscat was concerned, Livingston foresaw no difficulty in concluding an agreement with Sayyid Sa'id. This was evident from a letter that the "Imaum of Muscat," as the ruler was erroneously called by many Americans and Europeans, had sent to President Jackson. It had been forwarded through the medium of the Salem vessel *Complex*, whose shipmaster, Asa Burnham, had encountered Sayyid Sa'id at Mombasa, where the ruler was once again seeking to chastise the persistently rebellious Mazrui. That letter, Roberts was informed, had reiterated the sayyid's desire for the early conclusion of a commercial treaty with the United States. In transmitting the letter, the principals of the New York firm N. L. Rogers and Brothers stated, "We understand the Imaum [*sic*] is anxious to form a commercial treaty with the United States as he has with the English."[37] Roberts's earlier talk with him had manifestly made an impression, and the sayyid's letter suggested impatience that the promised envoy had not yet arrived.

Clearly, too, the State Department's aims had expanded once Roberts was under way. Livingston now also urged Roberts to obtain as much information as possible on how American trade with Japan might be opened and to ascertain the extent of Japanese trade with the Dutch and Chinese. In addition, Roberts was given discretionary authority to try to negotiate a commercial treaty with the "Birman Empire." Finally, it was suggested that perhaps a treaty with the king of Achin (northern Sumatra; "Acheen" in Livingston's letters), might provide greater security for the American pepper trade with Sumatra and help stop attacks by Malay pirates on American ships. What had come to be called the "*Friendship* incident" underscored the need for such arrangements. Further instructions would be sent to him at Canton, and Roberts was ordered to report at every opportunity.[38]

Captain Geisinger was under orders from the Navy Department to sail first to Sumatra to ascertain whether punitive action against the marauders of the *Friendship* was still necessary. If so, efforts were to be made to bring the perpetrators to the United States for trial and to obtain indemnification for losses sustained. Crossing the Indian Ocean turned out to be slow going. From the Cape of Good Hope, it was fifty-seven days to Java Head, whence the vessel bore away for Bencoolen (Bengkulu) on Sumatra. There it was learned that the *Potomac* had effectively chastised the Malay pirates of Quallah Battou — had, in fact, destroyed much of the village and killed some 150 pirates. Geisinger then sailed for Anger Roads, Java, where the vessel's depleted water and bread supplies could be replenished before proceeding to Manila.[39] The *Peacock* arrived at

Manila on September 30. Since the vessel had to undergo extensive repairs, Roberts took lodgings ashore and discreetly sought to engage a Chinese-speaking interpreter.[40] He was unsuccessful.

Arrival at Canton

On October 8, the *Peacock* arrived at Lintin (Nei Lingding Island), in the Pearl River south of Canton. The trip to Canton was made by native junk. Roberts found that one of the thirteen foreign factories (or *kongs*) in Canton was American, and that seven Americans already resided in that Chinese city. While in Canton, Roberts lived ashore at the American factory. From Canton he reported to the State Department that the *Peacock*'s crew had begun to be afflicted with "horrible diseases," and that eight crew members had died. Since the *Boxer* had not yet arrived with the presents ordered in the United States for use in Cochin China, Siam, and Muscat, he was required to purchase substitute presents in Canton. He had been told that presents for use in Cochin China and Siam had to be given in pairs. These goods, bought from Olyphant & Company, an American commercial establishment in Canton, consisted of teas, silks, watches, and silverware. They cost $3,199, considerably more than had been anticipated.[41]

To pay for these presents, Roberts informed the secretary of state, he had drawn a bill of exchange for $4,000 on John R. Latimer, another American merchant in Canton. This was a third more than he had initially estimated would be needed for this purpose. Not until many months later did he reveal to the State Department the exact amount spent on presents and local accommodations.[42]

The matter of presents prompted Roberts to revert to a subject that had increasingly troubled him during the voyage. The State Department, he had concluded, had allotted utterly inadequate funds for the overall expenses of such a mission. Judging from Shillaber's earlier estimate of likely costs, Roberts was right. Presents, the expenses of an interpreter, living ashore when necessary in a "decent" manner, Roberts wrote to Secretary Livingston from Canton, cost money. His diplomatic mission, he asserted, could not be effectively conducted for less than $3,000; indeed, he said, $10,000 would make but a "sorry figure" for dealing with the several Asian states he had been instructed to visit. By the time he arrived in Singapore after visiting Cochin China and Siam, Roberts predicted, he would be out of funds.

Roberts also related that the *Boxer* had still not arrived and was badly needed. In the current rainy season, the *Peacock,* because of her draft, would not be able to approach closer to Bangkok than twenty leagues (about 111 kilometers). The *Boxer*, with a shallower draft, could get closer.[43] Implicit in this observation was Roberts's conviction that the presence of an American warship off Bangkok would facilitate his mission.

The Morrisons

Equally important to Roberts during his Canton layover was engaging an efficient and discreet Chinese language interpreter. Through David W. Olyphant, the deeply devout American merchant in Canton who had long befriended missionaries and whose Canton premises were known as "Zion's corner," Roberts was introduced to the British missionary, the Reverend Dr. Robert Morrison, the first Protestant missionary in China.

Morrison, a Presbyterian, arrived in Canton in September 1807 on behalf of the London Missionary Society. Since the English East India Company was distrustful of missionaries, he had first traveled to the United States, where he obtained a letter from then Secretary of State James Madison commending Morrison to the American consul in Canton; Morrison then sailed to Canton aboard an American merchant ship. Becoming an accomplished Chinese linguist in his many years of service in China, Morrison had translated the Old and the New Testaments into Chinese and also prepared an English-Chinese dictionary. He was generally regarded as the most knowledgeable European in China. Although the English East India Company subsequently engaged him as interpreter and translator for Chinese documents, Morrison remained close to the few American missionaries in Canton and retained positive feelings toward the United States.[44]

Morrison's specific area of interest was China, but he was also considered the paramount authority on how best to deal with neighboring states heavily influenced by Chinese culture. Roberts now sought his advice on how to conduct his negotiations with the Cochin Chinese and Siamese. In a written private and confidential response to Roberts, Morrison provided some general rules of conduct for anyone dealing with Asian leaders.

One should always speak the truth, he declared. The Cochin Chinese should be told that Roberts had come to speak of "national affairs." In any interviews or audiences with senior Cochin Chinese or Siamese officials, the Westerner should decline to uncover his feet or to kowtow. His position should be that his visit was not intended to change local customs, but that the Western visitor wished to preserve his own customs as well. If Cochin Chinese or Siamese came to the United States, they could follow their own practices. Negotiations, Morrison continued, should not be on the basis of lord and vassal. Local usages should be avoided as much as possible, and reciprocal rights should be the foundation of all intercourse. Confidence should never be placed in apparently friendly natives. The Westerner should avoid making himself "cheap." He should be kind and courteous, but only "after some little formalities."

The U.S. warship, Morrison stated, should be anchored as close to the capitals of Cochin China and Siam as possible. Inferior local officials should be used as little as possible. Nothing would ever be gained by conceding to unreasonable local demands or in response to insulting local modes of conduct. Morrison concluded that a bit of pomp and show has "a certain weight which is impressive on the uncivilized mind."[45] That Roberts took Morrison's counsel to heart was evident by his subsequent conduct in Cochin China and Siam. He may at times have even overdone it.

Roberts deemed it necessary to confide the purpose of his mission to Morrison, even though the missionary was a British national and had an association with the English East India Company. Learning that Morrison had a son working in nearby Macao, who was knowledgeable of both the Mandarin and Fukien (Fujian) dialects of China, Roberts inquired whether the young man would be willing to accompany him to Cochin China and Siam as interpreter. After querying his son, John R. Morrison, the elder Morrison informed Roberts that the young man could do so and that he, the father, would stand in at his Macao work site during his son's absence.

The elder Morrison showed some concern, however, about his son's title. The designation "interpreter," he pointed out, was treated with considerable contempt by Asians. Morrison knew whereof he spoke. In 1816, he had accompanied Lord Amherst as interpreter on that English dignitary's abortive mission to Peking, and he had experienced the social odium of the title. Morrison proposed that his son be called private secretary, observing that the young man could help with copying documents. The missionary also stressed that, since his son was quite young, Roberts would have to act as his "protector and patron."[46]

Roberts readily accepted these terms. He had been on the verge of engaging a Portuguese, who also spoke English, but much preferred Morrison's son. Young John Morrison, Roberts assured his father, could have whatever title he wanted and could set his own terms. He would live in the ship's cabin with him and Captain Geisinger, and Roberts would consider any affront to the young man to be a personal indignity. But Roberts asked the elder Morrison to impress on his son the need for secrecy with respect to the object of the trip.[47]

Young Morrison was in fact designated "translator, interpreter, and private secretary." He would receive $500 for the voyage, together with expenses. The total cost of his employment, which would last five months, would come to $600.[48] Roberts made a brief trip to nearby Macao and brought the young man back with him. Although young Morrison generally served Roberts well, the American envoy subsequently became disenchanted with him.

While in Canton, Roberts also visited the small American missionary contingent.[49] He was impressed with its work to the extent that he sent Secretary Livingston a number of moral and religious tracts published in Canton by the American Missionary Society. These publications, he noted, were intended for a higher class of Chinese society.[50] He also sent some local seeds to Livingston and to the principals of Fish and Grinnell, for whom he had acted four years earlier as a commission agent.[51] It is at Canton that Commodore Geisinger first mentions Roberts in his journal of the *Peacock*'s cruise.[52]

3

Earlier Cochin Chinese and Siamese Contacts with Foreigners

Roberts would spend the next five months, first in Cochin China and then in Siam, endeavoring to negotiate commercial treaties with these neighboring but ethnically different Asian polities. Although a novice in the profession of diplomacy, Roberts suffered from no lack of self-confidence. Impressed with the importance of his diplomatic mission, he conceived it as furthering legitimate American commerce in the face of recalcitrant, sometimes duplicitous, and, as he generally thought, benighted peoples. By his standards, he found them dirty, arrogant, and barbarous. Their religious beliefs, largely Buddhism in Siam and an amalgam of Confucianism, Taoism, and Buddhism in Cochin China, were repugnant to his puritan Protestant upbringing.

In contrast, the indigenous inhabitants of Cochin China and Siam, especially their official elites who were legatees of proud cultural heritages, saw Roberts as but another in the continuum of unwanted yet seemingly unpreventable foreign visitors. They had experienced four centuries of intermittent European interlopers. It was thus inevitable that Roberts should encounter long-ingrained xenophobic antipathy toward "foreign devils," regardless of whence they came.

Such outside, non-Asiatic intruders were, by definition, untrustworthy. To the Cochin Chinese and Siamese, just as to the Chinese and Japanese, they were uncivilized, no matter what their technological accomplishments might be. Whatever protestations they might make of political disinterest or friendship, their motives remained suspect. Scorning as they did, through word and conscious or unconscious deed, the religious belief systems of the indigenous inhabitants, these visitors might have to be temporarily tolerated, but they were always regarded as unwelcome intruders.

Roberts, the latest in the genre of such non-Asiatic transients, might seek to contrast allegedly benign U.S. purposes with those of the often overbearing and territorially acquisitive British, French, and Dutch, but he could hardly hope to escape being stigmatized in local eyes as another undesirable. His own sometimes overbearing conduct, especially in Cochin China, contributed to that image. So did the generally malevolent counsel of well-placed Chinese merchants and Indian Muslim expatriate employees of the Cochin Chinese and Siamese governments. Whatever differences these categories of expatriate Asiatic foreigners might have between and among themselves—and most were there for personal profit rather than objective service, and they deeply distrusted one another—they shared a common desire to protect their privileged status and positions. They sought to do so by covertly imputing ulterior, even sinister, motives to visiting non-Asians. The times lent themselves to conspiratorial theories.

Moreover, Cochin Chinese and Siamese leaders alike had formed impressions of the relative strengths and weaknesses of the various Western nations whose official representatives had from time to time come to negotiate or whose shipmasters had touched their shores. The pomp and circumstance attending a visiting foreign diplomatic mission, regardless of its provenance, was a significant conditioning factor in conjuring local images of a foreign entity's power and purpose. Those perceptions, combined with Asian leadership elites' estimates of their internal strengths and of current external threats to their dominions, tended to dictate conduct toward any particular group of aliens at any given time. Roberts appeared with almost no diplomatic entourage.

Asian strategy, such as it was, called for playing off one group of unwanted foreigners against another, if possible, and reaping maximum security or economic gains from the rivalry. While Cochin Chinese and Siamese leaders equated their respective group interests with those of the state, the extent of concessions that either set of elites was prepared to grant to visiting non-Asian solicitors, official or otherwise, was based largely on their calculus of the aforementioned complex and often amorphous factors.

Structurally, both Cochin China and Siam were highly centralized despotisms. Minimal authority was deputed to provincial and district officials. Procedurally, norms derived from rigid Chinese protocol and bureaucratic styles pervaded the governmental systems of the two countries, albeit somewhat more so in Cochin China, by reason of its contiguity to China, than in Siam. They demanded strict and unquestioning compliance with the commands of higher authority. Innovation or the exercise of individual discretion by provincial or district officials was forbidden. Transgression of these inelastic rules, whether real or simply perceived as such by higher authority, mandated punishment for the hapless offender. Inevitably, in such circumstances local functionaries preferred to err on the side of negativism, rigidity, and procrastination in their dealings with foreign visitors. Referral of almost any question, no matter how trivial or routine, to a superior authority for decision was accepted operational procedure.

In both Cochin China and Siam, Roberts would experience these cultural patterns in full measure. By nature an aggressive, enterprising, and individualistic American entrepreneur, and imbued with that sense of self-righteousness and national superiority that characterized so many of his countrymen, he suffered what would today be called cultural shock. Even his experience in Zanzibar, difficult though it had been, had not prepared him for the refined Asian patterns of evasion that he encountered. Ever in a hurry, yet required to deal with ancient societies to whom time meant nothing, his interactions were sometimes marked by intolerance and manifest impatience. To the Cochin Chinese, in particular, and even to the Siamese, his comportment must have smacked of discourtesy and even rudeness at times.

At best, Roberts faced a formidable challenge. Yet had he been better attuned to Asian cultural mores and had he harbored greater empathy toward Asians, he might have handled some of his frustrations, especially in Cochin China, with greater aplomb. In considering the totality of his mission, its failures and successes, one might wonder whether Roberts interpreted some of the advice he received on how to deal with Asians far too literally.

Roberts's mission was a pioneering effort to establish U.S. relations with selected Southeast Asian political entities. To provide the essential backdrop for understanding Cochin Chinese and Siamese dealings with Roberts, this chapter presents detailed overviews of the historical experiences of these two Southeast Asian states with visiting European officials and American shipmasters before Roberts's appearance on the scene. In many ways, his experiences replicated those of previous visiting foreign diplomatic officials.

Cochin China

Roberts appeared on the Cochin Chinese scene as that country was slowly emerging from a destructive civil war. A massive peasant upheaval, known as the Tay Son rebellion, had devastated large parts of the southern, central, and northern parts of the country from 1771 to 1802. Nominally, the conflict ended with the military success of Nguyen Anh, a young prince from the south who later ruled the country as Emperor Gia Long. Nguyen Anh had been forced into exile in neighboring Siam at age fifteen, but after a decade of sporadic but bloody hostilities—and with the assistance of French Catholic priest Pigneau de Behaine, who helped recruit foreign volunteers to join the battle—he managed to regain his family's territorial patrimony. Yet even as the country slowly recovered, chronic insurgency characterized the ethnically polyglot political scene. Visiting Cochin China in May 1803, American ship captain Jeremiah Briggs of Salem confirmed the devastation of the Hué countryside.[1]

Emperor Gia Long, who had tolerated Roman Catholic missionaries in deference to the assistance his French friends had offered, died in 1820. He was succeeded by his fourth son, Minh Mang. Minh Mang did not share his father's tolerance. He was deeply suspicious of the motives of foreigners, resident or visiting, and soon commenced persecuting those of his subjects who had been converted to Catholicism. By the time Edmund Roberts arrived, Minh Mang's repressive policies had been in force for thirteen years. In 1833, the year of Roberts's arrival, an imperial prescript was issued declaring adherence to Christianity a capital crime. Consciously or unconsciously, the ruler's animosity to foreigners was bound to affect the reception given Roberts, the first U.S. emissary to appear on the Cochin Chinese scene. That he was American mattered not a whit; few Cochin Chinese had ever heard of America. To them, he was another foreigner, a Christian barbarian execrated by their emperor.

The French Connection

Cochin China had for centuries enjoyed limited trade relations with China and Japan. In the seventeenth century, Dutch and Portuguese traders were admitted into the country for the first time. The Portuguese location in nearby Macao, established in the sixteenth century, afforded a geographic advantage, but the steady erosion of Portuguese military strength in India and Southeast Asia soon made their residual influence politically negligible. In the eighteenth century, the French East India Company had shown a passing interest in encouraging commerce with the Cochin Chinese. It had sent an emissary, Pierre Poivre, to Annam to assess the state's economic potential, but little was done to follow up on his optimistic report. Successive Vietnamese rulers, Nguyen and Tay Son alike, had generally been willing to accept limited trade with foreigners, but had consistently been wary lest such commercial associations translate into foreign political domination. Although a high degree of xenophobia regularly suffused the Cochin Chinese governmental bureaucracy, Emperor Gia Long's attitude toward the French following his return to Cochin China in the late 1700s was curiously inconsistent, but also generally benevolent.

During Gia Long's almost twenty-year rule, some 400 French advisers were at various times employed by his government. Such expatriate Frenchmen were usually engaged on individual contracts, but were as a matter of policy barred from decision-making responsibilities.[2] Much as he might appreciate the counsel of his French expatriates, Gia Long sedulously guarded against their becoming, individually or collectively, an instrument of official French intervention in the state. Yet, whatever his purpose, their very presence projected an image of strong French influence in the Annamese state.

In August 1817 two French ships, *La Paix* and *Henri*, sent by the Bordeaux firms Balguerie, Sarget et Cie and Philippon et Cie, respectively, arrived almost simultaneously in Turan. Although their supercargoes were able to negotiate acceptable harbor charges, the overall commercial aspects of the ventures turned out to be failures. All the same, both supercargoes concluded that more carefully chosen outbound cargos could prove profitable. That judgment would prove erroneous.

Cochin China still had little need for foreign manufactures, and Chinese traders supplied most of its few external requirements. Within a few years, Philippon et Cie withdrew, leaving the field to its rival firm. In 1819, Balguerie, Sarget et Cie, despite marginal commercial success, opted to entrust one of its supercargoes, Auguste Borel, with the function of resident broker in Saigon.[3] Borel would remain for several years, but his commercial agency was eventually closed, as his principals finally concluded that the effort was unprofitable. But precedent now existed for a resident European commercial presence in Cochin China.

On the second visit of the two French merchant captains in 1819, during which they also visited Hué, they were entertained by two long-time French advisers in the employ of Gia Long, Jean-Baptiste Chaigneau and Philippe Vannier. Each had by then spent more than twenty years in Cochin Chinese service and had attained high mandarin status in the state. At a minimum, they were able to introduce their seafaring countrymen to important court officials. Vannier, in his youth, had been in the French navy and had been present when Lord Cornwallis surrendered British forces to the combined land and sea forces of George Washington and French Admiral de Grasse at Yorktown in 1780.[4] Visiting ship captains would often appeal to Chaigneau or Vannier for help with the Annamese bureaucracy because the two Frenchmen had become acculturated to Cochin Chinese society and customs. Their elite mandarin positions were essentially honorific rather than substantive and, although foreign visitors did not always realize it, their ability to assist their visiting countrymen or others was limited.

Two years earlier, as the first French commercial voyages to Cochin China were being undertaken, the French government, anxious to reestablish influence in Southeast Asia after the Napoleonic defeat, had dispatched a diplomatic mission to the area aboard the frigate *Cybèle*. Count Achille de Kergariou, who headed the mission, arrived in Turan Bay in December 1817. The appearance of the French warship with an official envoy alarmed Gia Long, notwithstanding his reliance on his numerous French contract employees. Denying an audience to the French envoy, the ruler refused Kergariou permission to visit Hué. Moreover, Gia Long declined presents from the French monarch Louis XVIII, ostensibly because the transmittal letter was written not in the name of the French king but in that of his foreign minister.[5] French, British, and American visitors were to learn that proper etiquette, based on Chinese models, was an Annamese cultural imperative.

Despite these diplomatic rebuffs, the French government determined to establish a consulate in Cochin China. In 1820 it designated Chaigneau, who had returned to France on leave the previous year, to be concurrently French consul at Hué and French (diplomatic) agent at the court of the ruler of Annam. He was specifically charged with negotiating a commercial treaty.

By the time Chaigneau returned to Cochin China in 1821, major political changes had taken place in the Annamese state. Gia Long, his longtime friend and royal benefactor, had died the previous year. The deceased ruler's son and successor, Minh Mang, was less well disposed to the French advisers and their activities in the state. The proposed French consulate was not accepted, as the new ruler preferred to keep French officialdom at arm's length. In any case, Chaigneau's new position meant a conflict of loyalties for him, which would sooner or later have been untenable. On the one hand, he continued to be a Cochin Chinese contract employee, from which he derived mandarin status and financial perquisites; on the other, he would now also have to serve as a French official. His credibility in Cochin Chinese circles, always somewhat suspect, inevitably eroded as he reappeared on the Annamese scene in a dual capacity. Soon thereafter he left Cochin China permanently and returned to his native land.

Some years later, in 1825, Emperor Minh Mang refused to receive Henri Baron de Bougainville, a French naval captain commanding the frigate *Thetis,* when his vessel put into Turan Bay. Once again, as with his father and predecessor, Minh Mang politely but firmly refused gifts from the French king.

Despite the reiterated snub, the French government once again decided to attempt to open a consulate in Hué, largely at the urging of Balguerie, Sarget et Cie, whose commercial agency was still in Saigon. Chaigneau had by then left Cochin China; his nephew Eugene was appointed French consul. The Annamese authorities, on Minh Mang's orders, refused to receive young Chaigneau in that official capacity, and in 1829 ordered him to leave the country. Eugene Chaigneau was shipwrecked when leaving Cochin China. In utterly destitute condition, he made his way back to Hué, whence he was rescued two years later by a French naval vessel. With his departure, the French consulate in Cochin China ended.[6]

English Interest

Predictably, perceived French interest in Cochin China aroused British concern. Exaggerated though that perception may have been, it was deeply ingrained and further ensconced when Napoleonic designs against the dominant English position in India were suspected.

The English East India Company, in its quest for Asian markets, had as early as 1800 considered the potential commercial value of Cochin China. In 1803, it had sent John W. Roberts, one of its twelve traders in Canton, to Annam to obtain Cochin Chinese agreement to establish a permanent English representative in Hué. After visiting Hué, the English emissary reported that the Tonkinese and Annamese markets, in the north and south of the country, respectively, offered trade prospects, but warned that chaotic internal conditions in Cochin China, where Nguyen Anh had just returned, would most likely preclude any immediate commercial agreements.

Sent on a second mission to Hué in August 1804, John Roberts was granted an audience with the newly proclaimed emperor, Gia Long, who informed him that English vessels would be received at any Annamese port if normal port charges were paid. The ruler declined to enter into formal arrangements with the English East India Company, contending that his need for foreign products was limited and hardly required a treaty. John Roberts's two missions took place before the appearance of French commercial interests in Cochin China, but at a time when Gia Long had already begun to engage French advisers.[7] Inevitably, in these circumstances, many Britons in India believed that French influence had aborted John Roberts's mission. Perhaps the French advisers may have tried to do so, but there is no evidence that anything but the strong-willed Annamese ruler's own inclinations influenced his decision.

In ensuing years, English firms in India occasionally sold goods to Annamese merchants, but no close or regular trade association developed between the two groups. Indeed, the French propagated a story, which may have been true, that in the early 1800s an English warship had threatened to bombard Turan for unpaid debts allegedly owed by the Cochin Chinese government to the Madras firm of Abbott and Maitland for a cargo of muskets. According to the story, Gia Long was incensed by the threat, which heightened his suspicions of British intentions.[8]

By 1821, French activity in Cochin China seemed to the British in India to have reached disturbing proportions. The governor general of India and president of the English East India Company, the Marquis of Hastings, determined to renew efforts to obtain formal commercial arrangements with Cochin China. Dr. John Crawfurd, a long-time employee of the East India Company, or what was colloquially called the "John Company," was designated as special envoy for this purpose. His choice seemed eminently wise. Crawfurd had extensive experience in India and Southeast Asia. He had spent five years in the Bengal Medical Service, had served elsewhere in Indian posts, and was a keen observer as well as a distinguished historian and naturalist.

Arriving at Hué on September 25, 1821, after a brief visit to Saigon, Crawfurd was received with manifest suspicion. He was refused an audience with Minh Mang, who also declined to receive presents sent by the governor general of India on the grounds that Crawfurd was not formally accredited by the king of England. Moreover, it was contended, the governor general's letter to Minh Mang had been inappropriately written and was contrary to Annamese custom. Although Lord Hastings's missive was addressed to "His Majesty, the Emperor of Cochin China," local Annamese officials complained that its formulation failed adequately to express expected "profound respect and esteem" for their exalted sovereign.

Textual alterations in the letter were demanded, which Crawfurd agreed to make, and both Chinese and Portuguese translations of the governor general's letter had to be provided. Equally unacceptable, Crawfurd was told, were references in the letter to Kamboja (Cambodia) and Laos. These ethnically different areas, parts of which had been conquered by Gia Long, were regarded by the haughty Annamese as utterly insignificant and therefore unmentionable, servile fiefdoms. Crawfurd spent a good deal of time endeavoring to craft an acceptable and sufficiently humble text that would satisfy Cochin Chinese mandarins.

Even after the correspondence problems had been resolved, the Cochin Chinese informed Crawfurd, as they had the French, that a commercial treaty was superfluous. They ultimately agreed, nevertheless, that English ships might trade at Annamese ports on the same basis as the Chinese and the French were allowed to do. Subsequently, ports in Tonkin and Cambodia were withdrawn from this concession, allegedly on the direct insistence of the emperor.[9] In fact, an American ship captain who had visited Cochin China some months before Crawfurd arrived asserted that the Cochin Chinese ruler, after conquering Cambodia, had deliberately forbidden foreign commerce with that entity in an attempt to make Saigon the entrepôt for all of southern Annam.[10]

Cultural rigidity, in the form of allegedly immutable indigenous custom, added to Crawfurd's difficulties. Since the governor general's presents for the emperor had been declined, Crawfurd insisted he could not appropriately receive proffered royal presents for his superior. Only minor presents offered to Crawfurd and members of the mission, in their personal capacities, could be accepted. This gave new umbrage to Cochin Chinese officials. They now announced that, in view of Crawfurd's refusal to accept royal presents for the governor general, a letter that the emperor had prepared for the Marquis of Hastings would have to be cancelled. They argued that Crawfurd's refusal to accept the gifts for the governor general, even though that dignitary was considered inferior to the emperor, grossly breached Annamese etiquette.

Crawfurd eventually agreed to take the royal presents to Bengal, if the emperor wished, but warned that he could not guarantee they would be accepted, a fresh protocol slight that the Cochin Chinese authorities considered unacceptable. The presents were withdrawn. Nonetheless, an official document, signed and sealed by the "mandarin of elephants," who functioned as a kind of foreign minister, was ultimately delivered to Crawfurd shortly before the English envoy's departure on September 25. It confirmed permission for English ships to visit Saigon, Han, Faito (Hoi An), and Turan.[11]

Crawfurd failed to obtain a formal commercial agreement, but he did manage to secure probably as much as was possible under the prevailing circumstances. Minh Mang was not prepared to allow broader English or any other foreign commerce, other than Chinese, into the country. Crawfurd was convinced that hostile counselors in the ruler's entourage—French, Chinese, and expatriate Indian Muslims—were largely responsible for the turndown.

Early American Interest

In the post-1783 scramble for Far Eastern trading ports, American merchants had shown early, though only sporadic, interest in Cochin China. In May 1803, at about the time the English supercargo John Roberts made his first mission to Cochin China, the Salem brig *Fame,* captained by Jeremiah Briggs, anchored in Turan Bay. She is believed to be the first American vessel to have visited Cochin China.

Finding trade prospects at Turan poor, Briggs took local officials' suggestions that he proceed to Hué and see the new ruler to explore longer-term commercial prospects with Annam. Briggs was particularly interested in purchasing sugar. At Hué, Briggs stayed for three days at the home of a French naval commander in the employ of the Annamese. The Frenchman told Briggs that he had never heard of a foreign ship loading a cargo of sugar on the Turan coast, and that he doubted that it was possible to do so.

Although Briggs did not meet with the emperor, he did, through the Frenchman's good offices, obtain a royal "passport" allowing the American captain to trade anywhere along the Cochin China coast. Emperor Gia Long, Briggs was told, had initially been "very jealous" and had not wished to grant any such privilege, lest doing so somehow strengthen his internal enemies, but he had finally relented.

The emperor subsequently sent a French priest to Briggs to point out on an old map in the cleric's possession where the United States was located and its boundaries. The priest, who had been in Annam for twenty-eight years, professed total ignorance of America. Returning to his ship, Briggs sailed along the Cochin China coast but made no effort to trade. He succeeded in preparing a large-scale map of the coast, which has unfortunately been lost.[12]

No records exist for fifteen years thereafter of another American vessel touching at an Annamese port. Then, in 1819, several vessels did so. In the spring of that year, the Salem brig *Beverly*, commandeered by John Gardner, called first at Vung Tau and then at Turan. Observing two French vessels already at Turan, the *Beverly*, after lying for a day in Turan Bay without anchoring, proceeded to Manila. Captain Gardner concluded that with two French ships already there, trade prospects were poor.

Two months later, in early June 1819, Captain John White of Marblehead, Massachusetts, master of the Salem brig *Franklin*, arrived at Vung Tau with the intention of proceeding up the Don Nai River to Saigon. White had prepared himself for the venture by reading a description of China authored by the aforementioned British reverend Dr. Robert Morrison of Canton and Macao, and he also scoured reports of unnamed, earlier French writers on Cochin China. These accounts, White's experience soon demonstrated, were wrong, or at the very least no longer valid.

His request for a pilot was refused by local officials, who demanded lists of the ship's company, number of guns, cargo, and the vessel's draft of water. The vessel was ordered to proceed to a more observable site at Can Gio, some seven miles upstream, but permission to proceed to Saigon continued to be denied. In view of the seeming intransigence of local officials, the *Franklin* sailed to Turan, where White was informed by local mandarins that the ruler, still Gia Long, had shortly before left Hué to lead another military campaign in Tonkin. Since the Cochin Chinese officials at Turan also seemed indisposed or unable to facilitate his trade objectives in the emperor's absence, White decided to proceed to Manila.

Shortly after the *Franklin*'s arrival in Manila, a second American vessel, the Salem ship *Marmion*, with Oliver Blanchard as master, put into port. The *Marmion*, it transpired, had arrived at Vung Tau shortly after the *Franklin*'s departure. Although she too had been re-fused a pilot, a ship's officer, Putnam, and a crewmember had been allowed to take a small boat upstream to Saigon. Finding trading conditions temporarily unpropitious, Blanchard likewise decided to proceed to Manila. Meeting there, the two Salem captains agreed to return to Vung Tau together for mutual protection and support, and to renew their efforts to be allowed to proceed up the Dong Nai River to Saigon.

The *Franklin* and *Marmion* returned to Vung Tau in late September 1819. There they learned that still another American vessel, the Salem ship *Aurora*, had recently visited but had then proceeded to Turan. Attempts to trade at Turan had been unsuccessful, so *Aurora*'s shipmaster, Robert Gould, had also opted to sail to Manila.

At Vung Tau, White and Blanchard requested a pilot to proceed upriver to Saigon. Local officials once again refused their request. Despite this refusal, Annamese port officials demanded a $100 anchorage fee for each vessel, which the American captains regarded as exorbitant and refused to pay. A demand that the ships' carronades (short, smoothbore cannons) be landed was likewise rejected.

As these issues were being debated, the two shipmasters decided to try to obtain permission for the vessels to go to Saigon. To that end, they sent Putnam—the officer from the *Marmion* who had been allowed some months earlier to travel upriver—to Saigon. Putnam's mission was successful. Permission was granted for the ships to enter that riverine port. Before anchors could be weighed, however, the Annamese "commissioner of marine," as White calls him, boarded the ship to demand crew lists, cargo lists, and an inventory of armaments aboard the vessels. It was deemed prudent to provide the thirteen copies of the data that the commissioner demanded. Four would be sent to the ruler in Hué, one to the viceroy in Saigon, and the rest were for distribution to other concerned madarins.[13]

This done, the two vessels proceeded upriver to Saigon. The *Franklin* arrived first on October 7, 1819, thereby gaining the distinction of being the first American ship to visit Saigon. The *Marmion*, delayed by adverse river currents, arrived in Saigon a day later. Once the two ships were anchored, a meeting with the acting viceroy was requested to enable the ships' captains to explain their purpose. Although they were welcomed, they first needed to come to agreement with lower-ranking officials on appropriate etiquette to be followed before the meeting with the acting viceroy could take place. As usual, Cochin Chinese and American customs were at variance, but a protocol compromise was reached. The two American captains, it was agreed, would render no more than three bows to the acting viceroy. There would be no kowtowing.

At the meeting on October 9, the captains offered the acting viceroy the customary presents and requested more moderate port charges. The presents were accepted, but the Annamese official insisted on deferring discussion of port charges for a future meeting. White observed that Cochin Chinese port charges were based on ship measurements; he and Blanchard urged that those charges be reduced.

At a second meeting with the American captains, the acting viceroy insisted that the laws of the country were immutable, but informed his visitors that he planned to send official word to the ruler in Hué about the vessels' arrival. Did they wish to send a present to the ruler? White and Blanchard readily agreed to do so, and also obtained permission to transmit a letter to the French mandarin Vannier (who they wrongly understood was the ruler's admiral), requesting his good offices to obtain a reduction of port charges and to facilitate their trading efforts.

While awaiting replies from Hué, the two captains busied themselves with obtaining information on Cochin China. Foreign commerce, they discovered, was virtually at a standstill. Only three Chinese junks had visited Saigon in the previous year. Two French ships, *La Paix* and *Henri*, the vessels that Captain Gould had earlier seen at Turan Bay, were still there. In five months, they had loaded only half cargos of sugar and some raw silk. Local merchants, including those engaged in the sugar trade, were described as rapacious. White and Blanchard would come to the same conclusion as they attempted to make sugar purchases from Saigon brokers. Appeals to the acting viceroy proved fruitless.

Other Annamese government officials were equally intransigent. Specie in the form of Spanish silver dollars, White and Blanchard were told, would be acceptable for payment of port charges, but at a locally set rate rather than at par. Believing this to be unfair, the two captains procured local copper currency, *sepecks*, to pay the official charges Their efforts to circumvent the bureaucracy failed. Local customs officials and guards colluded to make it utterly disadvantageous for them to pay in the indigenous currency. In the end, Spanish dollars had to be paid, but the Cochin Chinese officials accepted them only at a considerable discount.

The return of the viceroy to Saigon in December offered transitory hope to the American captains that their complaints might now be addressed. White and Blanchard immediately obtained an audience with the returned viceroy and proffered the customary presents. Their appeal for help, however, while met with polite sympathy, elicited the bland response that the viceroy could not interfere in local custom.

A reply from Vannier to White's earlier letter, received at about the same time of the meeting with the viceroy, asserted that the emperor had reduced anchorage charges the previous year and that presents were to be included with whatever amount was levied on visiting ships. Vannier added that the ruler, Gia Long, was ill and, in any case, rarely received foreign visitors. The viceroy, when apprised of Vannier's assertion that port charges had been reduced by the ruler, denied that he had ever received such royal instructions. He reiterated that he was required to adhere rigidly to legal requirements.[14] There was no recourse to higher authority.

By January 1820, the two American ship captains had experienced their fill of frustrations. Their repeated appeals having fallen on deaf official ears, they had no choice but to make the best arrangements they could with local sugar brokers. Despite lengthy negotiations, they could load no more than 1,700 Cochin Chinese piculs—a *picul* is an Asian unit of weight equivalent to approximately 60 kilograms—of sugar, less than half a cargo for each ship, at what they regarded as exorbitant prices. No more sugar was available locally, it was claimed, and a new crop would not be in until March. Moreover, the ruler had already preempted the larger portion of the new crop, as was his imperial prerogative. Additionally, incidents of harassment of the Americans were increasing, and crew members were often stoned by local youths, as was the house ashore in which White and Blanchard lived.

Eventually, ship measurement charges, together with numerous presents to all and sundry in the local mandarin hierarchy, were paid, as Annamese officials had initially demanded. The charges amounted to 7,200 Spanish dollars, a substantial port levy on so small a cargo. The viceroy was adamant that all officials entitled by established custom to receive presents be satisfied.

On January 30, 1820, the day Gia Long died, the *Franklin* and the *Marmion* departed Saigon, their captains and crews indignant over what White called the Annamese "harpies." At Batavia, their next port of call, the *Franklin* loaded the *Marmion*'s cargo of sugar because Captain Blanchard had decided to try to obtain a full cargo at Manila. But at Batavia, White and Blanchard discovered that Cochin Chinese sugar, despite the frustrations and expense they had encountered in Saigon, cost less than Java sugar.[15]

For many years thereafter, largely because of White's account of his visit to Saigon, which was published in Boston in 1823 and circulated among the Salem maritime and mercantile community through the East India Marine Society of Salem, American shipmasters avoided Cochin Chinese ports. Though White self-deprecatingly professed to be an "unlettered seaman,"[16] he clearly stated his intention of challenging what he termed unjustifiably "flattering" French and other reports on the profitability of the Annamese market. Such reports, he acknowledged, may once have been true, but had long since become obsolete. The Cochin Chinese, White had concluded soon after arriving in Turan, "were in many respects but little removed from a state of deplorable barbarism."[17] He persisted in that negative judgment. Most later foreign visitors, Edmund Roberts among them, shared or would come to share his view.

Siam

The kingdom of Siam—Thailand, since 1939—essentially straddles the river basin of the Menam River and its tributaries. Relations with its eastern neighbor, Cochin China, were generally peaceful. Over the centuries, Siam and Cochin China had divided Laos and Cambodia, areas geographically wedged between these two major states, between them. In contrast, Siam's relations with Burma, its western neighbor, were stormy. Siam and Burma regularly contested for hegemony over the minor sultanates of the Malay Peninsula and fought bitter wars with each other.

As early as the thirteenth century, various Thai principalities were already in existence. Persistent hostility between these entities and Burma was aggravated by deep and sharp ethnic differences. By the mid-fourteenth century, a Thai chieftain had established the kingdom of Ayudhya, in the Menam River basin, which endured for two centuries. In the early seventeenth century, however, much of Siam was conquered by the Burmese. Not until 1782 could a Thai prince, Phraya Taksin, after almost fifteen years of fighting, drive out the Burmese invaders and reestablish an independent Siamese political entity. The task completed, he was himself overthrown by one of his generals, Chulalok, who declared himself king, established the Chakri dynasty, and moved his capital southward and across the Menam River to Bangkok.

Styling himself Rama I, the new monarch revived the Thai kingdom and reestablished earlier Theravada Buddhist rites, which had fallen into disuse, as the moral and cultural basis of the state. The new Siamese polity's influence over neighboring Laos and Cambodia was expanded at the expense of Cochin China. When the ruler died in 1809 and was succeeded by his son, Rama II, a period of dynamic internal development ensued. It was marred only by continuing quarrels with the Burmese and, increasingly, with the British in India, especially over the vassal sultan of Kedah, who enjoyed a measure of British support. Siam's relations with the Western world were conditioned largely by growing suspicions of foreign intentions against its territorial integrity and continuing concern over an omnipresent Burmese threat.[18]

Early Siamese Contacts with the West

As early as the sixteenth century, the Portuguese, who under Afonso de Albuquerque had conquered Malacca, began trade with the kingdom of Ayudhya and its neighboring Thai-inhabited areas. In 1608, the Dutch also were permitted to open a factory at Ayudhya. The influence of the Dutch grew when they helped the Siamese monarch suppress a revolt by Japanese expatriates in Ayudhya and, subsequently, when they successfully wrested Malacca from the Portuguese. Tensions soon developed, however, between the Siamese and the Dutch. In 1656, trade disputes led the Dutch to threaten a blockade of the mouth of the Menam River.

This threat prompted the Siamese leadership to look for countervailing Western support, particularly from the French and the English. A French Catholic mission was established in Siam in 1664 by apostolic vicars, in return for help in constructing the fortifications of the capital against a possible Dutch attack. In retaliation, the Dutch implemented their earlier blockade threat, eventually requiring the Siamese ruler to conclude a treaty granting them various monopoly and extraterritorial privileges. In 1673, a French missionary persuaded Louis XIV to send letters to the Siamese monarch proposing the establishment of diplomatic relations. Any initial Thai interest in doing so waned when a Siamese mission sent to France to seek aid never reached its destination. Eight years later, in 1681, the first French trading vessel appeared off Ayudhya.

Concurrently, the French missionary establishment in Siam prevailed upon Constantine Phaulkon, a Greek adventurer who was also a disaffected employee of the English East India Company, to assist in its designs. Phaulkon had endeared himself to the Thai authorities with his denunciation of his erstwhile British employers. Through his intervention, the Siamese monarch was persuaded to send a second diplomatic mission to Paris in 1684, accompanied by French missionaries. After intensive negotiations, first at Versailles and later in Ayudhya, a secret agreement was reached under which more French missionaries would be sent to Siam. It was understood, at least by the French, that they would be appointed to provincial governorships and to military posts.

Three years later, ostensibly to carry out the agreement, a flotilla of six French naval vessels arrived. Two French representatives were aboard, Claude Céberet du Boullay, a director of the French East India Company, and Simon de la Loubère, as well as 500 French troops (1600, according to another source). Marshal Desfarges, who commanded the expedition, announced a change in the original plan.

To the Siamese monarch's distress, Desfarges declared that Bangkok would be occupied along with the commercially promising town of Mergui on the Bay of Bengal. The French threatened force if their demands were not met. A treaty was negotiated in December 1687, under duress, in which extraterritorial privileges were accorded French subjects in Siam, and the French were given the right to build trading posts anywhere in the country. The treaty was substantively similar to the one concluded two years earlier, but the new treaty ceded all islands within a ten-mile radius of Mergui to the French. For all practical purposes, Siam had become a French protectorate.

The Siamese public was outraged, and the French were increasingly viewed as enemies. Phaulkon, the Greek who had helped negotiate the treaty, soon had a falling-out with the French missionaries and military. During the Siamese king's serious illness in 1688, his master of elephants staged a coup d'état and had himself appointed regent. Phaulkon was then swiftly arrested and executed. French forces in Ayudhya and Mergui were quickly beleaguered by angry Siamese and had to negotiate or fight their way out of the country. An effort by Desfarges in the following year to reestablish the French position failed. A French missionary, Father Jachard, managed to arrange a peace with Phraya Phetracha, who had by now declared himself king, but the priest's efforts to reestablish the Franco-Siamese relationship was rebuffed. French missionaries were allowed to remain in Siam, but the monarch had learned his lesson: Europeans should be kept at arm's length.[19]

Siamese Relations with the English

As the English East India Company expanded its influence and control in India, and especially in Bengal, it was inevitable that its political activities would before long clash with those of neighboring Burma and Siam. Initially, however, relations were largely commercial in nature and cordial in tone. In 1612, John Company had established its first factories in Ayudhya and Pattani, but strong Dutch competition caused these posts to be closed ten years later. In 1661, with the direct encouragement of the ruler of Siam, the English factory in Ayudhya was reestablished.[20]

As long as the association remained largely commercial, Anglo-Siamese relations were fairly stable. Jurisdictional disputes nevertheless developed in the latter part of the eighteenth century, particularly over the Malay principality of Kedah. In August 1786, the British formally annexed Penang, a small island off Kedah. Its Muslim ruler was tributary to the king of Siam and, along with other Malay principalities, Penang was required to send the *bunga mas* (gold and silver leaves) triennial tribute to Bangkok to betoken fealty. The Malay sultan's efforts to solicit English assistance were fruitless. The Siamese leadership saw the appeal for British support as treasonable, and in November 1821 a Siamese fleet attacked Kedah, wiped out its Malay defenders, and seized the city.

The ruler barely managed to escape to the nearby British-held Penang Island. Peremptory orders from Siamese leaders that the Kedah sultan appear in Bangkok for trial were ignored, as the British, much to Siamese displeasure, had given him sanctuary and pleaded for his restoration.[21] This seeming British protection of the exiled ruler of Kedah persistently complicated Anglo-Siamese relations. So did the Anglo-Burmese war of 1824–1825. Although the Burmese were bitter enemies of the Siamese, the Thais closely observed the course of the war and factored its progress into their relations with the British.

These events formed the backdrop of the diplomatic mission sent by the governor general of India, the Marquis of Hastings, to Bangkok in 1825. The mission was headed by John Crawfurd, who, as mentioned before, was also tasked with negotiating a commercial agreement with neighboring Cochin China. Siam was his initial negotiating stop.

The Crawfurd Mission

On March 24, 1825, arriving off the mouth of the Menam River, Crawfurd sent a communication announcing his arrival to the *phra khlang*, the Siamese minister of finance, who was also responsible for dealings with foreigners. The *phra khlang* ranked fourth in the cabinet of the Siamese governmental hierarchy at that time. For the next three months, Crawfurd would be attempting to negotiate a commercial treaty with suspicious Siamese authorities.

A message from the district prefect of Paknam, located some two miles north of the mouth of the Menam River, welcomed Crawfurd, but asked that the ship's guns be landed before the vessel proceeded upriver—such was the custom of the land for visiting foreign vessels. Crawfurd protested against this requirement. Not until countermanding orders were received from Bangkok was the demand dropped and the vessel allowed to sail upriver to Bangkok. The prefect of Paknam also inquired what presents had been brought for the king, Rama II.[22]

To ensure that the appropriate forms were followed, the *phra khlang* sent a message to Bangkok asking that the governor general's letter to the king be delivered to Siamese government officers before it was presented to the ruler. The shape and quality of paper, the envelope, and all related matters, he emphasized, had to conform to local custom. The letter could not be personally presented to the exalted king by the envoy, but would be produced at the audience. At that time a Siamese translation would be read in the presence of the king. Crawfurd had no choice but to acquiesce.

The governor general's letter was placed in a gold vase provided by the Siamese and was ceremoniously saluted. The vase was then placed under a state umbrella on the boat that would take it to the minister's residence.[23] Such honors, Crawfurd discovered, were rendered in Siam to official documents rather than to the bearers of such missives. The governor general's presents for the king were also landed, at the court's request, to allow them to be examined and evaluated. A house ashore was made available to Crawfurd and his party.

After appropriate protocol arrangements had been agreed upon, a half-hour audience with the king took place on April 8. Three bows and obeisances were rendered rather than the customary prostrations. The king asked a series of perfunctory questions, and indicated that firearms were what Siam mainly wanted from the British. Crawfurd and his party were then shown the white elephants in the king's palace.[24]

In a subsequent talk with the minister, Crawfurd was asked whether the king of England had been or would be officially informed of his mission. Would the king of England then send a letter to the king of Siam? Although he had been told that the governor general of India had been delegated royal authority, Crawfurd explained that, if a letter from the king of England was wanted, one would doubtless be sent. The Siamese government, as a matter of pride, was wary of conducting official intercourse with the government of India or the East India Company, both of which it regarded as inferiors, and sought direct communication between sovereign equals.[25]

Negotiations with the *phra khlang* did not begin until April 17, when Crawfurd explained that the governor general hoped that Siamese levies on European goods would be lowered and that free and fair trade would be allowed for both sides. For his part, the Siamese minister indicated that he hoped more English vessels would visit Siam, and he sought specific agreement that at least four ships would be sent each year. To Crawfurd's rejoinder that conditions of trade would largely determine the number of ships that might visit, the *phra khlang* declared that Siam had two years earlier made a commercial treaty with the Portuguese that reduced import duties from 8 to 6 percent. Since then, however, no Portuguese ships had come, raising Siamese doubts about the value of commercial treaties. Instead of a treaty, the *phra khlang* indicated, a letter would be prepared for the governor general stating that "concessions" for English commerce had been explained to Crawfurd. The Siamese minister hoped this would suffice. Crawfurd pressed for a written agreement, setting forth the conditions applicable to English vessels visiting Siamese ports.[26]

Five days later, Crawfurd had further occasion to explain to the *phra khlang* the kind of commercial treaty that was sought: free and fair trade, fixed import and export duties and related charges, and security for British subjects who might come to Siam for trade and their properties. Moreover, since the Portuguese—and, Crawfurd wrongly believed, also the Americans—had recently obtained permission to establish a resident commercial agent in Siam, Crawfurd proposed that the English be allowed to do the same. The *phra khlang* stiffly responded that British subjects, like all others, were subject to the laws of Siam. Crawfurd did not demur.[27]

Negotiations were not helped when a vessel belonging to the king of Siam arrived in early May from Calcutta, by way of the Dutch settlement on Riau Island, near Singapore. At Riau, the Dutch had forced the Siamese captain to pay a balance claimed to be due for certain charges levied against Dutch vessels that had visited Bangkok in 1824. The royal venture was unprofitable, and

Crawfurd doubted that the Siamese would send a ship to Bengal anytime soon.[28]

It quickly became clear to Crawfurd that, despite the *phra khlang*'s seeming cordiality, Siamese in high places harbored deep suspicions of British motives. His objectives, he came to realize, were likely to be unattainable. Moreover, the arbitrary imprisonment of the Portuguese consul, Carlos Manuel da Silveira, persuaded him not to press for a British resident commercial agent.[29] There was no way of assuring the security of any English representative, he concluded. Given prevailing customs in Siam, the risk of such an agent suffering indignities at the hands of the Thai authorities was too great.

Crawfurd had given the *phra khlang* a Siamese translation of a draft commercial treaty. Although most points seemed to meet with assent initially, a provision for free and fair trade soon raised Siamese objections. The king, the *phra khlang* insisted, had the right of commercial preemption and had enjoyed it from time immemorial. Indeed, the *phra khlang* claimed, the very existence of that royal prerogative ensured the foreign merchant a fair return.[30] This was pure sophistry.

The appearance of an English brig, the *Phoenix*, from Calcutta in early May underscored the arbitrariness of the Siamese officials. The assurances given to Crawfurd—import duties would be reduced from 8 to 6 percent, and the ship's cargo could be freely sold—evaporated as soon as the ship anchored. The *phra khlang* had secretly sent orders forbidding all persons from dealing with the ship's master under penalty of a fine or imprisonment. Crawfurd's protest elicited the bland response that only when the number of English ships visiting Siam had reached five could duties be reduced.[31]

At his final interview with the *phra khlang* on the evening of May 26, Crawfurd reiterated his arguments for more favorable trade terms that would be of mutual benefit. Unfortunately, he was told, it was difficult to change the laws of the land. Two days later, Crawfurd was shown two draft letters in answer to the governor general's missive and asked to decide which should be sent. One was from the *phra khlang* to the governor general, the other from the *phra khlang*'s deputy to the secretary of the Indian government.

The Siamese had asserted that a direct reply from the king to the governor general was inappropriate, yet Crawfurd had let it be known that any letter from a Siamese minister to the governor general would, from a British point of view, be inappropriate. Hence, he chose the letter from the *phra khlang*'s deputy addressed to the secretary of the Indian government.[32]

A third document, from the Siamese superintendent of customs to Crawfurd, stipulated unlimited admission of English ships to Siamese ports and a reduction of import duties from 8 to 6 percent once the number of English vessels visiting Siamese ports each year had reached five. Crawfurd requested that import duties be lowered before five ships arrived, and he was assured that they would be reduced. The English envoy placed no weight on this oral acquiescence, however.

When nine days later Crawfurd finally received the promised Siamese commercial treaty document, the original draft had once again been altered. There was indeed a stipulation for free trade, but the reference to import duty reduction had been dropped. Crawfurd had no choice but to agree to the document as written. When the treaty and the reply to the governor general's letter were finally given to him on June 12, even the provision for free trade had been removed. The final form of the letter indicated that English ships, after landing their guns at Paknam, might proceed to Bangkok to trade and that customs would be no different than they had been.[33]

During his stay in Bangkok, Crawfurd also made several attempts to persuade the Siamese authorities to forgive the exiled sultan of Kedah. This, the *phra khlang* declared, was utterly impossible—the sultan had betrayed his Siamese overlord and had to surrender himself for trial and punishment.[34] Compromise on this score was impossible.

Crawfurd left in early August. His long mission had produced few results. He was convinced that local officials and merchants, and Chinese and Chuliahs (expatriate Indian Muslims) in Siamese employ, had worked against the success of the mission. He would be severely criticized by the governor of Bengal for his handling of the mission, but was lauded by the governor general in Calcutta. It would be left for Major Henry Burney, a longtime member of the

Indian military seconded to the Political Service, to make a new attempt to obtain a treaty with Siam.

The Burney Mission

Burney arrived at Bangkok aboard the brig *Phoenix* in early December 1825 and was ceremoniously received.[35] Developments in the previous five years made his mission more political than economic. With the outbreak of the bloody Anglo-Burmese war in 1824, the English in India had for a time hoped to obtain Siamese military support against Burma. To get it, the Supreme Government in Calcutta intimated a willingness to compromise on the Siamese demand for the extradition of the fugitive sultan of Kedah.

By the time Burney arrived in Siam, however, British military successes in Burma had caused the scope of his mission to be altered. He was now instructed to congratulate the new king, Rama III, on his accession to the throne and to reassure the Siamese leadership that they had nothing to fear from British military operations in Burma. No suggestion of English support for the reinstatement of the sultan of Kedah was to be made, other than a promise that, if the ruler were restored, the British would guarantee his triennial tribute to the king of Siam. Improvement of regulations for British trade with Siam was also sought.[36]

Burney spent almost six months in Bangkok discussing outstanding issues with the *phra khlang* and his subordinates. During that period, he was twice granted an audience with the king. The first meeting, formal in character, took place on December 16, shortly after Burney's arrival; a more informal meeting was held six months later, on June 16.[37]

In preliminary talks with Siamese officials, Burney asked for the immediate removal of all local impediments to trade. In British-controlled territories, he noted, Siamese ships paid no duties, whereas Siamese trade regulations discriminated against visiting foreigners. Even the Chinese paid no more than a simple ship measurement fee. The Portuguese paid only a 6 percent import duty. In contrast, the English (and others) paid 8 percent. In addition, they were arbitrarily charged excessive ancillary duties, depending on the size of the vessel, along with high export charges and special port charges at Paknam. They were likewise required to pay for vast numbers of customs clerks, whose nominal task was to weigh imported goods, but few of whom ever appeared at the custom-house to perform their duties.

The English wanted no particular or exclusive privileges, simply fixed duties and the right to buy and sell goods freely. It was the *phra khlang*'s expatriate Indian Muslim secretaries, the Chuliahs, Burney charged, who capriciously exploited British vessels. In place of prescribed ship-measurement charges, Burney proposed the adoption of the Chinese method of including anchorage and port dues, presents, and any import or export duties in a single comprehensive arrival fee. An aggregate levy of 1,500 ticals per fathom for the breadth of the vessel was reasonable, he suggested. Visiting merchants should then be free to buy and sell when and to whom they pleased. Customs-house weighers should be paid only for those amounts they actually weighed. Only powder and shot, not ship's guns, should be landed at Paknam by visiting vessels. Finally, Burney sought better treatment for those British subjects living in Siam who had had become debtors.[38] On March 29, he had a short draft treaty of fifteen articles incorporating his commercial and political proposals delivered to the *phra khlang*.[39]

For the next seven weeks, the Siamese ministers conferred about Burney's draft treaty. Arduous negotiations began on May 14, conducted in seven meetings with the ministers, the last of which was held on June 16. Although political issues were the primary focus of the talks, the Siamese negotiators considered Burney's proposal of 1,500 ticals on ship measurements to be too great a reduction. Burney ultimately agreed to 1,700 ticals for a vessel flying the British flag and bringing import cargo, and 1,500 ticals when such a vessel carried only specie. British subjects resident in or visiting Siam, the Thai ministers insisted, were to be subject to Siamese law. Although Burney obtained agreement that ships' officers and merchants were not to be subject to flogging, ordinary sailors and lascars could still be whipped or jailed. A general provision that English merchants could buy and sell freely was retained, but its vaguely worded text allowed diverse interpretations.[40]

The treaty, it was decided, should be written in three columns in Siamese, English, and Malay, with the seals of the ministers and

Burney appended to each column. Before signature and sealing could take place, discussions were renewed about whether it was appropriate for the king of Siam to conclude a treaty with the English East India Company, which lacked sovereignty. The Siamese eventually swallowed their doubts. With these and other minor points resolved, the document was formally sealed by six Siamese ministers and Burney on July 8. The treaty was subject to ratification by both sides.[41]

Although the governor of Prince of Wales Island criticized Burney's treaty on the grounds that it failed to protect the rights of the sultan of Kedah, the governor general in Calcutta approved it. A formal treaty of sorts, including commercial provisions, now existed between a European state and Siam. As Roberts would learn, the commercial parameters of Burney's treaty would constrain the scope of his negotiations.

Early American Experience with Siam

The earliest American commercial intercourse with Siam is obscure. With the rapid increase of American trade with both Canton and Calcutta in the early 1800s, it can be assumed that American masters and supercargoes soon showed an interest in Siam. Just when the first commercial vessel flying the American flag arrived at Bangkok is unrecorded, but circumstantial evidence suggests that it was somewhere around 1819. Extensive Salem ship records make no mention of voyages to Bangkok until much later, yet both Crawfurd and Burney refer to contemporary American activities in Siam. In his negotiations with Crawfurd, the *phra khlang* implied that various American vessels had already visited Bangkok, once noting that when Americans drank a toast to the king of Siam, they gave three cheers for the ruler.[42] The British, he pointedly observed, did not do so. Visiting Americans, the *phra khlang* also recounted, had encouraged the Siamese to grow coffee.[43] Their advice, if indeed given, was ignored. Crawfurd somehow also inferred that a Siamese promise had been given to Americans to establish a commercial residency in Bangkok.[44] This was not the case.

Moreover, on May 20, while Crawfurd was in Bangkok, the master of the Salem brig *Aurora*, Robert Gould, arrived in Bangkok.

His vessel had anchored off the bar of the Menam River. He had come for a small quantity of sugar to fill out his cargo. Unacquainted with Siamese business practices, Gould expressed the hope that his vessel might be able to leave in four or five days. He called on the *phra khlang* while that official was engaged in treaty talks with the English envoy.

In Crawfurd's presence, and clearly for the British envoy's benefit, the *phra khlang* pointedly stated that the Americans brought the Siamese what they most wanted, plenty of firearms and specie, and loaded cargos of sugar and other local produce. He claimed that he expected eight or ten American ships to arrive that year. Although Crawfurd considered this estimate fatuous, he concluded that the Siamese in fact found American trade "lucrative." In his view, this was largely because the Siamese dictated their own terms for such trade. Crawfurd caustically commented that the *phra khlang*, despite his optimism about American trade, had on another occasion expressed disappointment that "few or none" of the American vessels that had visited Siam in the past ever seemed to return.[45]

Like previous American shipmasters who had come to Bangkok, Gould was to learn Siamese commercial practices the hard way. The *Aurora* was detained in Siam for almost six weeks. The captain, although needing only a small amount of sugar and having paid for it in specie ("ready money"), had to endure "much vexation and imposition" from local officials before the cargo he had been promised was finally provided.[46]

Four years later, when Burney arrived, the situation remained unchanged. Burney, in suggesting commercial reform to the *phra khlang*, pointed out that because of the constant delays imposed on visiting foreign ships, many American as well as British traders left Bangkok determined never to return. He had learned that an American ship captain (unnamed) who had recently visited Bangkok had departed in a state of high dudgeon, averring he would tell all of his maritime colleagues about the "misconduct" of the Siamese officers as obstacles to free commerce.[47] As the image of Bangkok as an unpromising commercial port spread, American ship visits, always few in number, became increasingly sporadic. By the time Edmund Roberts arrived in Bangkok in February 1833, no American ship had visited there for the previous two years.[48]

If visiting American shipmasters and supercargoes railed against what they perceived as Siamese rapacity and dilatoriness, a small interdenominational Christian missionary establishment in Siam, including Americans, stoically accepted local hardships and quietly pursued its work. The first such American missionary, David Abeel, who belonged to the Dutch Reformed Church, had come to Bangkok in the late 1820s and had joined with English (Anglican) and Prussian (Lutheran) fellow missionaries in the hope of proselytizing among the Buddhist and Muslim peoples of Siam.

Their hopes almost died aborning.[49] The imprudent zeal of the Prussian, Karl Gützlaff, who within a few days of his arrival distributed large numbers of Christian tracts around Bangkok, aroused the immediate ire of the Siamese authorities and the Buddhist monks. The tracts were collected and burned; the Prussian missionary was ordered expelled. The friendly intercession of a respected English merchant in Bangkok with the *phra khlang* caused the expulsion order to be rescinded, but further distribution of Christian literature was forbidden. A translation of the affronting tract was shown to the king, who reportedly found it unobjectionable but also spiritually dull. Following the incident, Christian missionary efforts had to be conducted warily. Although an occasional Christian tract might still be given out, great circumspection had to be exercised in doing so. Instead, apart from Christian services unobtrusively held at the missionaries' cottage, considerable emphasis was placed on mission medical work. Badly needed in Siam, this missionary service was much appreciated. Abeel, in particular, earned high indigenous respect. He was not a trained doctor, but his medical knowledge was sufficient to deal with basic medical problems.

By the time Roberts appeared, Abeel and his English and Prussian colleagues had left.[50] In March 1833 the Reverend John Taylor Jones, a Baptist missionary, arrived in Bangkok with his wife and child and settled into what had come to be the missionary cottage. He had spent a number of years in Burma, but this did not seem to disturb the Siamese authorities.

Although Roberts extended hospitality to the missionary and his family until their cottage was habitable, he wisely made no special effort to commend Jones to the Siamese authorities. Doing so would simply have aroused suspicions that the American missionary enjoyed some kind of official status. The English merchant in Bangkok who had befriended other missionaries introduced Jones to the *phra khlang*, who reportedly received him well.[51] In a modest way, the respect that Abeel had enjoyed enhanced the American image in Siam, despite the paucity of local knowledge about the United States. Hardly surprisingly, however, the American missionaries would continue to find themselves the objects of local suspicion.

4

Abortive Talks in Cochin China

Doubtless much to the relief of Chinese officialdom, the *Peacock* left Lintin on December 29, 1832. Still without her escort, the vessel made for Turan Bay on the northern coast of Cochin China. This was the nearest point to Hué, the capital and residence of the emperor, where Roberts hoped to conduct treaty negotiations. Unexpectedly strong northeastern winds and currents in the South China Sea sent the ship southward beyond Turan Bay; ultimately, Geisinger had to put into the combined harbor of Xuan Dai, Vung Chao, and Vung Lam in the southern province of Phu Yen, where the *Peacock* dropped anchor on January 5, 1833. From there, Roberts dealt with astonished, distrustful, and hidebound officials of various grades in the hierarchical Annamese bureaucracy for the next six weeks.

Roberts, unknowledgeable of Southeast Asia, had sought to prepare himself for his negotiations with Cochin China and Siam. In addition to talking with the Reverend Robert Morrison of Canton, and obtaining that missionary's confidential letter of advice—which Roberts carried with him—he had examined Shillaber's pertinent reports. Roberts's library was later found to include White's book on his Annamese experiences, which the emissary had presumably read. There is no indication that Roberts and White had met before the *Peacock*'s departure from the United States. Since Roberts's mission was to be secret, this is scarcely surprising. As Roberts's frequent references in his official reports make clear, he had also carefully studied Crawfurd's published account of the British envoy's missions to Cochin China and Siam. Roberts was determined to avoid what he regarded as mistakes made and indignities accepted by Crawfurd in dealing with Asian interlocutors. In fact, he carried a copy of Crawfurd's published account with him, and both he and John Morrison sometimes cited it and showed pages to Annamese officials in support of their contentions. The Cochin Chinese were unimpressed.

Attempts to Satisfy Local Annamese Officials

The unexpected arrival of a strange vessel at Vung Lam, where foreign ships were rarely seen, puzzled and worried local Annamese officials. In the afternoon of June 5, the "assistant keeper" of the village of Vung Lam boarded the *Peacock* to inquire about the purpose of the vessel's visit. Was she on public business or had she come to trade? The exchange was conducted in part through John Morrison, orally, since the boarding official spoke some Cantonese Chinese, and in part through written Chinese ideographs—hardly conducive to effective mutual comprehension. The official was informed that the *Peacock* was a ship of war; a special envoy sent by the president of the United States was aboard, carrying a letter for the "king" of Cochin China. The American envoy wished to proceed as soon as possible, overland, to the capital to deliver the letter in person to the ruler.

Nonplussed and possessing no authority, the Annamese junior official asked for something in writing that he could present to his superiors. No explanatory note had been prepared, so he was grandly informed that the special envoy would write a letter to the capital to announce his arrival and to request an audience with the king. The local functionary's broad hint that the vessel could in three or four days sail north to the vicinity of Hué was, according to Roberts, inadvertently ignored. Instead, Roberts and his private secretary, Morrison, sought information from the assistant keeper about the structure of the Cochin Chinese regional and national governmental system. The official, at his request, was told the name of the envoy and the number of men aboard the ship. Arrangements were also made for the *Peacock* to exchange a thirteen-gun salute with the fort at Xuan Dai.[1]

Toward evening of the following day, a large party of Annamese officials, sent by the commandant at Xuan Dai, who ranked above the visitor of the previous day, boarded the *Peacock*. They were accompanied by two Chinese interpreters, both of whom spoke the Mandarin and the Cantonese dialects. This somewhat facilitated direct communication, but written Chinese ideographic exchanges were frequently required throughout the protracted talks. The new visitors stated that two officers of the ninth rank, dispatched by the Annamese provincial authorities of Phu Yen, had arrived earlier in the day. These more senior officials, the group spokesman explained, had sent them to ascertain the ship's origin and purposes.

They, too, were told that the *Peacock* was a U.S. ship of war with a special envoy aboard, charged by the American president with delivering a letter to the king of Cochin China. The envoy wished to proceed to Hué at once and, in the meantime, desired to send a letter to officials in the capital announcing his arrival.

Thus, in response to the Vung Lam officials' request for an explanatory note for their superiors, they were given a memorandum dated January 6, 1833, identifying the ship and her commander, David Geisinger, and Roberts, the special U.S. envoy tasked with delivering the presidential letter to the ruler. The purpose of the mission, the memorandum declared, was to conclude a treaty of friendly intercourse with Cochin China. The vessel had initially been headed for Turan Bay, but adverse weather conditions and currents had necessitated putting into Vung Lam. The ship's crew comprised 166 officers and men. A Portuguese translation was sent with the original English text.[2]

After receiving the memorandum, the Annamese group returned to shore. Asked before leaving if local provisioners could be urged to come out to the ship, they casually responded that the village market was open to all. They showed studied disinterest in encouraging sutler boats to come alongside the *Peacock* to sell provisions. To avoid possible offense, the Annamese were told that some members of the ship's complement planned to go ashore to purchase needed supplies. The Annamese interposed no objections.

The following morning, January 7, the same Vung Lam party once more came aboard, this time accompanied by the two higher-ranking deputies from Phu Yen and their retinues. The newcomers repeated the same questions that had twice before been asked, and they received similar answers. The two deputies were informed that the envoy was even then preparing a letter for the king. In about one hour's time, the missive would be taken ashore by American naval officers. The Annamese functionaries should be prepared to receive the official communication and to forward it immediately to the capital of the province.

When the two deputies inquired whether presents had been brought for the king and asked about the contents of the presidential letter to the ruler, however, Roberts dismissed their questions as "impertinent." Their requests to see the commissions of Roberts and Geisinger and a copy of Roberts's intended letter to the capital were likewise curtly refused. Reiterated queries about presents for the king were again parried. All things considered, the meeting did not go well. When pressed, however, the deputies grudgingly agreed to receive Roberts's letter and to forward it. With that, the Annamese were virtually ordered ashore to prepare to receive Roberts's letter formally.

That afternoon an American naval officer, in full dress uniform, carried Roberts's newly drafted letter ashore. Presented in the English original with a Chinese translation prepared by Morrison, the letter took the form of what Roberts called a "Chinese memorial" from him to the ruler. Dated January 7, 1833, Roberts's letter explained that President Andrew Jackson was anxious to promote friendly intercourse with Cochin China and had for this reason sent the U.S. warship *Peacock*, with Roberts aboard as special envoy, to arrange this. Roberts was the bearer of a presidential letter to the king and was vested with full powers to negotiate with the ruler for the "important objects" that the U.S. government had in view. Weather conditions, it explained, had prevented the *Peacock* from putting into Turan Bay, as originally intended, and had required her instead to enter Vung Lam. Since adverse climatic conditions still prevailed, he had to await the ruler's reply at Vung Lam, where the ship now lay. Folded and sealed, the letter was enclosed in vellum, and the outside wrapper was addressed "To His Majesty, the King of Cochin China."[3] Roberts's account indicates that he and Morrison were uncertain about proper Cochin Chinese correspondence forms. As events were to prove, their ignorance would prove troublesome.

Once the letter was given to the two provincial deputies ashore, and received by them, inquiries were made about onward travel to Hué. The Annamese officials showed a distinct reluctance to answer American queries about the road to Hué and how it might best be traveled. The vague responses offered seemed intended to discourage Roberts from proceeding overland. The officials' reluctance notwithstanding, they were informed that Roberts wished to travel to Hué, accompanied by a party of at least fifteen or sixteen persons and with considerable baggage.

On January 8, a Cochin Chinese Catholic priest unexpectedly boarded the *Peacock*. He explained that the Phu Yen provincial governor, apparently dissatisfied with answers provided thus far, had sent him to inquire whether the strange visitors were Catholics and whether they were French or English. The priest, it developed, had no knowledge of North America. He repeated, almost by rote, the series of questions that had already been asked several times about the mission's purpose.

He was given the same answers. There was a special U.S. presidential envoy aboard who wished to proceed to Hué to have an audience with the king. Twice the priest asked about presents for the king, and twice he was informed that this was a matter the envoy could not discuss. Although assured of the mission's friendly motives in response to his specific query, the priest laughingly observed that a warship coming with peaceful intentions seemed a bit dubious.[4]

While Roberts impatiently awaited a reply to his letter, John Morrison was sent ashore to collect data on the trade of Vung Lam and on the Phu Yen provincial administration. As he gathered information, it became increasingly evident that the continued presence of the *Peacock* in the harbor, especially as word spread that she was a warship, created uneasiness, even hostility, on the part of local villagers. A village official asked that crew members remain on the ship and not come ashore, except to buy provisions in the market. Roberts claimed that although there had been no trouble with the villagers, the village soldiery had indeed become increasingly harassing. Even he, when he once came ashore and was waiting for a boat to return him to the ship, had been almost physically forced to reembark without delay.

Meeting the Mandarins

On January 16, two mandarins from Hué arrived and came aboard ship in state, accompanied by their retinues. Like their predecessors, they asked about the *Peacock*'s nationality. To explain the provenance of the vessel and its mission, Roberts pointed out the U.S. flag to them on a large foreign flag sheet that they had brought with them. The mandarins were probably none the wiser for this identification. Once again, they asked the purpose of the mission, and once more general explanations were offered. When Roberts asked if his letter had arrived in Hué before their departure, they said that it had been received. However, inasmuch as the outside cover had been inappropriately addressed, the minister of commerce and navigation had concluded that he could not transmit it to the king. Their country, they averred, was no longer called Annam, as formerly, but Vietnam. It was ruled not by a king but by an emperor.[5]

Roberts assured them that no disrespect for the ruler had been intended—the error arose entirely from ignorance of proper forms brought about by inadequate intercourse—and asked them how the letter should properly be addressed. They proposed that it be addressed to the minister of commerce and navigation, whom they described as the chief minister, rather than to the ruler. It should request that the minister apprise the ruler of the mission's arrival and purpose. In this connection, they indicated that they had been instructed to examine all correspondence with the Hué authorities to ensure that no inadmissible words or phrases were included. Roberts's letter to the ruler was returned, at the American emissary's request.

The protocol error in addressing Roberts's letter reflected the paucity of American information about Cochin China. Roberts, and certainly Morrison, could have ascertained the correct form of address for the ruler before the letter was sent. The State Department, too, had sent Roberts what it understood to be the proper forms of address for Asian potentates on the itinerary, but that information was also in error. Annam was, of course, still known as such, although its formal designation and that of its ruler had changed thirty years earlier.[6]

The Hué mandarins repeated previous queries about the contents of the president's letter and the "particular and specific" objects of the special envoy's mission. Roberts responded that the letter introduced him, as envoy, to the emperor, and stated that he was prepared to negotiate "particular objects" of his mission once he had arrived in Hué. One general object, a treaty of "friendly intercourse," Roberts explained, was inclusive of all others. His reply was clearly considered ambivalent and failed to satisfy his Annamese interlocutors. They repeatedly, even if unavailingly, returned to the subject and sought more detail.

Asked to provide an explicit address for the proposed letter to the minister, the Hué commissioners drafted a short note, which in their view encapsulated the objects of Roberts's mission, as they understood them, and which stylistically conformed to Cochin Chinese linguistic decorum. To Roberts, it was utterly objectionable, servile in its phraseology, and implied disparity between imperial and presidential ranks. Various general expressions contained in the mandarins' draft also annoyed him. One that particularly outraged him was a reference to him as a "petty officer."

The mandarins' draft was summarily rejected. So were their protestations that there was no intention to demean the American side. By now, an irate Roberts had concluded that "truth does not form part of their [Cochin Chinese] creed." He portentously announced that he would write a letter the following day that would be respectful in content but without servility in tone. The Hué commissioners insisted they must see any such letter before it could be forwarded so that any improper words could be expunged. Roberts, despite his annoyance, had no choice but to agree that they might examine his letter, but he insisted that no "material corrections" could be made once a "fair copy" of the revised letter had been prepared. This first session with the mandarins had roiled both sides. To Roberts, the Hué mandarins seemed condescending and insolent; to the Annamese officials, Roberts must have seemed discourteous and demanding. Diverse cultural values virtually assured discordance.

The following day, January 18, the two Hué mandarins again boarded the *Peacock* and presented Roberts and Geisinger with a bullock, a hog, and other foodstuffs. Asked about the designation of the minister to whom they had suggested the letter be sent, they reiterated "minister of commerce and navigation of Cochin China."

That title was therefore inserted in the Chinese copy of the letter. In the English copy, however, it was altered to the "minister for foreign affairs, commerce and navigation." This, they assumed, was the official described by the English envoy Crawfurd twelve years earlier as the "mandarin for strangers."[7]

The redrafted letter, dated January 18, 1833, was shown to the Hué commissioners. After Roberts had agreed to alter a few "trivial" words in the Chinese translation, the commissioners declared the letter to be satisfactory. In the new letter, Roberts informed the minister that President Jackson, desiring to inaugurate friendly intercourse with the emperor of Cochin China, had sent the *Peacock* to the ruler's domain. The president had delegated Roberts to be special envoy "to his majesty's court," with full powers to negotiate the "important objects" that the president had in view. Roberts expressed the hope he might be granted a royal audience as soon as possible. Once more it explained that the ship had intended to go to Turan, but had been compelled by weather conditions to put into Vung Lam. An early reply was requested.[8]

In contrast to the strained atmosphere at the previous meeting, this one was more relaxed. The Hué mandarins even informed Roberts, amiably, that an American, whom they called "Leemesay," was engaged on an Annamese vessel as pilot.[9] The individual whose name Roberts believed to be Lindsay was in fact an Englishman in Annamese employ. He had apparently found it politic to present himself locally as an American, considering Cochin Chinese suspicions of the British. To Roberts, the prospects of getting early permission to proceed to Hué now seemed promising.

Deadlock at Vung Lam

For the next several days as Roberts awaited a reply from Hué, social contacts with the mandarins and local officials continued. On a visit to the ship, they asked questions about the structure of the U.S. government and economy. They showed particular interest in American production of ginseng, about which they appeared to have some knowledge. Earlier inquiries about why the *Peacock* had first visited Canton and why the vessel had spent so much time there were reiterated. In various forms, the matter of presents for the emperor was broached again and again.

Contending that Cochin Chinese ports were already open to foreigners, the Hué commissioners suggested that there was no need for an official mission. To this, Roberts responded that the commercial regulations of Vietnam were unknown to Americans and that, in any case, Annamese charges levied on visiting merchantmen were excessive and inhibited foreign traders from coming. His purpose, he emphatically declared, was to appeal to the emperor, not to them, for redress.[10]

On January 26, a feast was sent aboard the *Peacock,* allegedly on the orders of the emperor. This, the mandarins explained, had been prompted by the receipt of Roberts's letter by the minister in Hué; a reply should be forthcoming in two or three days.

The following day two additional senior officers arrived from Hué. Because the ship rolled heavily in the choppy waters of the bay, they could not board the ship, local officials contended, and Roberts was asked to come ashore to talk with them. Roberts declined, perceiving this request as an indirect effort to cause him to wait on the Annamese officials, but he sent Morrison ashore to deal with the new arrivals.

These newly arrived officials, John Morrison found, were brusquer than the officers with whom the Americans had previously dealt. In response to Morrison's queries, they indicated that the minister in Hué had sent no written reply to Robert's missive, but had instead delegated them to deal with the American envoy. They wished to converse with the envoy and those others who they assumed were associated with the mission. The Cochin Chinese, like the Chinese, seldom sent single envoys, hence their assumption that the official American party must include other members. It was already clear that the officials considered Captain Geisinger to be a member of the official party and, as a naval officer, perhaps more senior, something which did not sit well with Roberts and which he would later formally and categorically refute.

Told by Morrison that Roberts would for protocol reasons not come ashore, the Hué officials expostulated they had been sent to facilitate the mission's objective. For this purpose, the minister had instructed them to inform Roberts that he must have an advance copy of the president's letter to the emperor, along with a Chinese translation, to place before the ruler. Without such complete information, the officials declared, the minister dare not raise the matter with the ruler. Such was Cochin Chinese custom, and strict conformity with custom was essential. Alluding to the phrase "important objects," which Roberts's letter to the minister had indicated President Jackson contemplated, the minister needed clarification before the matter could be presented to the emperor. Morrison responded that letters from chiefs of state were not submitted to advance ministerial or other inspection. The original letter, and a Chinese translation, would be delivered to the emperor once Roberts reached the capital.[11]

In answer to the Hué commissioners' contention that in past Vietnamese intercourse with China, France, and England, copies of letters addressed to the emperor had always first been made available to the minister, Morrison insisted that European and Western practice demanded that letters to chiefs of state initially be presented to the leaders to whom they are addressed. He pointedly recalled that the English envoy, Crawfurd, had complied with the kind of request the Hué deputies were making, but had still been refused a royal audience.

Since Morrison was recognized to be no more than a junior messenger, he was asked to return to the ship and to urge Roberts to provide a copy of the president's letter, along with clarification of the objects of the mission. Presumably on Roberts's instructions, Morrison warned that if these demands were pressed, he feared the mission would soon have to leave. Such demands, he claimed, suggested that the emperor desired no relationship with the United States. Although the Hué commissioners insisted their sole purpose was to facilitate the mission and expressed surprise at the suggestion that the mission might leave, the meeting terminated on a sour note.

That afternoon, after receiving further instructions from Roberts, Morrison again met the Hué officials ashore. The U.S. government, he told them, would not allow compliance with their demands. The presidential letter was already sealed and could not be opened. Either it would be carried to the capital by the envoy, Roberts, or it would be taken back to the United States, where the reason for the envoy's inability to deliver it would be explained. The Hué officials now expressed doubt that a translation of the president's letter really existed. Morrison indignantly asserted that such a translation did indeed exist. The commissioners then asked for some indication of the scope of the president's letter. Morrison said he could not comply with this either, unless they could show written evidence that the ruler desired such an explanatory document. No such written evidence was adduced.

The exchange between Morrison and the Hué commissioners became increasingly acrimonious as each side sought to attribute the prevailing impasse to the other. The Hué officials, still contending that they wished to facilitate the mission, insisted that, on the minister's express instructions, they needed a translation of the president's letter and an explanation of what was meant by "important objects." They could not deviate from their orders. Their requests, they argued, were not unreasonable and were strictly in accord with local custom and precedent. The delay in effecting the mission's purposes, of which Roberts and Morrison complained, was entirely due to the obduracy of the American side, they charged. For his part, Morrison insisted that the presidential letter and an explanation of its contents could be given only to the emperor once an audience for Roberts had been arranged in Hué. Morrison repeated the warning that unless Roberts soon received permission to proceed to Hué, the mission would leave.[12]

On the following morning, January 28, all four Hué commissioners came aboard the *Peacock*. No sooner had they boarded when Roberts confronted them and abruptly asked why they had come. On the previous day, he recalled, they had been categorically informed that neither a translation of the presidential letter nor further clarifications would be given to them. Roberts also seized the occasion to instruct them that they should cease speaking of "two gentlemen" to conduct negotiations for the American side. There was only one envoy, and it was he, Roberts.

Rejecting the officials' rejoinder that their minister required clarification of the mission's objectives before being able to report to the emperor, Roberts angrily observed that the minister was fully aware that the objective of the mission was to establish "friendly intercourse" between the United States and Cochin China. He professed not to comprehend the minister's failure to report this to the emperor. Why, he demanded to know, had no word yet been received from the minister to proceed to Hué or, alternately, to leave the country? Roberts said he considered such conduct "uncivil." In the circumstances, he professed to have concluded that the emperor was unwilling to permit American commerce. If the commissioners had something new to say, fine; if not, he did not wish to rehearse Morrison's observations of the previous day.

Denying any desire to be uncivil, the Hué commissioners insisted that their government wished to treat visiting Americans with "liberality," but voiced concern at what they saw as an appearance of "secrecy" in the envoy's letter to the minister. It was this vagueness, they stated, that had given rise to the request for clarification.

Dismissing their claim as inconsequential, Roberts disparaged the assertion that the minister dared not report to the emperor. The detention of the mission at Vung Lam, as Roberts chose to interpret what was happening, he called "extremely rude." In justification of his position, he observed that Crawfurd had only a few years earlier been upbraided by a Cochin Chinese minister for having shown a provincial governor a letter from the governor general of India to the emperor. The Hué commissioners were shown the page in Crawfurd's published account where the reprimand was recorded. Roberts observed he was strictly following what he understood to be Cochin Chinese precedent. If he now had to return to the United States and report the affronts accorded the mission while at Vung Lam, Cochin China would be universally condemned as an "extremely rude nation." Should permission to proceed to Hué not be received soon, he would be forced to leave, as he still had eight or nine other places to visit in the current year.

The Hué officials responded as they had earlier to Morrison's similar representations. They knew nothing about the Crawfurd incident. They were simply conforming with the customs of the country. Other foreign envoys who had visited Cochin China had made available to the appropriate minister advance copies of translations of official letters to the emperor. They expressed a measure of offense at Roberts's refusal to deal with them when they had been specifically and officially deputed by the minister of commerce and navigation to conduct negotiations.

There had been, they now charged, numerous inconsistencies in the various statements that Roberts and Morrison had made about the presidential letter, the mission's purposes, and related matters. For example, Roberts had earlier stated that the mission had been sent solely to Cochin China; now he spoke of having to visit nine other places. There was something suspicious, they implied, in such conduct. They did not wish the presidential letter opened; they merely wished to know what the U.S. government wanted. Were such things as land on which to build factories or trade privileges sought, for instance?

Sharply denying there had been any contradictions in what he or Morrison had previously said, Roberts asserted that no favors or privileges were being sought. The United States did not build factories abroad. Only friendly intercourse, which embraced commerce for mutual benefit, was desired. In view of what he continued to term the "uncivil" conduct of the minister, however, Roberts now personally warned that he intended to leave shortly. Brushing aside the Hué officials' rejoinder that his obstinacy in refusing to comply with their legitimate requests was responsible for the delay, Roberts blamed the minister for presuming to take the business of the mission into his hands instead of referring it to the emperor. Roberts curtly told the newly arrived Hué officials, who had indicated that they planned to return to the capital in a day or two, that their travel plans were of no concern to him. He would leave when he was ready and, once ready to leave, he would write a letter of protest to the emperor with copies to other royal princes.[13]

As the appropriateness of Roberts's letters was still being discussed, the Hué deputies observed that the envoy's titles should be specified in detail, as were those of the minister. Showing himself up to the occasion, Roberts asked for several pieces of paper and, to the astonishment of his Annamese interlocutors and the amusement of his American hearers, proceeded with all solemnity to list the names of all New Hampshire counties; he would have continued with the names of rivers and cities, had not the deluged scribes asked for a halt. The Cochin Chinese deputies, Roberts recorded with satisfaction, accepted his bona fides without further question.[14]

Since word quickly spread that the ship might soon leave, Roberts sent Morrison ashore on January 29 with a written communication to the Hué commissioners, stating that if in six days he did not receive permission to proceed to Hué, the vessel would sail. The message added that the envoy strongly objected to the persistent failure of the minister to report his arrival to the emperor or to arrange an audience with the ruler in Hué.

Once again the Cochin Chinese interlocutors repeated their earlier positions. It was Roberts's obstinacy, they stated, that prevented a satisfactory conclusion to the business of the mission. If a translation of the president's letter would simply be provided, along with a statement of the complete objectives of the mission, a rapid conclusion of the emissary's business should be possible. Morrison also became aware that the two most recently arrived officials from Hué, who it transpired had not yet departed but remained concealed and listening inside the house during Morrison's talk with their colleagues, passed a note to their countrymen suggesting that the president of the United States, elected as he was by the people and not possessing a royal title, should appropriately write to the emperor in a more decorous and respectful manner. This clearly required a careful review of the presidential letter to remove any improper words. Morrison tartly responded that the president was the equal of any king or emperor and left.

Apprised by Morrison of what he regarded as an "insult" to the president, Roberts angrily sent Morrison ashore again, accompanied by a naval officer, to demand an apology. Failing this, he was to lodge a formal protest, for the information of the minister, against what he considered a denigration of the status of the U.S. chief of state. The Hué deputies denied they had made any such claim. Since they had previously been told that the president was elected by the public, they had merely asked whether he was really a king or not. As a separate matter, they had reiterated that letters to the emperor should be "humble and decorous." Although Roberts continued to fume aboard ship at what he perceived to be a gratuitous slight to the president, Morrison deemed their apology sufficient, and the prepared formal protest was not delivered.

This matter settled, Morrison and the ship's officer now asked for the costs of the refreshments sent to the ship, insisting that the mission wished to pay for them. Only if the mission were allowed to proceed to Hué could such culinary presents be accepted. These refreshments, the startled Hué officials remonstrated, were customarily provided to visiting ships, and no reimbursement for them was wanted, expected, or acceptable. The very suggestion struck another discordant note.

An Appeal to the Minister

On January 30, convinced by then that the Hué commissioners had no discretionary authority, Roberts addressed a new written message to the minister. Referring to his earlier letter, which had explained the purpose of his mission, he now sent a copy of the president's letter to the emperor, along with a Chinese translation, for the minister's perusal. The president's sole purpose, he again explained, was to ascertain whether American commercial intercourse with Cochin China, if placed on a most-favored-nation basis, would be welcomed or, alternatively, on what conditions and at what ports American vessels might be admitted. No exclusive privileges were sought and only a commercial treaty was desired.

Had the minister responded in writing to his earlier letter and requested additional information, Roberts complained, it would have been provided at once. But the persons sent by the minister, who Roberts implied had discourteously demanded information and a copy of the president's letter, could show no evidence that the minister had authorized them to do so. In saying this, Roberts conveniently overlooked his refusal to show the Hué commissioners his presidential commission. Observing that he had already been detained in Cochin China for some time, Roberts made a final appeal to the minister to arrange for him to visit Hué without further delay. Unless permission to do so was received within seven days, he now stated, the *Peacock* would have to sail.[15]

Substantial concession though this was, at least for Roberts, new difficulties arose when Morrison took the package ashore. The Hué commissioners insisted that Roberts's letter be opened for their inspection. Any corrections they might demand would have to be made before they would either formally receive it or agree to forward it. Morrison indignantly refused to do so and returned to the ship to receive Roberts's instructions.

That same evening, on Roberts's instructions, Morrison took copies of the Chinese translation of the president's letter and of Roberts' newly drafted letter to the minister and allowed the Hué deputies to examine them. The previously offered copy of the original English text of the president's letter was not sent.

Unbridgeable Protocol Issues

The Annamese officials immediately criticized almost every word and phrase used in the two letters. Among other things, the president's title, the Hué officials demanded, had to be placed lower than that of the emperor of Vietnam. Morrison rejected the numerous Cochin Chinese proposed alterations, viewing them as demeaning. On their part, the Hué officials adamantly stated that neither letter would be transmitted unless the alterations they proposed were inserted in the missives.

Taking another tack, they appealed personally to Morrison. He was something of a China scholar and knew Chinese customs. It was his responsibility, they argued, to make Roberts understand that the long-established Sino-Cochin customs had to be respected. If Morrison understood their point, as he probably did, he realized his position and did not fall in with their appeal. No agreement could be reached. Morrison finally returned to the ship, but left the sealed package addressed to the minister with the Hué commissioners. He hoped that the argument he had presented would persuade the commissioners to forward the package.

The following day, January 31, Morrison resumed negotiations on the form of the letters. The sealed package, he discovered to his chagrin, had not been forwarded. Nor would it be unless all of the alterations demanded by the Hué commissioners were accepted. Hence, the commissioners returned the package to Morrison, and he opened it in their presence. Although Morrison protested, the Hué deputies were shown the copy of the Chinese translation of the presidential letter; Morrison protested again when they said they wanted to change the text. (Crawfurd's account had undoubtedly made Roberts fully aware of the Cochin Chinese proclivity to make changes to official communications.)

For several more hours, the Annamese officials questioned the phraseology of the presidential letter, proposing alternative phrases and words consistent with Chinese stylistic practices. Morrison resisted proposed alterations that seemed to him to be degrading, but accepted *ad referendum* a number of what he thought were minor changes.

The Hué officials' reexamination of the Chinese version of the presidential letter raised new problems. The president, they now proposed, should address the emperor "with silent awe" or "with uplifted hands." Morrison peremptorily rejected those proposals. The Annamese officials saw the issue in a different light. They continued to argue that the sense of the letter could remain, but without adhering to the precise terminology of the original text. Again denying any desire to denigrate the U.S. president, they reiterated that established Annamese hierarchical correspondence styles had to be followed. Since neither party would budge, Morrison opted to return to the ship for further instructions.

Shortly afterward, as Roberts and Morrison were discussing what should be done, one of the Hué commissioners came aboard the *Peacock*. His first query again raised the matter of presents for the emperor. He also wished to know if, should an audience with the emperor be arranged, the envoy would submit to proper court etiquette. His query suggested that an imperial audience was still possible. Nonetheless, an irate Roberts replied that since the subject of presents was not mentioned in the presidential letter, there was no reason to refer to the matter. As for court protocol, he would make no prostrations, but would render whatever number of bows might be wanted.

Turning to the presidential letter, the Hué official again urged more humble and decorous phraseology consonant with Cochin Chinese practice, as had been the custom even before the ruler's arrogation of the imperial title. As before, Roberts indignantly rejected this suggestion as unfriendly and insulting. In that case, the Hué deputy sadly concluded, neither he nor his colleagues dared forward to the minister the letters from the U.S. president and his envoy.[16] Asked to repeat what Roberts interpreted as a refusal to forward the letters, the Hué deputy reaffirmed his comment and departed. Roberts saw this as a double refusal.

Three days later, by which time the situation was clearly adrift, one of the Hué officials boarded the *Peacock* to propose new introductory phraseology for the presidential letter. Roberts rejected the language. When Roberts asked for a copy of Cochin China's commercial regulations for the reference of American vessels that might come to trade, the Hué official refused. The divergent positions could not be bridged.

By February 7, eight days had elapsed since the return of two of the deputies to Hué and no further response had been forthcoming. Roberts and Geisinger therefore decided that the *Peacock* would sail on the following day. One of the remaining Hué deputies came aboard that afternoon and was informed of their departure plans. Obviously disturbed at the news, he again proposed alternative phraseology for the letters. Without such changes, he reiterated with some distress, neither he nor his colleagues could receive the American communications. His suggestions were turned down. In an effort to put the best face possible on the imminent breakdown of talks, the Annamese commissioner assured Roberts that, despite the inability to reach agreement, American vessels would be welcome in Cochin Chinese ports on the same footing as the ships of all other nations.

Disputing that assertion, Roberts observed that Chinese vessels were allowed to trade in Tonkinese and other ports, a privilege denied to other nations. He doubted American vessels would want to come under prevailing uncertainties. The Hué deputy's response was temporizing. But he adamantly refused to receive payment for the refreshments the Annamese authorities had provided the ship. Doing so would have constituted "loss of face." Before leaving the ship, the Hué deputy and Roberts drank toasts to the health of the president of the United States and the emperor of Cochin China. With that, the talks ended. The following morning, February 8, the *Peacock* weighed anchor and left Annam for the Gulf of Siam.[17] Almost two years would elapse before Roberts returned to Cochin China.

Behind the Abortive Mission

Roberts's mission to Cochin China was abortive. Indeed, substantive talks had never begun. That failure both galled and humiliated him. Cultural incompatibility unquestionably played a significant role in the diplomatic fiasco. The frustrations of dealing with Annamese officials were undeniably great, but one may wonder whether Roberts may not have been excessively haughty, self-conscious, and culturally insensitive. With all of the advantages of hindsight, he may perhaps have been too prone to see intended slights in different protocol practices, where none were consciously intended. There was no reason, for example, why Roberts, as solicitor of treaty arrangements, should refuse to pay a courtesy call ashore on senior Cochin Chinese officials. Young Morrison, who lacked any diplomatic experience, was hardly qualified to deal with ranking Annamese officials. Their sense of dignity was doubtless offended.

Moreover, the fact that the *Peacock* was a war vessel was bound to create suspicion. Nor could the *Peacock's* arrival at Vung Lam, hardly a customary port for a diplomatic mission, have reassured suspicious Annamese officials. Roberts's disregard of frequent suggestions to sail to Turan doubtless heightened their uneasiness. When the American envoy spoke of wanting to go overland to Hué, they may well have wondered if his government harbored secret territorial designs on southern Cochin China.

That Roberts felt keenly his failure in Cochin China is evident from what appears at times to be almost a defensive explanation of his method of dealing with the Annamese. Thus, in his posthumously published account of his mission, he recounts that before going to Cochin China, he had determined certain rules of conduct that he intended to follow in his transactions in that country and Siam. As with all Asians, Roberts asserted in that memoir, there should be no expressed or implied suggestion of American inferiority. Nor should there be any acceptance of anything that might imply degradation. Dealings with lower-ranking officers should be minimal, and a conscious effort should be made to impress through a constant show of dignity and reserve.[18] Or, as he put it in his preliminary report to the State Department, any suggestion of submission would be seen by Asians as weakness and would give them an advantage. "A dignified, yet unassuming conduct, jealous of its own honor, open and disinterested, seeking its own advantage, but willing to promote that of others," Roberts reported, "will doubtless effect such weak nations with the stamp of its character and must in the end be able to accomplish the object desired."[19] He was repeating the Reverend Robert Morrison's earlier counsel. The Cochin Chinese, in his view, had insulted American "national honor." He had defended it.

From Singapore, Roberts reported briefly to the State Department in early May that negotiations with Cochin China had been unsuccessful.[20] Not until six weeks later, following the *Peacock*'s arrival in Batavia to resupply the ship's victuals, did he write a longer report explaining the failure. In a five-page account, he outlined what in his journal is a fifty-page-long report. Had the *Peacock* been able to put into Turan Bay early in the southwestern monsoon, he now ruefully acknowledged, the results might have been different. In Vung Lam, he had simply been too far removed from the capital for effective negotiations. Conducting talks at that distance, and through lesser officials, was indeed a prescription for failure. He was right in that judgment, as far as it went.

Speculation is idle, but even had Roberts appeared in Hué, it is likely that he would have had to content himself with vague, oral assurances that American trading vessels might visit Turan and perhaps a limited number of southern Annamese ports. Nothing in Minh Mang's xenophobic reign suggests that the emperor would have acceded to a formal commercial treaty with the United States, or any other country, even if the procedural and stylistic obstacles that had so vexed Roberts had been overcome.

Given the past precedent of Cochin Chinese dealings with visiting foreign diplomats, it is unlikely that Minh Mang would have condescended to receive Roberts or to proffer any special concessions.

5

Negotiating a Treaty with Siam

Light winds delayed the *Peacock*'s voyage from Cochin China to Siam. Not until February 18 did the vessel arrive at the mouth of the Menam River, whence John Morrison was sent across the bar to Paknam to inform the prefect of that Siamese entry point of the arrival of an American official envoy. Roberts had prepared a letter to the Siamese minister of foreign affairs informing him of the object of his mission, but he sought information on how it should be correctly addressed. Since no one aboard knew Siamese, the letter would have to be in Chinese and the appropriate Chinese form of address for the minister was needed. Although several Chinese residents in Paknam were summoned by the prefect, they were unable to provide the needed information. They had no knowledge of so exalted an official.

Indicating that he had already sent word of the ship's arrival to Bangkok, the prefect stated that he would have to await a reply before forwarding any communication from the vessel. At his request, he was given the name and rank of every individual on the ship. The prefect expressed some surprise that no full naval captain was aboard.[1]

On the following day, Morrison again went ashore. In the meantime, a Chinese interpreter had been sent from Bangkok since the prefect claimed he could not rely on the interpreters of the previous day. Immediately asked by the prefect if there were presents for the king, Morrison responded that this was a subject he could not yet address. Since the prefect declined to give the name of the Siamese minister of foreign affairs, Roberts's letter was addressed in English and Chinese to the "Superintendent-General of Foreign Affairs and Commerce" and was handed to the prefect.

The letter, after explaining that the president of the United States had sent Roberts as "special envoy" to open "friendly intercourse" with Siam, and that Roberts possessed "full powers" to do so, asked that the king be informed and that arrangements be made for Roberts and a suite of about fifteen officers and servants to proceed to Bangkok in order to begin negotiations.[2] Only with difficulty could the prefect be prevailed upon to receive the letter and to forward it. Not yet having received instructions from the capital on how the unexpected foreign official visitors should be handled, he was fearful of being too accommodating.

Although he eventually consented to forward Roberts's letter, the prefect made clear that he would have to send a complete report on the vessel and her complement along with the letter, and he again solicited information on the numbers of sailors, soldiers, servants, and others who were aboard the ship. Informed of the size of the vessel's complement, the prefect suspiciously asked why there were more people aboard the *Peacock* than there were on other foreign ships that visited Siam. Morrison explained that the *Peacock* was a warship and that merchant vessels regularly carried smaller crews. Dismissing his query as levity, the prefect then insisted that the *Peacock* come over the bar and proceed to Bangkok. Only reluctantly did he accept Morrison's explanation that the vessel's draft precluded her from doing so.

Promising Developments

On February 20, Josef Piedade—a Portuguese employee of the Siamese government and self-styled "captain of the port" (harbor master)—arrived from Bangkok. An obviously much relieved prefect informed Morrison that henceforth Piedade would handle all matters involving the mission. Boarding the *Peacock*, Piedade indicated that the *phra khlang* had sent him to welcome the mission and to assure the envoy that both the king and the minister desired friendly commercial association with the United States. A few years earlier, he recalled, a treaty had been signed with a British envoy (Burney), who had been well received in Siam.

Piedade asked for details about Roberts's mission, the vessel, when the *Peacock* had left the United States, and where the ship had visited. He, too, was told that the *Peacock* could not cross the Menam River bar, and that Roberts needed suitable conveyances for himself and a suite of fifteen to proceed as soon as possible to Bangkok. Roberts stressed that he hoped to conclude his mission in no more than a month. Piedade opined that this was too short a period, but promised to be of all feasible assistance. Indicating that he must first to return to Bangkok to report to his superiors, he undertook to return in two or three days with the needed conveyances. Despite initial prefectural disquiet, Roberts could be gratified that his reception by the Siamese was vastly more positive than what he had experienced in Cochin China.

On February 23, two other Siamese officials boarded the ship, along with a Portuguese interpreter. They had been sent to inspect the vessel and to report to the government. Piedade, they stated, who had in the meantime been in Bangkok, had returned to Paknam with two barges and would make all the travel arrangements the next day. They reiterated the *phra khlang*'s welcome.

As promised, two state barges, bedecked with huge banners, anchored near the *Peacock* on the following day. Late in the day Piedade appeared with a well-dressed Siamese officer, a "person of some talent and a painter" whom the king had sent to look at the vessel and her guns, which previous visitors had found especially impressive. The envoy and his party could proceed upriver to Bangkok the next day, but protocol required that they first land at Paknam, where a feast had been prepared and a house stood ready to receive them for the night. Accordingly, Roberts, accompanied by Geisinger, Morrison, eight naval officers, and four servants, embarked on the royal barges for shore. A thirteen-gun salute was fired by the ship as they departed and was returned by the royal barges.[3]

The following day, February 25, Roberts and his party proceeded upriver for Bangkok, arriving there late in the afternoon. Although Roberts later learned that the *phra khlang* was at the landing site, that official chose not to show himself. He clearly deemed it inappropriate for a functionary of his rank to appear to be greeting the visiting American emissary. Piedade, on his part, immediately proceeded to the royal palace to announce the mission's arrival. There a "Moorish or Chuliah" secretary of the *phra khlang* (probably Khun Rachasitti, or Rassaty, as Roberts calls him) formally received the mission. As they were disembarking, the *phra khlang*'s eldest son also appeared to greet the party. The king had assigned a two-story house to the mission.

Roberts and his party, the naval officers in full uniform, were ceremoniously escorted to the house by the Siamese general of royal artillery (the *phraya visset*) and other military officers. Roberts observed that although the house was not built to the standards of comfort of Americans, it was spacious, well located, and had a protective wall around it. House servants were on hand and provisions were "partially provided." In contrast to Cochin China, the Siamese made all efforts to assure the well-being of the members of the mission.

Roberts Meets the *Phra Khlang*

On February 26, Piedade appeared with a message from the *phra khlang* asking Roberts to call on him that afternoon. It was the custom of Siam, Roberts was informed, for visiting foreign envoys to make an initial courtesy call on the *phra khlang*, who no longer had any superior in handling foreign affairs, as had been the case when Crawfurd was there. Acceding to this request, Roberts, accompanied by Geisinger, Morrison, and the naval officers in full dress uniform, went to the *phra khlang*'s home, which also served as his office, and paid their respects to that dignitary.

The Siamese minister asked the customary questions about the ship and the mission. All of these, Roberts noted in his published account, had already been set forth in his initial letter, which he assumed had been delivered.[4] Not included in his edited published account, but acknowledged in his private journal, is the fact that he had earlier acquiesced in the *phra khlang*'s request that the presidential letter to the king first be given to the minister. This, said Piedade, whose advice Roberts came to depend upon, was the unalterable custom of the country. Twelve years earlier, the British envoy, Crawfurd, had been required to follow this same practice.[5]

When the barges arrived to transport Roberts and his party to the *phra khlang*'s residence, Roberts took with him the originals of the president's letter, his full-powers document, and his letter of credence, along with Chinese translations of these official missives. Once aboard the barge, Siamese attendants of the *phra khlang* placed the documents in a "golden cup," or chalice. After the party arrived at the *phra khlang*'s home, the attendants placed the chalice opposite the *phra khlang*, who sat on a raised platform in the center of the room. After some desultory conversation about the *Peacock*'s voyage, including queries about why the voyage from the United States to Siam had taken so long, where the vessel had been, and where else Roberts had conducted negotiations, the *phra khlang* inquired about the presidential letter to the king. Although Roberts produced the document, the Siamese minister evinced no desire to look at it.

Instead, he asked Roberts if the American envoy wished to conclude a treaty quickly. Roberts responded that he did, since the *Peacock* would soon be out of various provisions that were not available in Siam, and he still had several other places to visit. Assuring Roberts that he would help, the *phra khlang* asked about the "object" of the desired treaty. Roberts responded that he hoped to place American commerce with Siam on a most-favored-nation basis. Mentioning that he understood English commerce had been placed on a most-favored footing, Roberts asked if he might be shown a copy of the Burney treaty. The *phra khlang* said yes, a copy would be shown to the American emissary the next day. Roberts also asked when an audience with the king might be expected. Not until the ruler had been shown a Siamese translation of the president's letter, the *phra khlang* explained, could such an audience be scheduled. The meeting concluded, Morrison was asked to stay behind to explain the various documents that Roberts had brought and to assist local interpreters with translating them into Siamese.

Translating the Documents

When Roberts and the rest of the party left, Morrison was taken to a small building near the residence, where a group of senior Siamese officials, interpreters, and the ubiquitous Piedade were already assembled. Now began the laborious task of translating the documents into Siamese. The presidential letter was first read aloud in English and explained by Morrison in Portuguese to Piedade, who then gave an oral Siamese translation to the *phra khlang*'s deputy, who in turn told a Siamese clerk what to transcribe, sentence by sentence. This completed, a number of Chinese attendants were summoned to read the Chinese translation of the letter. After the Chinese translation had been explained to the Siamese officials and was found to conform to the Siamese text translated from the English, through Portuguese, the Siamese translation was tentatively approved by the officials present. Roberts's full-powers document underwent a similar process, although in this instance the Chinese translators were not required to remain until a Siamese translation had been made.

The seal of the United States on the documents was closely examined by the Siamese officials, who expressed some surprise that the presidential letter had no official seal affixed to it. Morrison explained that although special documents might be signed and sealed, the president's letter represented an "introduction to the king," and such letters were carried open rather than enclosed in a sealed envelope. Morrison's response did not fully satisfy his interlocutors.

While the Siamese officials were consulting among themselves about the propriety of the documents, an urgent message from the *phra khlang*, who was at the royal palace, arrived asking for a translation of the documents. Although Roberts's letter of credence had not yet been studied and translated, the Siamese officials, when told what it was, saw no need to translate that document. The original of the presidential letter and the Chinese translation (and presumably the *ad hoc* Siamese translation, although Roberts's journal fails to mention this) were at once taken to the palace. Roberts's full-powers document was left behind.

Morrison was then escorted to the guest house by Piedade, who had been directed by his Siamese superiors to ascertain directly from Roberts why the presidential letter had no official seal and to report his findings immediately to the *phra khlang* at the palace. Roberts asked the captain of the port to assure the *phra khlang* that any doubts the Siamese minister might have were unjustified; the full-powers document was quite sufficient to authorize the envoy to conduct negotiations. The next morning Piedade informed Roberts that the *phra khlang* remained doubtful, but the king had expressed no objection when the matter was mentioned to him.[6]

Several days passed without further word, and Roberts was not allowed to make a copy of the English text of the commercial portions of Burney's treaty, although the *phra khlang* had promised he could. On February 27, in reply to Roberts's inquiry, Piedade informed him that one of the minister's secretaries would probably come by shortly with the Siamese text of pertinent commercial parts of the Burney treaty, which could then be translated into Portuguese and eventually into English.

Later that day, a Siamese deputation, including the *phra khlang*'s deputy, Rassaty (the Chuliah secretary), Piedade, and the general of artillery, called on Roberts ceremoniously to present him with a *catty* (or 80 *ticals*) of local money. This, they explained, was a gift from the king to enable the envoy to purchase locally whatever he might want.[7] The ticals amounted to slightly less than $50, so the gesture constituted symbolic rather than real munificence. Lest offense be given by refusing, the money—hardly enough to buy food for the party for more than a few days—was accepted. In thanking the messengers for the gift, Roberts indicated that he hoped to be able to reciprocate before he left.

Asked about the promised text of the English treaty, the Chuliah secretary Rassaty said he did not have it and asked, yet again, about the purpose of the mission and the type of treaty the U.S. emissary desired. The Chuliah explained to Roberts the previous mode of levying duties on imports and exports with Siam, and described how English commerce was regulated since the Burney treaty. He inquired whether either of these procedures would satisfy the American emissary or whether a new treaty was wanted.

Stressing that the United States was a distinct nation, Roberts made it clear that a separate treaty would be necessary. Roberts later learned that the Chuliah had interpreted his answer to mean that an agreement similar to the Burney treaty was not desired, hence there was no need to show Roberts the English document. The Chuliah, presumably on the *phra khlang*'s orders, also asked whether Roberts wished an audience with the king before or after a treaty was concluded? This, Roberts responded, depended entirely on the king's pleasure. The query clearly suggested, however, that the Siamese authorities expected a treaty to be signed.

On February 28, Roberts, accompanied by Morrison, again called on the *phra khlang* in hopes of preventing further misinterpretations on the part of the Chuliah secretary. When hearing Roberts's complaint that his comments to the Chuliah secretary had apparently been wrongly conveyed, the *phra khlang* asked if the American emissary wished to comment on the English treaty. The king, he observed, was prepared to conclude a treaty with the United States on the same terms as those accorded the British, but would not agree to anything more favorable.

Terms of the Burney Treaty

Roberts reiterated his request to be shown the commercial portions of the Burney treaty, which had earlier been promised him, before he could respond to the question. A copy of the Siamese version of six of the articles of the Burney treaty that pertained to commerce was then produced, read aloud by the Chuliah secretary and translated, sentence by sentence, into Portuguese, which Morrison in turn translated into English for Roberts's benefit. Roberts was not given a copy of the document.

The articles, as Roberts and Morrison subsequently recalled them from memory, required all incoming vessels to submit to Siamese regulations. Rice could not be exported. Munitions (and firearms) could be imported only for sale to the king and had to be reexported if he did not wish them. Otherwise, ship captains were free to buy and sell to whom and whenever they pleased (article 1).

Foreign vessels must first anchor outside the bar of the Menam River, from where crew lists, cargo manifests, and related documents were to be sent to the authorities at Paknam. Once these had been delivered and examined, the prefect of that locale would send a pilot to navigate the vessel over the bar into the Menam River. If the vessel had not previously been in Siam, the prefect would also send to the captain a copy of Siamese commercial regulations, along with an interpreter to translate them. Ships must anchor at Paknam, where Siamese officials would board to ensure that no contraband was carried. Ship's guns and ammunition had to be landed at Paknam and would be returned when the vessel left. These preliminaries completed, the prefect would authorize the vessel to proceed upriver to Bangkok (article 2).

At Bangkok, officials of the *phra khlang* would board the ship to determine its cargo (article 3). Ship measurement charges of 1,700 ticals per Siamese fathom of breadth would be charged for vessels carrying merchandise for import, and 1,500 ticals for ships carrying only specie. No other charges would be levied (article 4). Once an export cargo was ready, the ship's captain or supercargo should apply to the *phra khlang* for a "passport" to leave and, once it was obtained, the ship could proceed downriver to Paknam. There, she must anchor again to allow local examination to ensure that no fugitive, or anyone not included in the exit permission document, was aboard. Previously landed guns and munitions would be returned (article 5).

All persons on foreign vessels must comply with Siamese law and submit to legal punishment for any infraction of local law. For murder or manslaughter, the perpetrator's life would be forfeit, regardless of rank. For other offences, such as robbery, beating, maltreating, or speaking ill of Siamese government officers, the captain might pay a ransom (fine) instead of undergoing castigation, although seamen would be flogged for such offences (article 6).

While these articles were being read and translated, Roberts observed to the *phra khlang* that they seemed to be largely port regulations, which it hardly seemed necessary to incorporate in a treaty. Every nation had its own port regulations. The United States could not, however, agree to any treaty specifying punishment for one who spoke against a government official, nor could it agree to the payment of ransom in lieu of flogging or agree to the flogging of officers.

In Roberts's view, a number of important elements should be included in any treaty: First, vessels in search of a market, and required to return to a Siamese port after having already been there on the same voyage, should be allowed to leave free of charges; second, the United States should have the right to appoint consuls, if it deemed it advisable to do so; and third, most-favored-nation arrangements should be stipulated if another nation received better terms than those in force at the time with the United States.

The *phra khlang* readily agreed to the first and third of Roberts's suggestions, but strongly objected to the idea of resident consuls. The Portuguese consul, he complained, was useless. He was the only foreign consul in Siam. Despite a treaty concluded with the Portuguese some years earlier, and permission that they might establish a resident consulate, no Portuguese trading vessel had come to Siam in fifteen years. The Siamese government's experiences with the Portuguese consul, he alleged, had given it a "dread" of foreign consuls. Twelve years earlier he had made the same complaint to Crawfurd.

Disclaiming knowledge of or interest in the character of Carlos Manuel da Silveira, the Portuguese consul whom he in fact respected and who had given him valuable information on Siam, Roberts insisted that this should be no impediment to the appointment of an American consul. American trade in the Far East and Indian Ocean areas, he pointed out, was far greater than that of the Portuguese. More than two hundred American vessels were engaged in it, visiting various ports.

The *phra khlang* remained adamant in his dislike of even the mention of resident foreign consuls. Reverting to a position used earlier with Burney, he suggested that once substantial trade had developed between the United States and Siam, the appointment of consuls might be considered, but not until then. Despite Roberts's observation that this would require long, time-consuming negotiations for a second treaty, the *phra khlang* would not be budged. Roberts finally indicated that he would submit a draft treaty for the consideration of the *phra khlang* and the king.

On March 1, Piedade came by to ask about presents for the king. The monarch, he alleged, wished to know what they were. Before they could be taken to the king, however, they would have to be examined by Siamese officials to ensure their appropriateness. With some embarrassment, Roberts had to tell his interlocutor that the presents sent from the United States had not yet arrived, and all he had now were a few small articles he had bought in Canton. Should the king wish any particular items, he explained, they would be ordered and sent out with the treaty ratification document. As Roberts had predicted to the State Department, the problem of suitable presents had indeed become awkward. Piedade also hinted that sending presents intended for the *phra khlang* to that official right away might expedite treaty negotiations, even though Siamese protocol required that presents for the king be delivered before any others.

Proposed American Treaty of Amity and Commerce

By March 5, Roberts had drawn up a draft treaty of amity and commerce to present to the *phra khlang* and the king, along with a Portuguese translation of the document. A meeting had been arranged with the *phra khlang* for that morning to discuss the nine draft articles of the treaty.

Article 1 of Roberts's draft agreement called for perpetual peace between the two countries. Article 2 stipulated that U.S. citizens might enter Siamese ports to sell, buy, or barter products without hindrance. No prices would be fixed, and both sides would be free to buy or sell whenever and to whomever they wished. American ships would be free to depart when they wished and, should any Siamese officer seek to contravene the treaty provisions, that official would be severely punished. No rice could be exported, and the free sale of arms or munitions by Americans would not be permitted. Article 3 specified that American ships carrying merchandise would pay 1,700 ticals, and those carrying specie, 1,500 ticals. No other charges would be levied against American vessels. Should vessels come for supplies or to inquire about the state of the local market, no charges would be levied against them. If cargo intended to be landed in Siam was no more than half the ship's registered tonnage, only a "moiety" (half) of the regular measurement charge would be levied in proportion to the volume of cargo actually discharged.

Article 4 gave American citizens most-favored-nation privileges. Article 5 dealt with shipwrecked American sailors, and required that Siamese authorities succor them at the king's expense, which would be reimbursed by the U.S. government. The Siamese would deliver property from shipwrecked American ships to the owner, to an American consul, or to an "authorized agent." Article 6 stipulated that American citizens visiting Siam could not be imprisoned, enslaved, or subjected to physical chastisement for unpaid debts.

Article 7 specified that no special taxes or impositions would be levied against Americans coming to trade. Article 8 stated that, if persons or property aboard Americans vessels were seized by pirates and taken to Siam, the Siamese authorities would see to it that those persons were freed and that seized property was restored to the owners, American consuls, or authorized agents.

A final article authorized the president to appoint consuls to those ports in Siam where "principal commerce" was carried out. Such consuls would have exclusive jurisdiction over Americans and could receive American property or that of deceased Americans for transmittal to heirs, after first paying all debts due to the king or any of his subjects. Consuls and their households would be immune from arrest and their property would be inviolable. Should an American consul commit an offense against Siamese law, complaint should be made to the president, who would decide on appropriate action.[8] Roberts's draft treaty was based on the Burney agreement; it contained such additions as Roberts deemed necessary or desirable.

Having presented his draft treaty, Roberts and the *phra khlang* held preliminary discussions about the proposed provisions. There was no objection to the first three articles, but the Siamese minister objected to a phrase in the fourth article, "the nation most favored." Contending that Siam did not favor any nation over any other, he observed that all square-rigged vessels manned by Europeans were charged the same fees. Chinese junks admittedly were treated differently, but they could not be compared to square-rigged ships. The *phra khlang* therefore suggested a change in the article to the effect that if that situation changed and vessels of any other nation obtained lower duties than prevailing rates, American vessels also would be entitled to such reductions. However, if an American should own a junk-rigged vessel and send her to Siam with a Chinese crew, that vessel would be considered similar to Chinese and Siamese junks in terms of leviable charges. Although Roberts argued that the altered language gave other nations an advantage because of their proximity to Singapore, Batavia, Manila, and Macao, from which locations the English, Dutch, Spanish, and Portuguese could easily send junks to Siam, the *phra khlang* insisted on his amendment.

Roberts's fifth article was misunderstood by the Siamese nego-tiator. Siam, the *phra khlang* explained, distinguished between three classes of victims of shipwrecks: those who were poor and unable to pay, those who had some wealth but who were not known in the country, and those known by the Siamese authorities to be trustworthy. The poor were cared for without charge; those with wealth were required to pay costs of their "entertainment" before being allowed to leave; and known, trustworthy individuals were allowed to leave, but once they had returned to their homes, they were expected to repay any debts they had incurred in Siam. Roberts pointed out that the United States drew no such distinction. Regardless of the shipwrecked sufferer's means, it would pay all expenses. With this, the *phra khlang* seemed to accede to Roberts's proposed article.

A similar objection was advanced by the *phra khlang* to Roberts's sixth article, concerning treatment of debtors. If it were accepted, he indignantly asked, how would "evil-minded or dishonest men" be punished? They could evade Siamese law simply by secretly transferring their property to others and thereafter claiming des-titution. Roberts responded that if such misconduct was proved, just punishment could be meted out in the form of imprisonment or fining, but not through enslavement. Even without the inclusion of his proposed article in the treaty, Roberts stressed, the U.S. gov-ernment and people would most certainly resent the enslavement of an American citizen. It would be wise, he suggested, to guard against any such future dispute by embodying a provision like the one he had proposed in the treaty. In response to the *phra khlang*'s view that the treaty should specify punishment for various catego-ries of offenses, Roberts agreed that the laws of a country ought to be made known to strangers, but questioned whether they needed to be spelled out in the treaty. Foreigners in a strange land, he ac-knowledged, had an obligation to abide by local law. If they were unwilling to do so, they should not come. The Siamese minister made no comment.

Roberts's seventh article met the same objection that his fourth article had encountered on the issue of most-favored-nation treat-ment. Moreover, the *phra khlang* pointed out, trade was not per-mitted at some Siamese ports, hence foreign merchants could not reside there. Roberts replied that if a foreign merchant went to such a port, he should simply be told to move to one where trade was permitted.

Although Roberts's eighth article was accepted, the ninth, dealing with the establishment of consuls, was totally rejected. Not until considerable trade had developed between Siam and the United States, the *phra khlang* resolutely maintained, could the idea of consuls even be entertained. Roberts's efforts to persuade him to reconsider were unavailing.

The draft articles having been preliminarily reviewed, the *phra khlang* now stated that once a Siamese translation of the draft treaty had been prepared, he would inform Roberts in writing of the changes he wanted made. He also undertook to send Roberts the standard measure of a Siamese fathom, the critical element in assessing duties on incoming foreign vessels.

Roberts took the occasion to observe that if 1,500 ticals per fathom were charged on vessels carrying only specie, this would not induce American ship captains to carry such "ready money." If the Siamese government really wished to provide an incentive for specie importation, the charge should be reduced. The *phra khlang*, while acknowledging that Americans were more likely than the English to carry specie, insisted that the duty on bullion-carrying vessels had to be the same for all nations. To Roberts's suggestion that if Siam wished to encourage the importation of specie, charges should be reduced for all nations, the *phra khlang* offered no "decisive" answer.

A brief discussion was also held on the language of the treaty. The *phra khlang* wished it drawn up in Chinese, English, and Siamese. Chinese, he observed, was widely known in Siam. Roberts asked that a Portuguese version also be made. All four languages were agreed upon. The *phra khlang* added that two signed copies of the treaty would be needed, one to be kept in Siam and the other to be carried by Roberts to the United States for ratification. The ratified copy should be brought back to Siam, after which the king would affix his seal to the retained copy and exchange it for that returned from the United States. Roberts objected that such a procedure was contrary to general usage, but the *phra khlang* insisted it was Siamese practice. Roberts asked for time to consider.[9]

The Matter of Presents for the King

On March 6, Piedade came for a "half private, half official" call. He told Roberts that no audience with the king could be fixed until the presents for the ruler had been sent and a report on them rendered. Officials would be sent that morning to examine the presents. An embarrassed Roberts again explained that the presents were trivial and that he had been required to buy them "in consequence of the loss of the presents originally sent from the United States." He repeated his earlier offer to arrange to send, along with the treaty ratification document, whatever items the king might want. On the following morning, a delegation of three, including the *phra khlang*'s eldest son, appeared to examine the presents. They were given two lists, one of presents for the king, the other of presents for the *phra khlang*.

For the king, Roberts had bought in Canton three pairs of worked and enameled silver baskets, a pair of gold watches set in pearls and enameled, sixty pieces of slate-colored pongee, and twenty pieces of black crepe. For the *phra khlang*, there were two pairs of worked silver baskets similar to those for the king, one gold watch set in pearls and enameled, forty pieces of slate-colored pongee, eight pieces of silk lusting (closely woven cloth), some grey silk, and various sweetmeats.

The Siamese examiners did not conceal their disappointment with the presents. They complained the gifts were of Chinese, not American origin. After the lists had been taken to the *phra khlang*, Piedade reappeared, this time to hint that the *phra khlang* wanted a meeting to receive the presents intended for him. Roberts presented them that afternoon to the Siamese minister, who received them with "little ceremony." The *phra khlang* apologized for not yet having provided the alterations he wished to make in Roberts's treaty draft, but promised to do so the following afternoon. They could thereafter meet again to discuss the proposed changes.

Not until March 9 were the Siamese proposed alterations completed, and a Portuguese translation was not ready until a day later, when the revisions were finally delivered to Roberts. To his chagrin, he found that almost every word of his earlier treaty draft had been changed or recast. When Roberts protested, the *phra khlang* blandly observed that this was the way treaties were negotiated—one party prepared a draft, the other altered it—and that the process continued until agreement was finally reached. It was like bargaining over the price of an article. Denying the analogy and lamenting the delay, Roberts protested that he had understood most of the articles in his draft treaty had been agreed upon in their meeting of the previous week. "What was to last as long as Heaven shall endure," the *phra khlang* told him, could not be hastily concluded. Other senior Siamese ministers had had to be consulted and their views taken into account. Roberts was asked to study the proposed revisions and told that another discussion might take place the following day.

The Siamese Counterdraft

The Siamese counterdraft consisted of a preamble and twelve articles. Reciprocity was introduced throughout to allow Siamese who might visit the United States the same privileges as Americans visiting Siam. On this reciprocal basis, freedom of commerce was stipulated, as was a mutual obligation to obey the laws of both parties. Ship measurement charges, as previously agreed upon, were set forth. American merchants who might contract debts in Siam were first to sell all the goods they possessed and use the proceeds to discharge the debt. Should the proceeds of such sales prove insufficient, they should contract to pay the balance in a specified period of time to be fixed with the creditor. Americans might not, however, be imprisoned, enslaved, or whipped for indebtedness.

Export of rice or paddy (for producing rice for export) was prohibited, and arms or munitions could be sold only to the king, not to private Siamese merchants. Should the king decline to buy such arms or munitions, American merchants would have to take them out of the country. Ship arrival and departure procedures at Paknam were stipulated, as was the method of measuring visiting ships for the purpose of levying charges. Siam undertook to succor seamen or property from wrecked American merchant ships, or from American ships taken by pirates, if they landed in Siam, and would continue to do so until the United States sent someone to take charge of the persons or American property for repatriation. American merchants should trade only with Siamese merchants having a "floating house," a brick house, or an established reputation, not with unknowns. Information on reputable Siamese merchants could be obtained by newcomers from "competent [Siamese] officers," who would also assist American merchants if officially designated Siamese merchants should default on payment to Americans. However, should a Siamese defaulter abscond, or should an American merchant contract with an unknown local trader who defaulted and absconded, there could no claim against the king's officials for reimbursement. Once American trade with Siam was "extensive" and it seemed desirable to appoint consuls, the president of the United States should write to the "court of Siam" and request permission to send a resident consul. The king of Siam retained the right to acquiesce or to refuse.[10]

On the occasion of a visit by Piedade, who had acted as interpreter in most of the talks, Roberts expressed his exasperation with the *phra khlang*'s counterdraft. He considered the title and preamble of the Siamese draft inadequate. The Siamese draft also omitted various matters that should be specified, including the length of a Siamese fathom and precisely how ship measurements would be made. The debtor provision, in his view, failed to provide adequate protection if the debtor's assets had been liquidated. He thought several articles were redundant, others diluted in force. Still others, he contended, should textually revert to his first draft.

In a seven-hour meeting with the *phra khlang* on the evening of March 10, it was initially agreed to use the Siamese counterdraft for purposes of discussion. After going through the preamble and the first two articles and hearing Roberts's objections, the *phra khlang* unexpectedly reverted to the American emissary's original text as the negotiating document.

Agreement was quickly reached on the title and the language of the preamble, consistent with Siamese practice. Although the *phra khlang* declared ratification to be unnecessary, he accepted Roberts's contention that American constitutional requirements mandated such approval if the United States were to consider a treaty valid. After extensive haggling, articles one, five, six, and seven of Roberts's draft were accepted as written or accepted with minor modifications. Reciprocity was introduced into article one. In article two, however, the *phra khlang* refused to countenance any language that required the king to punish Siamese officers. He contended that this would take place as a matter of course and need not be set forth in a treaty. He also insisted on retaining language requiring American merchants to take back arms and munitions if the king did not wish to buy them.

In article three, the *phra khlang* objected to Roberts's prescription on how duties would be determined on partial cargoes. He contended it would mean frequent quarrels between port officers and visiting American captains on the matter of what proportion of their cargoes had been landed. He was not satisfied with Roberts's explanation that the availability of the ship's register of tonnage and cargo manifest should resolve the matter. Instead, the *phra khlang* proposed that ships landing partial cargo pay 1,500 ticals, like vessels carrying specie. Roberts proposed instead a duty of 800 ticals, but the Siamese minister insisted he could not agree to anything less than 1,300 ticals. Both sides agreed to consider the matter further.

A provision was added to Roberts's original article seven allowing visiting American merchants to rent a local place of residence, inasmuch as Siamese law forbade foreigners to buy land. Roberts's final article on the appointment of consuls was again peremptorily rejected, and the *phra khlang* insisted on a provision that American citizens coming to trade in Siam had to conform to local law.

These points presumably agreed upon, Roberts was promised a copy of the treaty in the next day or so, with only minor changes in phraseology, which would be worked out by the *phra khlang*'s deputy and his Indian Chuliah. On March 12, Morrison and Piedade were sent to the *phra khlang* to measure the standard Siamese fathom, which turned out to be 74-1/4 English inches. Roberts had also instructed Morrison to propose to the *phra khlang* a 1,000 tical charge on vessels carrying partial cargos; Morrison was also to propose that the final article of Roberts's initial draft treaty be altered to allow American consuls if any other nation was allowed to establish consulates in Siam. Because the Siamese minister was out and a destructive fire had broken out in Bangkok that same day, these proposals could not be conveyed to the *phra khlang* and the conclusion of Roberts's business was further delayed.

On March 15, Roberts received the promised translation of the draft treaty, along with what he expected to be the final alterations sought by the *phra khlang*. To his annoyance, the new version again altered the document beyond what he and the *phra khlang* had agreed upon five days earlier. Piedade attributed these changes to the Chuliah secretary, Rassaty.

Morrison was immediately sent to remonstrate with the *phra khlang*'s deputy about the new changes. The Chinese expressions for American and Siamese governmental authorities also caused problems: To Roberts's mind, they implied that U.S. authorities were inferior. That these terms had been used in Siamese treaties with the British in Bengal and with Portugal, as the Siamese deputy claimed, did not make them acceptable to the United States, Morrison insisted. Burney, the Siamese deputy countered, had come with great pomp and a large retinue; Roberts had arrived with no pomp and virtually unattended. Morrison insisted that U.S. custom dispensed with pomp and pointedly observed that Roberts had come aboard a U.S. warship.

Morrison on his own agreed to minor textual changes in the first two articles of the draft treaty. In article three, he proposed a charge of 1,000 ticals on visiting American vessels carrying partial cargos. Automaticity in benefits for Americans from prescribed most-favored-nation privileges was inserted in article four, and—at Siamese insistence—reciprocity for Siamese was included in article six on the treatment of debtors. Morrison also explained that in article seven, American merchants who might wish to reside permanently in Bangkok, rather than visiting ship captains or supercargoes, were intended in the reference to local house rentals. The *phra khlang*'s deputy agreed to refer these points to his superior for a decision. He had no authority to accept them.

On the following day, Roberts received word that most of the alterations previously agreed to by the *phra khlang* were confirmed, but that the Siamese minister could not agree to lowering charges on vessels carrying partial cargos to less than 1,300 ticals, and he also wanted no mention whatsoever of consuls. Some philological and orthographical problems remained to be settled in the treaty text. These were discussed when a Siamese delegation called on Roberts on March 17 to make arrangements for an audience with the king. The discussion was not without acrimony: The Chuliah secretary was overheard to say to his colleagues that "the treaty they [the Americans] are making will be no better than a treaty with the wind." Roberts sharply rebuked Rassaty for such impertinence. The *phra khlang*'s deputy, who was present, pressed Roberts to agree to a 1,300 tical charge on partial cargos, and the envoy reluctantly assented. As it transpired, however, even this provision did not appear in the *phra khlang*'s final version of the treaty.

The Royal Audience

In anticipation of the royal audience, Roberts and his colleagues were instructed on appropriate protocol. Outside the audience chamber they should take off their hats, and when they entered the audience hall, they should make three bows. They should seat themselves with their feet turned behind them and, from a seated position, make three bows. These should consist of joining the hands at the forehead and then bending forward as low as possible. When the name of each member of the mission was read, the designated member should make a bow or nod. At the conclusion of the audience, three Siamese bows should again be made and, as the party walked out, its members should bow to the princes and ministers on each side. Roberts refused to agree to the Americans' removing their shoes when entering the audience chamber. The Americans were also informed there should be no loud talking or laughing during the audience. Barges, a palanquin for Roberts, and horses for the other members would be provided.

The audience was scheduled for March 18. At the appropriate time, Roberts and his party were conducted to the royal palace where soldiers, drummers, and musicians of various sorts were lined up outside and in the anteroom. The cacophony was deafening. Directed into the audience chamber, the American party found King Rama III seated on his throne on an elevated platform. Every effort was made, as Roberts later described the event, to impress the Americans with the magnificence of "His Golden-Footed Majesty." The Siamese princes, ministers, and other dignitaries were prostrate before the royal presence. Roberts's presents for the king had been placed before the throne. Roberts and his party, after rendering three bows, were seated behind the presents, feet pointed backwards.

Communication between Roberts and the king was conducted through the medium of the *phra khlang*'s deputy, who crouched between the king's throne and the American party. The king's questions were asked in an audible voice, they were then repeated by the deputy *phra khlang* in a lower voice to the senior Chuliah secretary, who next whispered them to Piedade, who in turn interpreted them in a whisper to Roberts. Replies were returned in the same fashion. The king's questions were banal and had to do with the length of the *Peacock*'s voyage and the health of U.S. leaders. Some were answered by Roberts, others by Geisinger. Expressing gratification at the safe arrival of the mission, the king said that American vessels were always welcome at Siamese ports. The end of the audience, which lasted no more than twenty minutes, was signaled by a curtain being drawn in front of the throne. Roberts and his suite were then shown around the palace grounds, where they viewed the white elephants, the monkeys, and the king's special temple.[11]

On March 19, a day after the royal audience, the *phra khlang*'s deputy called to make the final alterations in the treaty. To Roberts's surprise, it now appeared that the amended treaty draft nearly matched the one that he had initially proposed. However, reciprocity for Americans and Siamese was stipulated in the various articles, and a new ninth article was inserted to permit American merchants to rent factories in Siam for warehousing purposes. A tenth article, which the *phra khlang* accepted with great reluctance, gave both the United States and Siam most-favored-nation status with respect to future consulates in each other's country. Portuguese, Siamese, and Chinese copies of the document were promised as soon as possible.

The Final Treaty

The following day the final version of the treaty was presented to the king and given royal approval. Although formal sealing did not take place until later, the treaty is dated March 20, 1833. The preparation of three Siamese language copies began that day, without Roberts's involvement. At an earlier meeting, the *phra khlang* had reversed his earlier objection and agreed that three copies of the treaty might be signed and sealed. Two would be given to Roberts, one to take with him and the other to be sent on a different vessel in case the *Peacock* should suffer an accident en route to the United States.

A Portuguese translation, brought to Roberts on March 22, proved to be generally satisfactory except for some seemingly inadvertent minor omissions. Morrison was sent to the *phra khlang*'s deputy to arrange for the corrections. There he found that large portions of the Siamese copies had already been prepared, hence the scribal mistakes made in those copies had simply been passed on to the Portuguese translations. Morrison insisted that corrections be made in both Siamese and Portuguese texts, to which the Siamese official eventually acquiesced.

A Chinese translation was brought to Roberts four days later. On the emissary's instructions, Morrison submitted that translation to a local Chinese merchant for review and revision. With a few minor corrections in phraseology, the Chinese consultant determined the text to be satisfactory, but observed there was no reference in the treaty forbidding the importation of opium. The Chinese merchant quickly brought the matter to the attention of the *phra khlang*, who, much to Roberts's unhappiness, directed that an opium importation ban be inscribed in all language versions of the treaty. Omitting this provision, he insisted, had been an oversight. Roberts was aware of the thriving opium trade and wished Americans to be able to participate in this lucrative business.

The examination and collation of the four language texts continued to be a problem. Three Siamese language texts prepared by the Siamese, brought to Roberts on March 24, were found to be imperfectly done, with numerous erasures and words or phrases simply crossed out. Morrison was sent to the *phra khlang*'s deputy to ask that the texts be more carefully prepared and that seeming mistakes be corrected. The *phra khlang*'s deputy asserted that the changes were not mistakes—they had been added at the direction of his superior.

On March 30, three copies of the treaty, with collated Siamese, Portuguese, Chinese, and English texts in four parallel volumes, were delivered to Roberts. They were found to be satisfactory, and a signing and sealing ceremony was arranged for April 3. The document was twenty-one inches wide and nine feet long. Now, however, despite his earlier agreement to sign and seal three copies, the *phra khlang* would sign and seal only two. Rebutting Roberts's contention that two copies should be sent to the United States lest one be lost en route, the Siamese minister insisted that it was impossible for an American warship to be lost at sea. Roberts should not even entertain such an idea. It was contrary to Siamese custom to provide more than two copies. Roberts retained the third prepared copy, but it remained unsigned and unsealed.[12] It would eventually become part of his personal collection of memorabilia.

Signing and sealing completed, and with a written statement by Roberts about Senate advice and consent and ratification requirements attached to the document, the *phra khlang* inquired how the U.S. government planned to send out the treaty ratification. Would an official agent carry it back? The ratified treaty, he insisted, should not be sent back with an American merchant captain. Roberts was unable to provide information on this matter, but he used the minister's query to urge again that a second signed and sealed copy of the treaty be sent to the United States. Should the ship carrying the single copy to the United States be lost, he once more pointed out, there was no assurance the treaty would be brought back at all. The *phra khlang* was not swayed.

Geisinger and most of the naval officers had returned to the ship after the royal audience, but Roberts and Morrison were invited to attend on the following day the formal cremation ceremony for the Siamese so-called second king, who had died ten months earlier. A Cochin Chinese delegation was also present for the ceremony, but Roberts had no contact with its members.

A day later, the *phra khlang* asked Roberts to call so he could be told what presents the king and he wanted sent out with the treaty ratification. Roberts used the occasion to try one final time to persuade that official to sign and seal the third copy of the treaty, but to no avail. With that, and having received the list of desired presents, Roberts took final leave of the *phra khlang*. He had been detained in Siam longer than he had expected.

The king wished to have five pairs of stone statues and men, some life-size and others of greater size, all dressed in various American costumes; ten pairs of plain glass vase lamps of the largest size; one pair of curved gold hilted swords with gold (not gilt) scabbards. The *phra khlang* asked for one or a pair of mirrors, three cubits long and two in width, fixed in a screen stand and with frames carved and gilt, with the back painted green; some soft, hairy carpeting, and some flower and fruit trees, planted or in seed, with flower pots.[13] Before leaving, Roberts wrote the *phra khlang* that the statuary desired by the king was likely to be unobtainable, but that the other items would be brought.

On his last day in Bangkok, the *phra khlang*'s deputy presented Roberts with various gifts. These included elephants' teeth, sugar, sugar candy, pepper, sapan wood, and other items. Roberts described them as "all of very inferior quality and little worth." Robert surmised that the poor quality was attributable to embezzlement by the Siamese officers charged with buying the presents. They were given adequate funds to purchase good-quality presents, but instead bought tawdry items and pocketed the bulk of the funds.

On April 4, Roberts and his remaining party embarked for the trip downriver to the *Peacock*. They made a brief protocol stop at Paknam. Two days later, on April 6, the *Peacock* sailed. Roberts's mission to Siam was successfully completed.

The Siamese Mission Completed

In a brief letter to the State Department sent from Singapore, the next stop on the *Peacock*'s itinerary, Roberts reported that a treaty had been signed with Siam.[14] Not until June 22, 1833, after the *Peacock* had arrived in Batavia, could he arrange to send the unsigned copy of the Siamese treaty to Washington, where it was received in November of that year.

In his transmittal letter, Roberts lauded the treatment accorded him by the Siamese authorities. Knowledgeable people in Bangkok, he explained, had expressed surprise at how expeditiously the treaty had been negotiated, contrasting that period to the six months Burney had needed to conclude the British treaty. Roberts and his party had been received by the king and, in accordance with expected custom, presents had been presented to the ruler and to the *phra khlang*.[15] He would explain the treaty at greater length later.

Despite the frustrations he had encountered in negotiating the treaty with Siam, Roberts was manifestly pleased with his success.

This was particularly true after the Cochin China failure. He had learned useful lessons from that failure. Though still determined to allow no slights to himself or to his nation, and despite his view that the Siamese were disingenuous, fickle, and given to intrigue, Roberts had shown much greater flexibility in his dealings with Bangkok than he had in Vung Lam. He had also come to understand, however reluctantly, that local custom had to be taken into account and that reasonable accommodation to it had to be made. True, the precedent of the Burney treaty existed, but he had bargained hard and well and had achieved most of his objectives.

Moreover, lacking suitable presents for the ruler and the *phra khlang*, he had been required to negotiate at a disadvantage. Many Siamese officials, accustomed to pomp and ceremony, made invidious comparisons between the material modesty of Roberts's mission and the considerably more imposing Burney mission four years earlier.

In a sense, Roberts was fortunate. The Siamese leadership recognized that the United States had no political or territorial interests in their country, and in principle, at least, they were eager to encourage what had become stagnant foreign commerce. And the few American Baptist missionaries who had been in Siam for four or five years before Roberts arrived, while suspect in the eyes of Buddhist monks, were generally respected by the authorities. These advantages notwithstanding, Roberts deserves credit for his effective talks and negotiations in Siam.

6

On to Arabia and Home

From Siam, the *Peacock* sailed to Singapore, arriving on May 1, 1833.[1] Part of that island entity had been ceded to the British by a Malay sultan in 1819, and its English governor was anxious to make it a place of free trade. In accordance with his contract arrangements, John Morrison left the mission in Singapore and arranged passage by private vessel back to Canton and Macao.

Also awaiting Roberts in Singapore, in the custody of the local English firm of Thompson, Roberts [no relation] and Company, were twenty-three packages of merchandise. They contained the long-awaited presents intended for presentation in Cochin China, Siam, and Muscat. The goods had been sent on a Salem ship, the *Eliza*, to Canton. Finding that Roberts had already left that port and would not return, the master had transported them to Singapore, which was known to be on Roberts's itinerary.

A disappointed Roberts observed that the presents, except those for Muscat, had arrived too late. To make matters worse, the English authorities in Singapore had levied a 1 percent *ad valorem* import duty on the landed packages. Since the *Peacock* lacked hold space to transport the bulky packages back to Brazil, as Roberts would have liked, it was finally arranged that only five boxes would be taken aboard for use in Muscat. The remaining packages were left with the English company in Singapore with instructions that they be sent back to the United States on the first available American vessel.

Next Steps

With the successful conclusion of his mission to Siam, Roberts had to plan the rest of his next negotiating itinerary. Should he now proceed to Japan, Burma, and Achin, as the secretary of state's earlier instructions had suggested? Should Japan be dropped, but visits made to Burma and Achin, or to only one of the two? Or perhaps he should go directly to Arabia before returning home. Various factors weighed in his ultimate decision to proceed directly to Arabia and to forgo other stops.

He had by then been away from the United States for almost two years, and visits to Japan, Burma, and Achin would extend his absence for at least another year. Prospects of success at those places were highly uncertain. Moreover, as he had previously warned the State Department, he was running out of funds. At Singapore, in fact, he had been required to draw a bill of exchange for over $850 on the New York firm of Fish and Grinnell to pay expenses associated with his diplomatic mission.

It was impossible to proceed to Japan, Roberts wrote the secretary of state from Batavia, where the *Peacock* arrived on June 5, because he lacked funds to purchase the kind of presents that the Japanese emperor and his senior officials were accustomed to receiving from the Dutch. Anything less than the Dutch offered would make a poor showing in Japan and would militate against success. In any case, he had been assured by "merchants of the first respectability" in Batavia that before long all Japanese ports would be opened to Americans and that Americans were the only people who could achieve this.[2]

Apart from the Dutch, who had their trading factory at Deshima (Dejima), Europeans were generally distrusted by the Japanese. The Portuguese and Spaniards were, by Japanese law, excluded. Ever since the "unprincipled" action of an English naval captain, Fleetwood B. R. Pellew of the ship *Phaeton*, who had in 1808 threatened to bombard Nagasaki, the British were likewise rejected.[3]

During the Napoleonic Wars in 1808–1809, when Napoleon was using Dutch outposts to operate against British shipping interests, the Dutch in Batavia chartered neutral ships, several of which were American, to transport goods to their factory at Deshima. Roberts was informed that the American shipmasters had encountered no

difficulties with Japanese officials in Deshima. This, those in Batavia generally believed, was because the vessels flew the American
flag. That notion encouraged a concomitant belief that American
ships would continue to be welcomed. It was simply a matter of
time.

By then, too, the urgency for Roberts's visit to Japan seemed to
be diminished. At Batavia, Roberts received new letters from the
secretary of state, dated July 23, 1832, superseding his earlier instructions. They had been brought by the *Boxer*, which was finally
able to rendezvous with the *Peacock*.

A separate U.S. treaty mission was now contemplated for Japan, Roberts was informed. Nevertheless, if he considered prospects favorable, he was still at liberty to try to open that country
to American trade. Should he opt to do so, Roberts should not go
in a U.S. naval vessel, which could not submit to the indignity of
being disarmed on arrival, as the Japanese required of all foreign
vessels visiting their ports. A Russian naval vessel, the State Department had learned, had earlier condescended to accede to such
a degrading demand. Nor was Roberts to go to any extraordinary
expenses for any mission to Japan. A postscript to the secretary of
state's letter added that news had just been received that an English
vessel from New Holland had shelled and burned a village on the
northeast coast of Japan. There had been Japanese casualties. Roberts was instructed to do all he could to ensure that the Japanese
would not attribute this outrage to Americans.[4]

To Roberts, as he pondered this information, an immediate visit
to Japan hardly seemed propitious or feasible. The idea of going
to Japan on a treaty mission on other than an American warship,
as the State Department was suggesting, was preposterous. To go
aboard any kind of vessel with cheap trinkets as presents, as the
State Department seemed to be hinting, spelled failure. It strength-
ened his decision to forgo a Japan trip.

As for a visit to Burma, Roberts was informed by merchants in
Batavia that the trade of that country was adrift. Although there
were reports that quantities of Burmese sugar would shortly be
exported, an official American mission to Ava, Burma's capital,
seemed hardly necessary at present. As far as Achin was concerned,
he was told that the "once powerful" king of that Muslim state in

Sumatra was reportedly scarcely able to control his own limited territory. In any case, the current king, Muhammad Syah, was described as a "savage" who would not respect any treaty.

Geisinger provided yet another compelling reason for not extending the mission indefinitely. The terms of enlistment of many members of the *Peacock*'s and *Boxer*'s crews would before long expire. Thus, it was desirable that the ships return to Brazil, their designated stations, to discharge these men and obtain replacements.[5]

Much of the information on Japan, Burma, and Achin that Roberts gleaned in Batavia came from an American merchant who lived there, a Mr. Forestice, whose hospitality Roberts enjoyed during his two-month sojourn there. Although the State Department had sent an official letter to the American consul at Batavia, John Shillaber, asking him to provide all possible assistance to Roberts, there is no indication that Shillaber communicated with Roberts or even that the consul was still at Batavia when Roberts arrived.

In any event, the die was cast. Roberts decided to proceed to Arabia and, following the completion of his mission there, to return to the United States. He must have been amused to know that on those concluding parts of his mission, he finally had specific and written guidance from the State Department on what was wanted in the commercial treaties it had sent him to negotiate. The new instructions from the secretary of state that Roberts received in Batavia included a draft treaty document, prepared in Washington, for use in treaty negotiations. It had not been ready by the time Roberts left the United States, although he had obviously been orally briefed on what was optimally desired. The draft treaty document had taken almost a year to reach Roberts.

The draft treaty called for perpetual peace between the signatories; free trade, allowing ships of both states to enter each other's ports to buy and sell merchandise; most-favored-nation treatment for visiting American citizens; local succor, at the expense of the U.S. government, for shipwrecked American seamen; reciprocal protection of persons and property of the signatory states that had been seized by pirates, and the conveyance of such persons or property to the respective consuls for repatriation or return to the owners; and, finally, the right to appoint American consuls in the ports of the other's signatory state, with exclusive, extraterritorial jurisdiction over disputes between Americans resident in the other state's domains. Such American consuls and their residences would be inviolable, and any complaint against them would be made to the president of the United States, who would take whatever action deemed appropriate to remove or reprimand offending American consuls.[6] Despite the absence of a model treaty document when negotiating with Cochin China or Siam, the treaty Roberts had concluded with Siam generally conformed to the desired basic provisions. He had reason to be pleased with his achievement.

Yemen

After stopping at Batavia and briefly at Anger Roads, the *Peacock* and the *Boxer* sailed for Arabia on July 28, 1833.[7] During the long haul across the Indian Ocean, the *Boxer* had difficulty keeping up, frequently requiring the *Peacock* to shorten sail so that the ships could remain within sight of each other. An impatient Geisinger ordered his subordinate, Lt. Commander Shields, to keep on course at night. Should the ships become separated, the *Boxer* was to proceed to Mokha, in the Red Sea, where she should remain until September 10, 1833. If the *Peacock* had not rendezvoused with her there by that date, the *Boxer* should sail to Muscat.[8]

On August 20, the two vessels reached Cape Guardafui, at the northeastern tip of Somalia. Seven days later, Cape Aden (in Yemen) was in sight. Off Aden, they spoke to the East India Company cruiser *Nautilus,* which was en route to Surat from Mokha, convoying smaller brigs. From her captain, they learned that a revolution had recently taken place at Mokha, and that the "Turks" were now in possession of the port.[9] Two days later, they transited the Bab el-Mandeb into the Red Sea. On August 31, the *Peacock* stood two miles off Mokha, and the *Boxer* appeared that evening. An officer from the *Peacock* was sent ashore the next day to visit the new pasha and to make arrangements for a gun salute. Not until early afternoon did the *Peacock* salute, with fifteen guns, the "authority on shore." A like number of shots was returned by the shore batteries.[10]

While the American naval vessels obtained brackish water, some livestock, and vegetables from Mokha ship chandlers, a meeting was scheduled with Mohammed Agha, better known as

Turkchi Bilmas. Turkchi Bilmas was the Georgian head of the Albanian mercenaries who had a month earlier marched overland from Jeddah to the Yemeni Tihamah and seized its towns, including Mokha.[11] Roberts was anxious to discuss possible Yemeni interest in concluding a commercial treaty with the United States.

Accompanied by Geisinger, Roberts landed at the Mokha stone jetty. The two were taken to the "palace," which had previously been the residence of the imam of Yemen. Roberts later graphically recounted the scene:

There were, lounging about the grand entrance, a goodly number of his [Turkchi Bilmas's] cutthroats, whose trade and pastime are blood, armed to the teeth, and ready for service. We were conducted through long dark passages, up a precipitous staircase, wide enough for only one person to advance at a time. Landing places were frequent, and heavy doors at each, so as to cut off all communication: wherever a soldier could be placed on the narrow landings or passages, either above or below, there was no space left empty. … He [Turkchi Bilmas] plac[ed] himself in the corner of the settee, probably as a precautionary means against treachery. … [His guards] were principally Turks [Albanians]: some wore the turban, and others the red military cap. They were heavily armed about the waist, with two pair of horse-pistols, a cimeter [scimitar], and perhaps with one or two daggers; the handles being fancifully inlaid with silver.[12]

Although the setting was hardly propitious for negotiations, Turkchi Bilmas received the Americans affably. Expressing his gratification at the visit of the two American warships, he offered any assistance needed. But Roberts's attempts to obtain agreement for a treaty reducing Mokha customs charges and anchorage and harbor fees for American vessels were politely parried. Doubtless keenly aware of his already precarious position—he would in fact fall victim to an Asiri bedouin attack only two months later and barely escape with his life—Turkchi Bilmas promised to do what he could to equalize the charges with those of English vessels visiting the port, but cautioned that Yemen was at the time in a highly unsettled state. He professed to be awaiting instructions from the Ottoman sultan on what administrative measures should be taken in Yemen.[13] Turkchi Bilmas showed no awareness of the recently concluded U.S. treaty with the Ottoman Porte (the government of the Ottoman Empire), nor is there any indication that Roberts mentioned it to him.

Recognizing that no firm commitment could be obtained from Turkchi Bilmas in the prevailing circumstances, Roberts had to be content with these vague promises and determined to remain no longer. The two naval vessels departed Mokha for Muscat on the following morning. On the way, they stopped briefly at Aden for water and supplies, an action quickly reported to the English authorities in India. The stopover, brief though it was, gave rise to suspicions among at least some English officials in India that the United States might be contemplating seizing that south Arabian port as a commercial outpost.

Treaty with Oman

The *Peacock* and *Boxer* arrived in Muscat on September 18, 1833, eighteen days after leaving Mokha. A seventeen-gun salute was fired by the ships and was returned by the Muscat forts.[14] Two days later Roberts, accompanied by Geisinger and Shields in full dress uniform, paid a formal call on Sayyid Sa'id. In contrast to the slow and agonizing negotiations with Cochin China and Siam, those in Muscat were conducted with astonishing rapidity. After presenting President Jackson's letter, Roberts outlined to the ruler, through the latter's interpreter, "Captain" Sa'id bin Khalfan (a trader and former naval officer in the Omani navy), American ideas for the commercial treaty that they had discussed five years earlier. Also present at the audience were Sayyid Khalid, the ruler's eldest son; the governor of nearby Birka; and ten ranking members of the ruler's *diwan* (council of state)

Roberts reported that, after hearing his presentation, Sayyid Sa'id at once agreed in principle that American shipmasters visiting his ports should enjoy most-favored-nation privileges and pay only a single charge of 5 percent import duties. The presence of the two American warships in the Muscat harbor, a new experience for

Oman, may well have influenced the ruler to grant so readily such generous terms. But he had earlier indicated his desire for a treaty with the United States.

At a second meeting with Sayyid Sa'id, held on September 21, 1833, the American eight-article draft treaty was formally presented. It reflected the document that the State Department had belatedly sent to Roberts. After its articles had been orally translated into Arabic by the interpreter, according to Roberts's subsequent account, Sayyid Sa'id accepted the document with only minor modifications. In the fifth article of the draft treaty, which dealt with the treatment of shipwrecked American seamen, he insisted that he would pay any expenses incurred in supporting them and arranging for their repatriation to the United States. Such treatment, the ruler grandly averred, was required by Arab usage and customary rights of hospitality. The draft treaty was amended to reflect his wish. It was further agreed between Sayyid Sa'id and Roberts that the date of the treaty would be September 21, 1833, and that both English and Arabic versions would be signed.

The Arabic translation was done by Sa'id bin Khalfan and, unaccountably, took some ten days to complete. Actual signing did not take place until October 3, 1833.[15] There was no way Roberts could check the accuracy of the Arabic text. The treaty document, almost five feet long and eighteen inches wide, was drawn up in two parallel columns, Arabic on the left and English on the right. The principals signed and sealed three copies. Sayyid Sa'id retained one, and Roberts took the other two for transmittal to Washington for ratification. To each copy, Roberts appended a statement in English reserving the treaty for U.S. Senate "advice and consent" to ratification. Roberts promised Sayyid Sa'id that the ratified treaty would be sent to the ruler at Zanzibar, where the ruler expected to be the following year.[16]

There is some uncertainty whether an actual signing ceremony, at least one in which both Sayyid Sa'id and Roberts participated, ever took place. Roberts's reports imply that it did. Sometime later, however, Sayyid Sa'id told a British naval officer that the document had simply been placed before him and that he had signed it without careful study. The latter account seems disingenuous and was obviously intended to mollify critical British interlocutors after the event.

With treaty negotiations concluded, the vessels could prepare to sail. But before that, on October 4, 1834, Sayyid Sa'id visited the *Peacock*, along with his large retinue, and was received aboard with full honors. Two ship's officers escorted him, and the Omani flag was hoisted on the *Peacock's* mainmast. After an hour aboard ship, during which refreshments were offered, the sayyid and his party departed. A twenty-one-gun salute was fired in his honor, the yardarms were manned, and the assembled crew gave three cheers for the ruler. As his boats passed the *Boxer* that vessel rendered similar honors. In each case, the Muscat shore batteries returned the gun salute, as did the ruler's ships in the harbor.[17]

Before the ships' departure, Sayyid Sa'id indicated his wish to send along two stud horses and two mares for the president of the United States. Roberts declined the offer, explaining that any presidential acceptance of presents was "in violation of the Constitution of the United States." Sayyid Sa'id gave Roberts a letter addressed to President Jackson, dated 22 Jamadi 1249 A.H. (October 7, 1833), expressing appreciation for the president's earlier letter and gratification at the conclusion of the treaty. The princely missive was in due course forwarded, through the secretary of state, to the president.[18]

Return to the United States

On October 6, Roberts and Geisinger went ashore to take leave of Sayyid Sa'id. The next day, after again firing twenty-one-gun salutes, the *Peacock* and *Boxer* weighed anchor.[19] After touching briefly at Mozambique and rounding the Cape of Good Hope, the vessels arrived at Rio de Janeiro in mid-January 1834.

Because the *Peacock* needed repairs, which would delay her departure, Roberts transferred to the USS *Lexington*, captained by Isaac McKeever; the *Lexington* sailed on March 1 for the United States. While on board, Roberts composed much of his extensive journal report, using draft copies of letters that he had written during the long voyage. The *Lexington* arrived in Boston harbor on April 24, 1834. Roberts, while still on board, wrote to Secretary of State Louis McLane, who had assumed that office on May 29, 1833. Roberts informed McLane of his imminent arrival in Boston and his intention to proceed to Washington, D.C., with the Siam and Muscat treaties.[20] A year of controversy with his government awaited him.

The *Peacock*, with Geisinger aboard, had to refit in Rio de Janeiro and did not return to New York until May 25, 1834. Geisinger would have his own problems with the Navy Department.

7

Interlude at Home

Back in the United States, Roberts had pressing personal and official responsibilities to discharge. Having been away for over two years, he had to reestablish paternal ties with his children. In his absence, the Roberts family had subsisted in part on meager residual family assets and in part on a modest financial allotment that Roberts had arranged with the State Department before leaving.

On the official front, the treaties with Siam and Muscat had to be submitted to the State Department, along with a series of expected supplementary or explanatory country reports. Moreover, while still en route to the United States, he had heard that certain provisions of both treaties were being criticized in the media; he would need to respond. Roberts also had to seek reimbursement for what he considered legitimate official expenses of the mission, which had been grossly underfunded from the outset.

The extensive personal journal that Roberts kept throughout the long voyage, and which he hoped to publish as a means of earning income, had to be collated and edited and a publisher sought. Inevitably, these official and private activities became intertwined, causing occasional controversy.

From Boston, Roberts proceeded immediately to Washington, where he arrived in the second week of May, to report to the secretary of state on his negotiations. He clearly entertained hopes that he might be designated to exchange treaty ratifications, once Senate approval had been obtained. Writing five weeks later to one of his daughters, he apologized for not having yet returned to

Portsmouth. "The president and the secretary of state," he explained, had expressed themselves as "decidedly and unequivocally my friends." He feared it might mar his future prospects if he left Washington at once. Although he was uncertain whether he would be sent abroad again, he believed that the president and the secretary of state wished to ask him to do so if the treaties were ratified and if resources could be found to send a second mission. If sent, such a mission would probably leave in November of that year. Should he be asked to conduct the exchange of ratifications, Roberts emphasized, he would insist on a more senior diplomatic rank and a higher salary. Another purpose in remaining in Washington, he plaintively added, was to obtain adequate compensation for the mission he had just completed.[1]

The Treaties

Perhaps not fully aware of established governmental procedures on submitting treaties to the U.S. Senate for that body's requisite advice and consent, Roberts had apparently believed that he, personally, would present his handiwork to the Congress and explain the treaties.[2] By the time he returned to the United States with the signed and sealed originals of the Siam and Muscat treaties, that impression had been corrected. Accordingly, after arriving in Washington in May 1834, Roberts formally transmitted the two treaties to the secretary of state, along with sundry observations on Siam and Muscat.[3] A month later, on June 12, 1834, President Jackson presented the two treaties to the Senate.

By then, Roberts's negotiations and some of the contents of the treaties had become public knowledge in parts of the United States. On October 31, 1833, six months before Roberts's return to the United States, the *Daily National Intelligencer* of Washington had carried an extensive account of Roberts's negotiations with Siam.[4] This was republished from a New York newspaper, which had in turn copied it from an issue of the *Singapore Chronicle* dated six months earlier.

The Singapore story was attributed to an unidentified correspondent residing in Singapore when the treaty with Siam was concluded. Roberts, who had apparently met the man in Singapore, never identified him but scathingly dismissed him as a "worthless

Scotsman." The account factually related the arrival of Roberts aboard the *Peacock* in Siam. The Siamese leaders, the correspondent stated, had been surprised that the presidential letter to the king of Siam bore no official seal and had questioned its authenticity. Nevertheless, the presence of the *Peacock*, a warship, had caused the Siamese to swallow their doubts, and Roberts undertook treaty negotiations. Although Roberts had allegedly sought a treaty more advantageous than the English treaty (Burney), the Siamese had insisted that Americans could trade in their country only on the same footing as the English. A treaty had eventually been signed, after arduous negotiations, but the "foolish old [Siamese] *phra khlang*" would not agree to sign a duplicate copy so that Roberts could take two copies back to the United States with him.

Roberts's presents, the correspondent averred, had failed to produce the desired effect, even though they were of some value. To the Siamese court, given the ignorance of local officials, the fact that they came from China rather than the United States had reduced their impact. The Siamese could not credit that presents originally intended for Cochin China and Siam, but sent separately, had not arrived in Canton before the *Peacock* left that port. The correspondent estimated the value of the presents presented by Roberts in Bangkok at about $2,000 to $2,500. In return, Roberts had received "a little sugar, sticlac, pepper, tin, gambouge, benjamin, Anguella wood, Sapan wood, and inferior Cardamons" valued at between $1,000 and $1,100. The correspondent's information was rather accurate, suggesting a reliable source.

At Robert's request, the account continued, an article had been inserted in the treaty providing for the reciprocal treatment of defaulters. If either an American or a Siamese bought from a citizen of the other country or owed that person money, the debtor would be required to pay with whatever assets he possessed and would thereafter be given a discharge. The correspondent decried this proviso as "liberty and bankrupt law with a vengeance." Because of the way business was transacted in Bangkok, it was almost impossible, he asserted, for a foreigner to become indebted to a Siamese. In contrast, a Siamese merchant could take advantage of the reciprocity provision on debtors and benefit from it. This had been explained to Roberts, who had thereafter endeavored to cancel the clause altogether, but the Siamese would not consent. The correspondent questioned Roberts's claim that a most-favored-nation proviso in the treaty alleviated any danger of the defaulter provision being abused by the Siamese.

When introducing this Singapore report of the Siamese treaty, the editor of the Washington paper caustically opined that Roberts had been "out-generaled" by the Siamese *phra khlang*. On the issue of the personal responsibility of debtors, he charged, Roberts had committed an "obvious error." Since the Washington newspaper reflected the views of the Whig opposition, Jacksonian Democrats assumed its criticisms were purposely partisan, but were also anxious to counter them.

Roberts first heard of the story when the *Peacock* put into Rio de Janeiro in January 1834. Vexed and chagrined, he immediately sent an explanatory letter to Secretary of State Louis McLane. Roberts contended that the reciprocal debtor provision had been introduced as a result of the "intrigues" of Chinese merchants in Siam, who had great influence with the authorities of that state. He insisted that he had not introduced it, although he had indeed objected to prevailing harsh Siamese laws that allowed American debtors, along with other foreign and native Siamese debtors, to be imprisoned, sold, or tortured for being in default of payments. He had been unable to obtain removal of the objectionable reciprocal clause and could not tarry to continue such efforts because the *Peacock* needed provisions and had to leave. The president could, if he considered it desirable, reject the objectionable clause.[5] Roberts's written explanation from Rio de Janeiro arrived at the State Department in March 1834, before his return to the United States.

Still concerned about negative reaction to the reciprocal debtor clause, Roberts, shortly after arriving in Washington in May 1834, explained at greater length his reasons for wanting some kind of debtor proviso in the treaty. A "highly reputable individual" in Bangkok, the Portuguese consul, Carlos Manuel da Silveira, had informed him that debtors could be mistreated under Siamese law. Da Silveira himself, Roberts dramatically claimed, had almost lost his life and had been imprisoned because of a "trifling" debt he owed to merchants in Goa or Macao.

Motives of humanity, Roberts insisted, had prompted him to

introduce the debtor provision in order to protect Americans. The Siamese, after initially accepting the proviso, had later insisted on making it reciprocal, and he could hardly object. No American, he was confident, would enslave a Siamese debtor. This time he accused a Singapore trader in Bangkok, along with Chinese merchants and Indian expatriate secretaries in Siamese employ, of intriguing to defeat his treaty mission. The king of Siam, on the other hand, had expressed gratification that an American "envoy" had been sent. In his letter, Roberts underlined the term envoy.[6]

Still later, Roberts would conclude that the story must have come from John Morrison or from officers of the *Peacock*, despite his express instructions that nothing be said to the press about the negotiations in Siam.[7] John Morrison was henceforth on Roberts's blacklist. Querying an American merchant whom he had met in Canton about the younger Morrison's actions after disembarking in Singapore, Roberts was reminded, "You are aware that I never liked him."[8] This judgment bolstered what had by now become strongly negative views of Morrison.

Criticism of the Siamese treaty continued to rankle Roberts. Although most of the furor about the debtor provision of the Siam treaty had subsided by the time he arrived in Washington, he lost no time in sending the secretary of state a detailed exposition of advantages allegedly derived by Americans from the treaty with Siam. The treaty had removed all obstacles to a "lucrative" American commerce with Siam, he claimed, and Americans were henceforth free to sell and buy wherever and from whom they pleased. The previous system of royal or governmental preemption of incoming cargos, and ruinous price fixing, often inflating costs of goods purchased by visiting Americans by 20 to 30 percent, had been corrected. So were the vexations of costly delays for American shipmasters, which often lasted two to four months. They could now sell, buy, and expeditiously leave.

Capricious and fluctuating import duties, and undefined but often exorbitant port charges and exactions, had been eliminated. Export duties on high-quality sugar, which had sometimes been 25 to 30 percent, were no longer permitted. And the ubiquitous system of presents for high- and low-ranking officials alike was now subsumed in charges based on a single ship's measurement.

Adducing a comparative model of pre- and posttreaty charges on a hypothetical 250-ton vessel, Roberts argued that the treaty significantly reduced local overhead charges for American shipmasters visiting Siam and "has secured for us a valuable branch of commerce which was entirely destroyed, and which will continue to increase vastly."[9]

Roberts's spirited defense of the treaty overreached somewhat. The treaty provisions were sufficiently vaguely worded that Siamese officials could—and did—continue to try to circumvent or interpret them to their advantage. Nor did he mention that the system of designating allegedly reputable local merchants with whom visiting Americans might deal would not prevent covert preemption of imports and exports by the Siamese court and governmentally favored elite. Posttreaty American commerce with Siam was slow to develop and never reached the levels glowingly predicted by the treaty's author. Nevertheless, Roberts's contentions appeared on the surface to be persuasive. They could be used by proadministration senators to urge approval of the Siam treaty.

Word of the Muscat treaty's signature had also preceded Roberts's return to the United States. The *Essex Register* of Salem, Massachusetts, published on March 20, 1834, a curious letter by a Boston shipmaster, John Webster, addressed generically to "captains of American vessels at Zanzibar." Webster, master of the Boston brig *Rupee*, owned by Silsbee, Pickman and Stone of Salem, found himself stranded at the East African port of Lamu in May 1833 by heavy surf that prevented his return to the *Rupee*. Believing Webster had perished ashore or in the surf, the *Rupee*'s crew sailed without him. While waiting at Lamu for another passage, the captain encountered Sayyid Sa'id, who visited that port in November 1833, and learned from the ruler of the signed treaty and its provisions. As he had promised Roberts, Sayyid Sa'id sent one of his vessels from Lamu to Zanzibar, carrying the ruler's copy of the treaty. With this knowledge, Captain Webster wrote to American shipmasters at Zanzibar to alert them of their right, pursuant to the treaty, to request customs reimbursements. The text of Webster's letter eventually reached Salem and other eastern U.S. ports.[10]

By then, an erroneous report was circulating that the Muscat treaty banned American vessels from trading with Zanzibar. Because Zanzibar was considered a more promising commercial site than Muscat, the report evoked both surprise and distress. When apprised of this situation at Rio de Janeiro, Roberts wrote the secretary of state to explain that reports of a ban on trade with Zanzibar were entirely erroneous. Through a scribal error on the part of the sultan's secretary when preparing Sayyid Sa'id's letter to President Jackson, Zanzibar rather than Mombasa had inadvertently been specified as the place where trade was banned. The sayyid, on learning of the error, had been embarrassed and offended. His purpose had been and continued to be banning trade at Mombasa, where the Mazrui remained truculent, not Zanzibar.[11] When the explanation was received in Washington in March, it occasioned satisfaction and relief.

Some initial concern indeed existed that the two treaties might not receive requisite Senate approval. This was prompted not by any serious dissatisfaction with the contents of the treaties, but because various opposition Whig senators viewed Roberts's designation as deliberate presidential circumvention of their constitutional right to give advance advice and consent to diplomatic appointments. A similar senatorial objection had arisen in connection with the 1830 treaty with the Ottoman Empire. Supporters of the president contended now, as they had on the earlier occasion, that such a procedure was necessary to allow the chief executive to send temporary agents to foreign countries to conduct secret negotiations. Although the legality of Roberts's diplomatic appointment was debated for several days, Senate resolutions of advice and consent for both the Muscat and Siam treaties were passed on June 30, 1834. The controversial debtor provision in the Siam treaty remained intact. For no apparent reason other than a lack of any sense of urgency, presidential ratification of the two treaties did not occur until six months later, in January 1835.[12]

As these events were taking place, back in Canton John Morrison was unaware of Roberts's censure. Writing to Roberts in July 1834, young Morrison recounted that his mother and sister had returned to England, but that his father would remain in Canton. In Canton, he had recently and unexpectedly encountered one of the Cochin Chinese commissioners with whom they had unsuccessfully dealt in Vung Lam. That official, then on an Annamese mission to China, had informed him that permission for the Americans to proceed to Turan to trade was received the day after the *Peacock* left Vung Lam. His Cochin Chinese informant had specifically asked that Roberts be advised of this development.[13] Roberts did not deign to reply to the letter.

Even if the comment of Morrison's Cochin Chinese informant had been taken at face value, it signified very little. Given the history of limited Cochin Chinese intercourse with foreigners, some element of foreign trade at restricted locations was allowed, but the unresolved issue was and remained the terms of such trade. Nor did the remark reported by Morrison suggest any Cochin Chinese readiness to conclude a commercial agreement with the United States.

Country Reports

In his initial instructions from the secretary of state, Roberts had been asked to investigate the products of the countries he would visit and to ascertain the military and maritime capabilities of those countries. He was conscientious in his pursuit of the desired information, which he eventually submitted to the State Department in a series of country reports. Most were sent after his return to the United States. Until the posthumous publication of Roberts's memoir in 1837, with its wealth of material on all the places he had visited, the State Department perforce relied heavily on his country reports. Private American merchants in the New England and mid-Atlantic coastal cities, as might be expected, had their own sources of information from shipmasters, supercargoes, and local marine societies.

Roberts submitted country reports on Siam, Muscat, and Japan. Although he had not visited Japan, the recurrent American interest in opening that country led him to collect, mainly in Batavia, such information on the empire of the rising sun as he could. He did not submit a country report on Cochin China.

Siam

The kingdom of Siam, Roberts wrote, had in 1832 brought most of the Muslim sultanates of the Malay peninsula under its political control, as well as a large part of the former kingdom of Laos. It had also seized the Cambodian province of Batabang, with the exception of a small part of that province in the south. The people of these conquered lands were allowed a continuing measure of local autonomy, but they were subjects of Bangkok and were nominally prohibited from conducting independent foreign policies. Siam's boundaries extended in the east from about 105 degrees longitude, northward to 15 degrees latitude, the dividing line between Laos and Cambodia, and southward to the Gulf of Siam.

The Siamese government maintained no standing army, but every male capable of carrying arms was required to serve in the military establishment for three months of each year. The militarily eligible male population of the country was divided into four parts, each of which served sequentially for three months and without pay. Rations consisted of a small quantity of rice. Firearms were issued to the soldiers only in time of war and even then, for security reasons, not until troops were at least one day's march out of the capital. When on duty at the royal palace, soldiers were armed mainly with heavy staves. A few had spears and shields. They were thus hardly a formidable fighting force.

Nor did the Siamese have any regular ships of war. Instead, however, the state had some five hundred or more war canoes. Made of a single, hollowed teak tree, some were as long as one hundred feet. The Siamese navy also had between fifty and sixty three-masted vessels, each carrying between three and eight guns. Though well and sometimes even elegantly built, the largest of these vessels did not exceed one hundred tons burden. Some were regularly engaged in commercial voyages. Probably no fewer than thirteen thousand persons were employed in foreign and coastal voyages. Ship construction, especially of Chinese junks—some as large as a thousand tons burden—was considerable.

Siamese imports consisted of English piece goods, white and printed, and some woolens. Indian goods of all kinds, including coarser Bengal and finer Surat materials, were popular. Silks, teas, porcelain, quicksilver, and almost anything else of Chinese production were brought from China. From elsewhere, arms, cannon, powder, glassware, crockery, some drugs, and alcoholic beverages of various kinds were regularly imported. The importation of opium was strictly forbidden, but it was smuggled into the country in large quantities by Chinese and others.

Other items that, in Roberts's view, could be sold in Siam included cotton twist, Siamese dresses in cases of 400 dresses, prints, chintz of long ell (from elbow to elbow) length, and steel. He urged that samples of goods be taken to Bangkok to facilitate sales.

Inland trade also flourished, especially with Laos and the Chinese province of Yunnan. Flatboats and bamboo rafts plied the Menam River. Boats might leave Laos in August or September, when the river was in flood, and arrive in Bangkok two or three months later. All manner of items were brought, including benzoin resin, raw silk, ivory, beeswax, horns, hides, and timber. Siamese exports to China, through Laos, included coarse woolens, cutlery, broadcloths, gold, copper, and lead. Although Chinese merchants resident in Siam were the principal foreign traders, native Siamese were also involved in coastal trade with China, Cambodia, Cochin China, Singapore, the Malay states, and the eastern coast of Sumatra.

The Siamese coined no money, but used bent bars of silver, stamped with a star, as a medium of exchange. This unit of currency, called a *baht*—or, by Europeans, a *tical*—also existed in halves (*salings*) and quarters. Siamese weights were similar to those used in China.[14]

Muscat and Oman

Still impressed with Sayyid Sa'id, his princely acquaintance of four years earlier, Roberts reported to the State Department that the ruler's possessions in Africa extended from Cape Delgado to Cape Guardefui, and in Arabia from Cape Aden to Ras al Hadd, and from there, along the coast of Oman to the entrance of the Persian Gulf. Sayyid Sa'id, he indicated, claimed all of the seacoast and islands in the Persian Gulf, including the Bahrain islands and their contiguous pearl fisheries, and along the Makran coast of Persia (Iran) as far as Sind. Only a small part of these territories were garrisoned, but all were tributary to him. In East Africa, the sultan owned the ports of Monghow, Lindy, Kilwa, Melindi, Lamu, Pattu, Brava, Mogadiscio (Mogadishu), and the islands of Mafia, Zanzibar, Pemba, and Socotra. This, it may be observed, was grossly overstating the sayyid's effective hold on these far-flung territories.

Again lauding Sayyid Sa'id's reputation for justice and his power, Roberts effused that the ruler possessed a more efficient naval force "than all the native princes combined from the Cape of Good Hope to Japan," and appended a list of fifteen Omani-owned vessels, noting their names and place of origin, and the number of guns carried by each. The sayyid also owned some sixty large sailing vessels (with a capacity of 150 to 400 tons) and smaller craft. These vessels performed a dual service. They were mainly used in trade, but could when necessary be utilized to transport military forces. The ruler's ships visited East African, Red Sea, Persian Gulf, and Indian Ocean ports. His naval officers practiced lunar observations and possessed good chronometers. With his naval force, he could control the ports of East Africa, the Red Sea, Abyssinia, and the Persian Gulf.

Although there was no shortage of Omani sailors, he had few regular troops. He could nevertheless call out large numbers of bedouin tribesmen who, if furnished with provisions and clothing, would fight for his cause.

Sayyid Sa'id's resources, Roberts commented, were more than adequate to his needs. His trading activities flourished. From his African domains, gum copal, aloes, gum Arabic, columbo root and various other drugs, ivory, tortoiseshell, rhinoceros horns, hides, beeswax, coconut oil, rice, millet, and ghee were exported. From Muscat, wheat, dates, horses, raisins, salt, dried fish, and various drugs were sold abroad. Muscat, because of its location, was the key to the Persian Gulf and an entrepôt where the products of Africa, the Red Sea, and the Arabian coast could be bought and sold.

Omani currency differed from that of the Persian Gulf, and Roberts provided conversion rates for the universally accepted Spanish milled dollar into local *mamoodies*, as they were called, and its subunits. Weights in Muscat were measured in *maunds*, which differed in customhouse and local bazaar practice.

Roberts's information on Muscat was derived largely from the sayyid's interpreter, Sa'id bin Khalfan, whose home was much frequented by European and American visitors. In part factual, in part impressionistic, his information inflated Sayyid Sa'id's assets. The ruler was indeed a remarkable man, especially for his time, but much of his presumed power was superficial, and his domains in both Oman and East Africa were undergoing considerable internal turmoil.[15]

Japan

Roberts's report on Japan was based on secondhand sources; he never visited there. It nevertheless offers some useful contemporary insights on that island empire.

Only the Dutch and the Chinese, Roberts observed, had direct trade with Japan. Such trade, he had been told, was limited to a certain number of ship visits each year, and then to only a single Japanese port, Nagasaki. The Dutch government monopolized trade with Japan and conducted it entirely from Batavia. One voyage was made each year, leaving Batavia in the southwest monsoon and returning from Nagasaki during the northeast monsoon.

Dutch exports to Japan included diverse products such as cotton and woolen goods, cotton thread, raw sugar and sugar candy, tin, various spices, sandal and sapan wood, ginseng (often American ginseng, purchased in China), alum, quicksilver, ivory, paints, drugs, glassware, tortoiseshell, and sundry other items. What the Japanese seemed to want, judging from what Roberts had been told, would "perhaps embrace all that a manufacturing, commercial people could supply." Roberts was not given an estimate of the aggregate value of Dutch exports to Japan, but he estimated that average Dutch imports to Batavia from Japan amounted to between $600,000 and $800,000, including individual "adventures." Japanese exports included copper, camphor, silks, lacquerware, gold, silver, iron, high-quality teas, beeswax, gold thread, porcelain, silk robes, and soybeans.

Batavian estimates of the volume of Chinese trade with Japan differed. Estimates of the number of Chinese commercial voyages, for example, ranged from ten to seventy a year. Some of the Chinese junks involved in the trade were said to be quite large. The proximity of China and Japan enabled multiple trips each year.

Reverting to a pet subject, Roberts emphasized that the emperor of Japan, his principal courtiers, the governor of Nagasaki, and some of his subordinates all expected presents. What seemed to be most appreciated were "natural curiosities," broadcloth, fine-cut glassware, velvets, handsome firearms, and optical instruments. He estimated that about $20,000 would be needed for appropriate presents.

Roberts recounted that when the British had briefly held Java in 1814, the governor had sent a mission to Japan under Dr. Daniel Ainslie.[16] Ainslie's report had indicated that the Dutch, obviously for ulterior reasons, had greatly misrepresented both the character of the Japanese people and the difficulties encountered in dealing with them. Ainslee had found the Japanese "entirely free from any prejudices which would interfere with a free and unrestricted intercourse with Europeans; they are remarkable for frankness of manner and intelligent enquiry."[17]

According to the Britons in Batavia with whom Roberts had talked, no effort had been made to follow up on the Ainslee mission because the English East India Company had not been prepared to license private traders to probe the Japanese market; moreover, at the time, it had its hands full with other enterprises. The Dutch, of course, offered other reasons why British trade had not developed. British naval officer Fleetwood Pellew's high-handed capture of Dutch trade representatives in Nagasaki and demand for supplies, they asserted, had permanently alienated Japanese officials and prevented trade with Britons. The Dutch were clearly not unhappy that, whatever the real reason, the British had been kept out of the Japanese market.

A respected American merchant in Batavia, a Mr. Forestice, and a British merchant, Mr. Davidson, also resident in Batavia, had conducted discreet inquiries on Roberts's behalf about the prospects of opening Japan to American commerce. They were convinced that an official U.S. mission, conducted by a person of discretion and perseverance and having suitable interpreters and "rich presents," should be able to negotiate a commercial treaty with Japan. Should such an approach be made, Roberts cautioned, strict secrecy should be maintained. Otherwise, the Dutch government, again in control of Java, would do everything in its power to subvert the object of the mission. For reasons that he had mentioned earlier from Batavia, possible Spanish, Portuguese, and British competition could be ignored. None of these countries had any standing in Japan. Nor was there any need to worry about the Russians, who had seriously antagonized the Japanese authorities by seizing some of the northern Japanese islands and committing various other offenses.

Only Americans, Roberts predicted, could open Japan. Americans had never committed any offense against Japan, hence the Japanese harbored no prejudices toward them. Presciently, Roberts concluded, "My opinion is that we are destined to break down this Dutch and Chinese monopoly and open the eyes of the [Japanese] government to a free and unrestricted commerce with all nations."[18] Success in such an endeavor would mean that Americans would also soon be able to establish "a most valuable trade" with the eastern and northern coasts of China, the coast of Korea, Tartar (northern and central Asia), and the island of Formosa. And, Roberts now speculated, if a treaty could also be effected with Cochin China (as he had attempted to do), and if America offered to trade with Tonkin, "we should speedily possess an invaluable trade with the southern coast of China."[19]

Although Roberts might wax eloquent on American trade prospects in the Far East, especially those that would flow from opening Japan, the difficulties of establishing that trade were considerably greater than he realized. The State Department, no less than Roberts and American merchants, was anxious to encourage the opening of Japan to Americans. More than Roberts, however, it recognized the need for diplomacy and a show of U.S. naval force to achieve that objective. In the meantime, the department was doubtless gratified to have Roberts's pertinent report as it contemplated ways to negotiate with Japan.

Financial Vexations

While on his long voyage, Roberts had several times complained in dispatches to the State Department about the financial stringencies under which his mission had to be conducted. By the time he reached Singapore, the funds initially advanced to him for the mission had been spent, and he had been required to dip into his own meager resources or to borrow money to make ends meet. It was his hope that, once he returned to the United States, the financial problems of the mission would be recognized and he would be re-imbursed. To his bitter disappointment, he found little sympathy in the executive branch of the government to redress what he considered a great wrong. For the next eleven months, he would vainly seek an equitable settlement of his accounts.

Although Roberts's final instructions from the secretary of state had stipulated $6 per diem for the period of the mission and all necessary expenses—whatever that might mean—he had also been cautioned that any such expenses were intended only for "unforeseen circumstances," since his subsistence aboard the *Peacock* had presumably already been arranged.[20] Such vagueness was bound to lead to differing interpretations.

The initial suggestion that Roberts's identity could be concealed by the fiction of listing him as the captain's clerk was unrealistic. Nor did it conform with Roberts's ebullient personality or his conviction that any special emissary of the United States designated to negotiate treaties with Asian potentates had to display not only dignity but a certain status. To Asian eyes, this was essential to success. The Reverend Robert Morrison had emphasized the importance of making a good showing in dealing with Asians. The inadequacy of funds for presents had troubled Roberts throughout the mission.

Upon his arrival in Boston, he immediately informed the secretary of state that he had been required while he was in Rio de Janeiro to draw a draft on the State Department for $800 to pay the *Peacock*'s purser for mess expenses incurred since leaving Singapore. The draft, to his distress, had sold for a 14 percent discount, netting him only $680. Similarly, he had had to draw a second draft for $170, in favor of Captain Isaac McKeever of the USS *Lexington*, to cover mess expenses incurred on the voyage from Rio de Janeiro to Boston.[21] Although these expenditures may have been necessary, Roberts's unexpected, unauthorized drafts did not sit well with State Department or Treasury officials. He soon also learned that the U.S. Treasury Department had disallowed a part of Captain Geisinger's account for having provided Roberts with two rations a day while aboard ship when, Treasury contended, he was entitled to only one such ration.[22]

Cabinet changes in Washington just prior to and after Roberts's return complicated the problem. Livingston, who had participated in the planning of the mission, had retired as secretary of state on May 29, 1833. McLane, who assumed that position but was not knowledgeable of the mission's background, remained in office only a year or so. Moreover, he had come from the tight-fisted Treasury Department. On July 1, 1834, as Roberts was in the midst of attempting to straighten out the controversial financial aspects of his just-completed mission, John Forsyth became secretary of state. He, too, was unfamiliar with the mission's antecedents. Levi Woodbury, Roberts's friend, resigned as secretary of the navy in June 1834, just after Roberts returned, and the new secretary of the navy, Mahlon Dickerson, had no background on what understandings had been reached between the State and Navy Departments when the mission was dispatched. Although Woodbury became secretary of the treasury on June 27, 1834, he was loath to involve himself in Roberts's tangled official finances.

Roberts appealed, first to McLane and then to Forsyth, for an additional compensatory allowance for personal expenses incurred on the mission; the appeals resulted in further misunderstandings. Although Forsyth, the new secretary of state, agreed to submit the claim to President Jackson, Roberts gained the impression that this was largely a matter of form, lacking in commitment. He expected the claim would be included in a list of unanticipated contingency expenses, for which the president would ask Congress to appropriate necessary funds.

In early August, however, Secretary Forsyth informed him that the president could not allow Roberts's claim and therefore was not prepared to submit it to the Congress. Nevertheless, the president would not object if Roberts chose to make a direct appeal for relief to the appropriate congressional committees.[23] In response, Roberts acknowledged his misunderstanding of what had been said and spoke of "memorializing" the Congress.[24] The president eventually acquiesced in Roberts's plea that he be allowed a commission of 5 percent of the value of the presents he had bought in Canton for Cochin China and Siam, but refused to consider any other claims for alleged expenses in Siam in the absence of documentary proof.[25] Documenting a wide array of contingency expenses was virtually impossible.

A special appeal Roberts made to the Treasury Department for an additional $1,000 allowance for official expenses incurred on the mission was likewise disallowed on the specious grounds of "reports prevailing that you [Roberts] were an ambassador."[26] Roberts did not seek to use the title of "ambassador" on his mission, but he did regularly refer to himself as "envoy" rather than special commissioner or emissary. The implication in the Treasury's letter that a less-exalted official designation would have reduced expenses was nonsensical. It was bureaucracy at its myopic worst.

Frustrated in his efforts to obtain relief or even help from the executive branches of the federal government, Roberts had no alternative but to petition Congress for additional compensation. For this purpose, he solicited the aid of Congressman Samuel Bell of New Hampshire, to whom he complained that only a part of his legitimate expenses had been paid. In the Senate, he sought the help of Senator Edward Everett of Massachusetts. Both agreed to assist. True to his word, Bell introduced a resolution into the House of Representatives authorizing an additional $7,297 for extra expenses Roberts incurred while on his official mission.[27] Unfortunately for Roberts, the lateness of the date prevented the resolution from coming up for a third and final reading before Congress adjourned. By the time the next Congress convened, Roberts was already on a new mission. His future son-in-law, Congressman James Parker of New Jersey, would seek to pursue the claim in the next Congress, but eventually the matter lapsed.

Captain Geisinger, too, sought an additional $1,500 for special expenses that he had incurred on the *Peacock*'s long voyage.[28] When Roberts was informed of this claim, Roberts attempted to assist. In a supporting statement for Geisinger's use, Roberts pointed out that the captain had been required to extend hospitality to John Morrison for five months, and that the ship's entertainment expenses at Muscat, where Sayyid Sa'id and his extensive retinue had boarded, had been considerable and could not have been foreseen.[29]

Like Roberts's appeal, Geisinger's was fruitless. A full year after the appeal was submitted, he was informed by the secretary of the navy that there was no naval regulation under which his claim could be paid. The claim should, in the first instance, be submitted to the State Department, which should appropriately reimburse for special expenses occasioned by Morrison or in entertaining the ruler of Muscat. If the State Department could not help, Geisinger would have to apply directly to Congress for relief.[30] Geisinger's claim was never paid. He was promoted to full captain in May 1838, which may have offered some symbolic satisfaction but was cold comfort for the personal out-of-pocket expenses he had incurred during Roberts's first mission.

The Journal Controversy

Throughout the long voyage, Roberts kept a detailed personal journal of places visited, persons met, events experienced, and sights and ceremonies encountered. He seems to have jotted down notes and, during the long days at sea, referred to these to prepare fuller accounts, both for dispatches to the State Department and for his private journal. There is an overlap of material in his official communications to Washington and in his journal entries, although, generally speaking, the journal is considerably more replete in detail. It includes descriptions that would not have been of interest to U.S. government officials, but which reflect environmental and societal aspects of the still little known places that Roberts visited.

Even before undertaking his treaty mission, Roberts had been meticulous in maintaining family and business records and correspondence, as his voluminous collection of personal papers in the Library of Congress attests. But there is no indication that Roberts had earlier kept a journal or personal diary. What prompted him to do so is uncertain, but it may well have been his perusal of John Crawfurd's published account of his official missions to Siam and Cochin China and a realization that a similar publication on the mission upon which he, Roberts, was about to embark offered prospects of financial gain. Businessman that he was, Roberts always had an eye for promising economic opportunities.

For Roberts, keeping the journal became a labor of love. Few things of possible interest escaped his perceptive eye. By the time his return voyage to the United States had begun, not all parts of the journal had been completed or rewritten. He hoped to prepare a final draft of the journal, one which could be submitted to a publisher, once his official mission had been completed and he had relocated in Portsmouth.

Roberts's series of dispatches to the State Department provided no hint that he was keeping a separate journal for his own use, nor was there any reason that State Department officials needed to be informed of his chronicles. He would soon discover, however, that the existence of his journal stirred additional controversy.

Roberts brought portions of the journal that had been completed with him to Washington after he returned to the United States, ostensibly to show them to his friend and benefactor, Secretary of the Treasury Levi Woodbury, and to seek his counsel on publication. Roberts showed portions of his journal to Asbury Dickens, the chief clerk of the State Department, and, at Dickins's request, lent them to him. Dickens, Roberts later recounted, wished to show them to Secretary Forsyth and promised to return them in two weeks.

Three months went by and the journal portions had not yet been returned. After making informal inquiries, Roberts was notified by the secretary of state, in early August 1834, that the journal represented an official document and should properly belong to the department. Yet, apparently recognizing the tenuousness of his claim, Secretary Forsyth added that Roberts might of course have use of the journal, but he expressed concern about possible publication in its present form.

Forsyth recommended that if indeed publication was contemplated, it should be delayed until after treaty ratifications had been exchanged with Muscat and Siam. Implying that some of the contents of those portions of the journal he had seen were sensitive, the secretary of state feared that premature publication might interfere with the exchange of ratifications or with a possible renewed attempt to negotiate a treaty with Cochin China. Moreover, Forsyth reminded Roberts, the State Department had only those parts of the journal dealing with Cochin China and Siam. The Muscat portion should likewise be submitted. As these exchanges were taking place, Roberts was told that the president had not yet decided whether to send another diplomatic agent to "Asia" for further negotiations.[31] Thus, the matter of a second diplomatic mission remained nebulous.

An annoyed Roberts responded at once. In a letter to the secretary of state, Roberts reiterated that he had lent the journal portions to Dickins at the latter's request, and that Dickins had acknowledged the document was Roberts's private property and would be returned. Roberts insisted that he had never deposited it with the State Department as part of the records of his official mission. His dispatches to the State Department, sent from the *Peacock*'s various itinerary stops, were on file. These represented his official reports. He was, of course, prepared to allow the State Department to copy the journal, if its contents were considered useful, but the original was his "private property." He badly needed the journal, which "Governor Woodbury" was urging him to publish. He offered assurances that nothing detrimental to possible future negotiations with Cochin China would be included in any publication. In any case, since neither the Siamese nor the Cochin Chinese could read English, there should be no cause for concern.

Moreover, Roberts pointed out, accounts of the negotiations had already been published in newspapers in Singapore, Canton, Calcutta, and Batavia, thus no harm would result even if the whole of his journal were published. Roberts asked that the secretary of state reconsider the injunction not to publish the Siam and Cochin China parts of the journal since failure to do so would defeat the purpose of publication. "The Government," he lamented, "have left me in a very crippled condition." Publication of the journal, he hoped, would help redress his straitened financial circumstances.[32] Considering the negative responses to his request for additional official remuneration, Roberts's desire to publish his journal as a means of earning money was understandable.

To this appeal, Secretary Forsyth replied that either the original of Roberts's journal or a copy should be filed with the State Department. Roberts could retain a copy for his own use, and Forsyth reiterated his request for the Muscat portion of the journal. Regrettably, the secretary asserted, because of indiscretions in "some quarters," the substance of Roberts's negotiations had been published abroad, "to the great hazard of the success of your mission."

Roberts's journal, the secretary of state opined, contained matters which it might, for the time being at least, be inexpedient to publish. Secretary Forsyth pressed that even if Roberts's personal interests mandated early publication of the journal, only those parts that would not pose political problems should be published. Specifically, references to Japan, Cochin China, and other Asian countries, except Siam and Muscat, should for the time being be omitted. Perhaps as a spur to inducing Roberts to acquiesce, Forsyth hinted that if the president decided to pursue the original purposes of the mission, it was "probable" that Roberts would be chosen for the task.[33]

If Roberts's acquiescence was the purpose of Secretary Forsyth's hint, it had the desired effect. Three weeks later, Roberts replied in a much calmer tone. A copy of the entire journal, including the Muscat portion, would be sent to the State Department as soon as possible. He had not yet received from the State Department the promised copy of the report that he had submitted on his mission, he pointedly observed, and hoped that it might soon be sent to him. He assured the secretary of state that he would exercise great care not to say anything about the Cochin China negotiations that might prove to be politically embarrassing. Nor would he mention anything about the putative missions to Japan, Burma, Achin, or Borneo.[34] Borneo had not been specified in his instructions, but had apparently been discussed with State Department officials.

With this exchange, the journal controversy seemed for the moment to be over. Roberts was slow in submitting to the State Department copies of the various revised portions of his journal. Some were delivered before he embarked on the second mission. The final portion was sent from Rio de Janeiro in January 1835, after Roberts had already departed on his second mission.

A New Assignment

Roberts clearly believed he was best qualified to undertake any follow-up diplomatic mission to exchange treaty ratifications with Muscat and Siam, but he was uncertain whether he could afford it. From a personal, financial point of view, his first diplomatic mission had been anything but auspicious. He had come away from a two-year diplomatic voyage scarcely able to make ends meet. Nor did the criticisms he received from State and Treasury Department officials about alleged extravagance and exaggeration of his diplomatic status please him. His controversy with Secretary Forsyth over his private journal, he must have assumed, had strained relations with that cabinet officer. But he still had a friend in the person of Secretary of the Treasury Levi Woodbury, who retained influence with President Jackson. Roberts, his frustrations notwithstanding, had little choice but to allow matters to take their own course.

Whatever uncertainties may have existed earlier, by mid-August President Jackson was again contemplating a second diplomatic mission to the East. It must be assumed that both Forsyth and Woodbury helped bring this about. In any event, exchanges of instruments of ratification were essential if the signed treaties were to go into effect. In mid-August, the secretary of state informed Roberts that the president was actively considering sending a U.S. naval vessel to Muscat and Siam with the requisite treaty ratification documents, and with presents for the rulers of those countries. If the president decided to pursue the purposes of the original mission, he added, Roberts would probably be chosen for the task.

Once President Jackson had signed the ratification documents for the Muscat and Siam treaties, he authorized the dispatch of a new diplomatic mission to exchange the respective instruments of ratification with the rulers of Muscat and Siam. As Secretary Forsyth had earlier suggested, Roberts was selected for the follow-up mission. Roberts was manifestly the best-qualified person for the job. This time Roberts was formally designated "special agent of the United States."

The USS *Peacock*, now with C. K. Stribling as acting commander, was again designated to convey Roberts on his new mission; the *Peacock* would be accompanied by the U.S. sloop of war *Enterprise*, captained by Lieutenant Commander A. S. Campbell. Captain Edmund Kennedy would be in command of the naval squadron, and was authorized to fly the broad commodore's pennant for the duration of the cruise.

Roberts was informed that the *Peacock* would be ready to sail from New York on March 25, 1835.[35] Perhaps belatedly recognizing the financial burdens imposed on Roberts during his previous diplomatic mission, the State Department initially promised him a salary of $4,400 per year, paid quarterly. After Roberts pressed for a greater sum, the salary was increased to $5,000 per year.[36] The higher figure represented a generous salary for government officials at the time. Ample provision was also made for gifts to Eastern potentates. Some $5,000 was spent on gifts to be carried to the rulers and senior officials of Muscat, Siam, Cochin China, and Japan, and

Roberts was given discretionary authority to promise the leaders of Japan and Cochin China additional presents valued at $10,000 once treaty ratifications were exchanged. Rarely had the U.S. government shown such generosity.

The primary purpose of Roberts's mission was to exchange treaty ratifications with Muscat and Siam. Thereafter, according to the instructions he received from the State Department, he was authorized "to make such commercial arrangement with other powers whose dominions border upon the Indian Ocean, as may tend to be to the advancement of the commerce of the United States in that quarter." The ratified treaties were forwarded to Roberts in Portsmouth, along with gifts to be presented to the rulers of Muscat and Siam. He was to inform these rulers of the friendly feelings of the American people toward them and of the president's satisfaction over the conclusion of the treaties and the amicable relations they portended between the United States and those polities. Muscat would be the first official port of call, followed by Bangkok.

From Siam, Roberts was instructed to proceed to Cochin China to attempt to conclude a commercial treaty with that state. Thereafter, he was to proceed to Japan for the same purpose. Because the Dutch still had their factory at Nagasaki and might be expected to seek to thwart Roberts's purpose, it was suggested that he try to enter Japan through some other port, perhaps Owari, but he was given discretion as to his overall itinerary.[37]

Citing his previous experience with potentates, Roberts continued to emphasize to the State Department the importance of a higher diplomatic rank for himself and of suitable presents for the success of treaty negotiations. He was curtly informed by the secretary of state that $4,000 had been allocated for presents. This, in the secretary's view, should suffice for the rulers of Cochin China and Japan. The presents for the rulers of Muscat and Siam, Forsyth pointedly observed, had cost less. Should Roberts consider it absolutely essential to give more valuable presents in Cochin China and Japan, however, the allowance for such gifts might be raised to $5,000, half for Japan and half for Cochin China. Secretary Forsyth rejected Roberts's request to be named envoy or minister, contending such higher diplomatic status was unnecessary and might convey the wrong impression of U.S. intentions. Strict secrecy was again enjoined. No treaty with Burma was contemplated.[38] Achin and Borneo were not even mentioned.

Roberts had to be content with these instructions. But even as they were being written, he had more queries to answer about his first diplomatic mission. He was reminded that he had not yet submitted to the State Department either the original or a complete copy of his journal, and he was asked to do so before his departure.[39] The State Department also wished to know what had happened to the two blank full-powers documents, one for the king of Cochin China and the other for the emperor of Japan. These should be returned to the State Department. Finally, the State Department alluded to the aforementioned report in the *Daily National Intelligencer* that Roberts had received from the king of Siam gifts valued at $1,100. These, the department claimed, had not been mentioned in Roberts's correspondence. The implication was that they properly belonged to the U.S. government. Roberts should provide an explanation before he left.[40]

A disgruntled Roberts responded that he had earlier informed the secretary of state that the Siamese presents had been "very ordinary." They had come from the *phra khlang*, not the king. Some of these "miserable presents" were still with a Batavia merchant because they were "totally unsalable." John Morrison had taken the rest to Canton and sold them there for $34.25. The gum benzoin had been stolen. If necessary, he was prepared to give the proceeds to the State Department, but he had been advised that no official claim could be made on them.[41] Roberts had not returned the two full-powers documents, seemingly regarding them as his personal property. Fortunately for Roberts, there was insufficient time before departure for the State Department to pursue these outstanding matters.

Roberts's initial instructions were reconfirmed in mid-April, at which time a copy of Jonathan Elliot's two-volume *The American Diplomatic Code* was also sent to him. Published in 1834, *Diplomatic Code* was the first semiofficial diplomatic and treaty compilation published in the United States. New letters of credence for Cochin China and Japan, dated March 20, 1835, and signed by President Jackson, along with new full-powers documents, were likewise forwarded to him.

In preparing the papers, the State Department sought to correct some of the inadequacies of the documents that Roberts carried on his first mission. Thus, one of Jackson's letters was addressed to the "Emperor of Wietnam [sic]." Moreover, that letter and a similar presidential letter to the emperor of Japan were issued under the Great Seal of the United States. This was highly unusual, but was doubtless prompted by earlier Siamese and Cochin Chinese puzzlement as to why the American president's letter had no seal affixed to it. The *Daily National Intelligencer* article may have helped open official Washington eyes to the importance of such protocol formalities.

The documents for Cochin China included French and Portuguese translations. Those for Japan had Dutch and Latin translations. The inclusion of a Latin translation was equally unusual. The State Department had never before used Latin as a language of diplomacy.[42]

Inasmuch as Roberts's departure was now imminent and the issue of his private journal had not been fully resolved, Secretary Forsyth informed Roberts that there would in principle be no objection to the publication some months after his departure of those portions of the journal that would have no bearing on his present mission. Since the Muscat portion of Roberts's journal that he had earlier been asked to provide to the State Department had not yet been received, the secretary of state stated he was unable to make a judgment on which portions of the journal should be omitted. Forsyth nevertheless recommended that publication be delayed as long as convenient, lest Roberts's new mission be somehow impeded through disclosure of some of the things he had written in his journal. In fact, official permission to publish any parts of the journal that might adversely affect his upcoming negotiations was withheld.[43] That injunction was vague, however, and subject to different interpretations.

Still dissatisfied with the pecuniary arrangements of his new mission, Roberts asked for a commission on any official presents that he might purchase along the way. He recalled that President Jackson had (belatedly) allowed this for his first mission. His request was curtly rejected. He was informed that, in the secretary of state's view, he had already been generously dealt with in connection with compensation for his upcoming duties.[44] In a sense, Roberts's request was not unreasonable, inasmuch as supercargoes regularly received commissions for purchases made. But he would travel as a U.S. official, not as a mercantile agent. His salary was considerably above what a shipmaster or supercargo would receive. As so often happened, Roberts intertwined his official diplomatic interests and his personal business interests.

The State Department completed its final contingency planning before the mission departed. Recognizing the perils of a protracted voyage and the possibility that Roberts might succumb during the trip, the secretary of state authorized Commodore Kennedy to exchange treaty ratifications with Muscat and Siam in the event of Roberts's incapacitation.[45] Although Kennedy proposed to the secretary of the navy that he also be given contingent authority to take over any of the other duties entrusted to Roberts,[46] his request was ignored. It is uncertain whether the secretary of the navy ever sent it to the State Department.

Family Matters

The Roberts daughters in Portsmouth had expected that their father would be sent abroad again on a diplomatic mission at some time, though they could hardly have anticipated the event with any sense of pleasure. He had been absent when their mother died, he had been away for over two years on his first diplomatic assignment, and he would doubtless be away on the new mission for at least another two years, if not longer. Much as they had become accustomed to their father's absence, it weighed heavily on the family. In writing to his daughters of the new mission, Roberts put the best face possible on his upcoming voyage. He emphasized it should result in financial gains that should enable him to cease his wandering life—he would never have to leave home again. This reflected wishful thinking on his part, but it may have provided some emotional comfort for his daughters. Harriet, the third eldest daughter, even expressed a desire to accompany her father on the voyage, but Roberts gently pointed out that this was patently impossible.

As Roberts was awaiting departure from New York, he was informed that his daughters in Portsmouth had moved to a new and smaller home. Maintaining the old homestead in which they had grown up was more than the Roberts family could afford. Their new home had belonged to Roberts's deceased uncle Joshua. Their furniture, Catherine happily wrote, had been moved without suffering a scratch. Roberts could depart in the knowledge that his family was at least resettled in new quarters. In their father's constant absences, the older Roberts daughters showed extraordinary resourcefulness.

8

British and European Concerns

During Roberts's yearlong interlude in the United States, and as he prepared himself for a second diplomatic mission, European officials who dealt with Asian and Indian Ocean areas learned of his successful treaty negotiations with Siam and Muscat. Predictably, they showed some concern and puzzlement at this official intrusion by the United States into regions so remote from the North American continent.

To be sure, American merchantmen and whalers had long since ceased to be a novelty in eastern seas. But the presence of two U.S. warships, with an official American diplomatic emissary aboard one of them, was something new. Did it portend an expanded official U.S. interest in these regions? If so, what was intended, and how might this affect European and especially British interests? Since Great Britain had by then become the predominant European power in the area, some English officials, in particular, showed an almost paranoid concern about American activities.

Dutch, French, and British Interests in Southeast Asia

From the inception of Roberts's first mission, the U.S. government had enjoined strict secrecy on him and on others involved in the diplomatic enterprise. It will be recalled that he was warned that premature disclosure of the mission's purposes might cause the British, French, or Dutch to attempt to thwart its objectives. Such American concerns, while perhaps exaggerated, were not entirely without justification.

The Dutch, from their position in Batavia, were beginning their efforts to achieve political control over the East Indies archipelago. Moreover, they had a special, even if very limited, position in Japan. Although frequently willing to charter an American merchant vessel to transport the annual supply of Dutch manufactures and presents to their factory at Deshima, they jealously guarded their exclusive trading privileges in Japan. It was not until the 1840s that the Dutch accepted the idea that Japan should seek wider contacts with the outside world, and began to encourage Japanese officials to do so. As events would show, however, their political influence was negligible.

The French, it was assumed, had influence in Cochin China, which they would try to use to exclude or to sharply limit anticipated American trade with that country. Like the British authorities in both Calcutta and London, State Department officials held exaggerated impressions of the intimacy of the Franco-Annamese tie. Wrong though they were in their assumption, they were not alone in failing to fathom the Cochin Chinese predilection for self-imposed isolation.

Although the Portuguese were no longer a significant commercial or political power, their residual, strategically located colonial foothold at Macao offered them advantageous geographic opportunities to trade with Southeast Asian states. Except in a negative way—that is, through sometime hortatory cautions that other foreigners harbored ulterior intentions—their political influence in Southeast Asia was nil. They were no more than tolerated. Their fall from political ascendancy had been precipitous and fast.

The State Department rightly viewed the British in India as the greatest potential threat to any expanded American interests. The long-established English East India Company, with its headquarters at Fort William, Calcutta, and with military and naval forces to support its objectives, fused commercial and political objectives into a single powerful institution that already showed signs of aspirations to dominate not only India but also neighboring Southeast Asian and Indian Ocean entities.

A parliamentary act of 1833 put the heretofore autonomous John Company under British governmental control, and thus the firm became an arm of the British Crown.[1] Under either arrangement, British political and economic tentacles were everywhere: in the Malay sultanates, Burma, Siam, Ceylon, the Persian Gulf, Muscat, and Zanzibar. Although American trading vessels were, according to the Anglo-American treaty of 1794 (the much criticized Jay's Treaty, as it came to be known), admitted to seaports and harbors of British territories in the East Indies, the British attitude toward a more official American presence in what they saw as its broader Indian Ocean preserve was in doubt.

Roberts's failure in Cochin China was doubtless welcomed by expatriate Europeans in the area. In Singapore, Roberts called on British governor Robert Ibbetson, and English officials in that port also offered their hospitality. However much he might have tried to conceal his recent doings, Roberts most likely apprised them in general terms of the treaty with Siam. Moreover, however he may have instructed John Morrison, he must have realized that Morrison, as an English subject, would doubtless speak of the mission to his fellow countrymen.

Unsurprisingly, therefore, a fairly detailed account of Roberts's mission was published in the *Singapore Chronicle* of June 6, 1833. In quick succession, it was republished in the *Bengal Hurkaru* (Calcutta), the *Canton Register,* and the *Dutch Gazette* of Batavia. Roberts, as previously indicated, attributed the media account to Morrison's indiscretion.

The news was out, and it predictably evoked at least some British concern. Media accounts seemed to suggest that Roberts had obtained a number of exclusive privileges in Siam and Muscat. Whatever initial British concern may have been aroused by such reports, some of it quickly abated when it became clear that Roberts had obtained no concessions in Siam other than those accorded to the English in Burney's treaty.

When he learned in Rio de Janeiro in February 1834 of the British concerns, Roberts vehemently denied that he had sought any exclusive privileges for Americans visiting Siam. He insisted that he had not even sought the right to establish factories, which had been granted to other nations and which he could have obtained, had he been authorized to do so. His instructions, he recalled, had prohibited seeking exclusive concessions and he had strictly abided by them.[2]

British Representations to Sayyid Sa'id

A more serious British furor flowed from Roberts's treaty with Muscat. As early as November 1833, hardly a month after the treaty had been concluded with Sayyid Sa'id, the British provincial government of Bombay was informed by its native agent in Muscat and its "political resident" in the Persian Gulf that two American warships, the *Peacock* and the *Boxer*, had recently visited Muscat. During the visit, these sources had learned, a treaty had been concluded with the ruler. The agreement would, among other things, permit American agents or consuls to be established anywhere in the sayyid's domains, reportedly in return for U.S. help against the rebellious Mazrui in Mombasa.

Midlevel Bombay government officials at once broached the legal question of whether such a treaty with the United States contravened the preemptive agreements of 1798 and 1800 that Oman had concluded with the government of India. These earlier agreements, taken together, had given the British a special position in Oman and had bound the rulers of Muscat to prohibit French or Dutch consuls in their domains.[3]

In fact, few senior Bombay officials were seriously aroused by the news. Addressing the issue raised, the legal officer of the Bombay government opined that, on the surface at least, there was nothing in either of the earlier British agreements with Oman that precluded or would prevent the ruler of Muscat from entering into a treaty with the Americans. Nevertheless, it was considered prudent to bring the matter to the attention of the governor general of India for his review. In due course, after studying the issue but without having the text of the United States–Muscat treaty, the governor general informed the Bombay government that in his view the ruler of Muscat was not prohibited by his agreements with the government of India from entering into any such engagements with foreign nations. The treaty of 1798, he observed, had only forbidden Omani commercial intercourse with the French and the Dutch during their war with the British.[4]

While the subject was still under consideration in India's governmental political circles, the British naval commander-in-chief in the Indian Ocean, Vice Admiral Sir John Gore, decided to take matters into his own hands. In December 1833, without informing the

British political authorities in India, Gore instructed Captain Henry Hart, commander of His Majesty's ship of war *Imogene,* to proceed immediately to Zanzibar, where Sayyid Sa'id had gone shortly after signing the American treaty. The goal was to ascertain exactly what had transpired during Roberts's visit to Muscat. Hart, as it turned out, was hardly qualified for such a delicate diplomatic mission.

Departing Bombay on January 5, 1834, the *Imogene* arrived at Zanzibar at the end of the month. An English and an American merchant ship were in the harbor. Sayyid Sa'id had already been told of British concern over the American treaty, and he was clearly worried about the sudden appearance of an English warship. He went out of his way to be hospitable to Hart and to the officers of the *Imogene,* greeting them on the steps of his palace at Mtoni with assurances that he had always regarded the English "as his best friends."

In a series of three meetings, the sayyid and Hart discussed the American treaty at length. The sayyid raised the matter. His agent at Bombay, he asserted, had written to him about alleged British distress over the treaty. He had indeed signed such a treaty, but he insisted that he had done so without any intention of injuring or forgetting his English friends. On the contrary, he sweepingly announced, he was willing to give the English everything, even the entire country if they asked for it. As for the Americans, "He cared nothing for them, they were nothing to him," or so Hart reported. He would show Hart the agreement. If it contained anything objectionable to Hart, he would at once alter or break the treaty and send it back to the Americans. The treaty, like the Americans, meant nothing to him.

On the following day, Sayyid Sa'id gave Hart the American treaty and asked the British naval captain to read it. Hart should then advise him whether to alter or to break the treaty. But, the canny ruler asked, would the British support him if, presumably in response to his altering or breaking the treaty, the Americans attacked him? Taken aback, Hart agreed to study the document.

As for the sayyid's query about British support in the event of an American attack, the British naval captain hastily explained that higher authorities would have to make that determination. All the same, Hart stated, it was a great pity that the ruler had concluded the treaty with the Americans without first consulting the British. There had been no need to sign such a document. Instead, the ruler could simply have told the Americans that they were welcome to trade with his dominions, but that a treaty with the United States was not possible without prior consultations with his English friends. Sayyid Sa'id agreed, but pointedly observed that he now had the treaty. What was to be done? He reiterated his offer to cancel the treaty, but again asked Hart whether he could count on British support if he unilaterally renounced the recently concluded treaty and the Americans consequently attacked his domains.

Later that same day Hart read the English text of the treaty. It permitted the United States, he observed, to establish agents (consuls) anywhere in the ruler's domains. As yet, the British enjoyed no such privilege. Hart also expressed surprise that Sayyid Sa'id had agreed to a single 5 percent import charge, thereby waiving all export duties and pilotage or other dues, and that American shipmasters were allowed to fix the value of their cargos. These privileges, in the eyes of some English traders, enabled American merchants to buy copal, for example, on the eastern coast of Africa for between sixteen and twenty Spanish dollars, including a duty of eight dollars per *rasila* (thirty-six pounds), when British merchants had to pay thirty dollars in Zanzibar. The American treaty, Hart concluded, was "most far-fetched and over-reaching."

Hart subsequently went through the document, paragraph by paragraph, with Hassan bin Ibrahim, the ruler's agent and interpreter in Zanzibar, explaining to his interlocutor the precise meaning of the English phraseology. Averring he had not been in Muscat when the treaty was signed, Hassan bin Ibrahim disclaimed all responsibility and opined that the ruler must not have comprehended the meaning of the treaty language.

The next day Sayyid Sa'id made a formal call on the British warship. While aboard, he offered the British navy, through Hart, his seventy-four-gun warship *Liverpool*. The canny ruler had two objectives in doing so. He hoped that this gesture on his part would mollify what he perceived to be official British displeasure over his signing of the American treaty. He also wanted to get rid of a vessel that was far too large for his purposes and had become a white elephant in his fleet.

At a third meeting with Hart, Sayyid Sa'id recounted his version of the origins of the treaty with the United States. He allegedly related that, on his first visit, Roberts had asked the ruler to reimburse him for monies due from one of his subjects as a result of a commercial transaction of five or six years earlier, when Roberts had been trading on the East African coast. The sayyid claimed he had refused to do so. Roberts had then broached the subject of a treaty, contending that the ruler allowed other foreign vessels and agents to visit and to settle in Zanzibar. What fault had the Americans committed, he had asked, that they should not be allowed to do the same? Americans, Roberts had pointed out, traded everywhere.

Sayyid Sa'id, according to Hart, unflatteringly described Roberts as "an old, fat, blustering man." The ruler averred he had signed the treaty simply to be rid of Roberts and had not considered the matter to be of any importance. He denied having seen Roberts or anyone else actually sign the treaty. Nor had there been any witnesses to the signing. "They brought the paper to me and I signed it," the sayyid reportedly stated.

Remonstrating that the sayyid had erred in signing the treaty, Hart repeated his earlier comment: American trade could have been welcomed, but treaty negotiations should not have been undertaken without British concurrence. Once more Sayyid Sa'id agreed, but this time he observed that it would have taken a long time to get a reply from Bombay.

Had it been the admiral, the ruler artfully remarked, a quick answer would of course have been forthcoming. But expeditious replies were not, unfortunately, the practice of the Bombay authorities. Expressing exasperation with the problem of dealing with British officialdom in India, Sayyid Sa'id complained that when he wrote to the British political resident in Bushire (Bushehr), he was told that his letter would have to be sent to the Bombay government; when he wrote to Bombay, he was informed that any princely communication should first to go the British political resident in Bushire. His last letter to the resident, he complained, was still unanswered after six months. As a result, he had incurred the ire of the "King of Persia," his father-in-law. In such circumstances, could he really have expected a prompt reply had he submitted to the British authorities the American request for a treaty?

Never in the future, the ruler pledged, would he conclude another treaty with a foreign power without advance British consent. In fact, the French governor of Bourbon wished to come to Zanzibar to conclude a treaty, but the sayyid would inform the French that they must first consult with the Bombay government before he could enter negotiations. Whatever was agreed there would be satisfactory to him. Sayyid Sa'id reiterated that, if the British promised to support him, he would send the American treaty back to the United States and refuse to comply with it.

Hart, perhaps by then aware that he was out of his depth, acknowledged that he had no authority to make a treaty and that breaking a treaty was a serious matter. A commitment from the ruler that, in the future, no treaty would be made without prior British approval would suffice. He also sought a written pledge that Sayyid Sa'id was prepared to break the American treaty if the British wished, and he asked for a copy of the document. The ruler readily assented to these demands. Further, in order to mollify the British, Sayyid Sa'id asked Hart to inform the Bombay authorities that he would welcome an English resident representative in Zanzibar.[5]

On the following day, an Arabic language document, drafted by Hassan bin Ibrahim and signed by Sayyid Sa'id, was given to Hart. In it the ruler pledged to cancel the American treaty should this be the desire of the governor general of India and if the British would support him against a possible retaliatory American attack. The letter also promised that the ruler would conclude no future treaty without British acquiescence. The original of the U.S. treaty in Sayyid Sa'id's possession was given to Hart.[6]

After returning to Bombay, Hart submitted, through Royal Navy channels, the sayyid's offer to cancel the American treaty. A subsequent letter from Sayyid Sa'id, sent through his agent in Bombay, was also submitted to the governor general of India, apprising the British authorities of the expected arrival of a French brigantine, with a commissioner aboard charged with concluding a treaty. The French, so the ruler claimed, wished both an offensive and a defensive treaty. Specifically, they sought Sayyid Sa'id's help in attacking Bembalooka. In return, the French promised to assist him in any way he might require. They also wanted permission for a French agent to reside at Zanzibar. He had responded to the French request that he could do nothing about a treaty without prior approval from the Bombay government.

The governor general, while appreciating Sayyid Sa'id's offer, stood by his earlier judgment that there were no tenable grounds on which the British could interfere to modify or annul the American treaty. He doubted the propriety or the expediency of accepting the ruler's offer to break it. The sayyid should be so informed. Since the offer had come through naval rather than political channels, the reply should be sent in the same fashion. Captain James H. Plumridge of the British Navy was instructed to sail directly to Zanzibar, bearing a letter from Vice Admiral Gore setting forth the British view. The original of the American treaty should be returned. Sayyid Sa'id was doubtless relieved when he eventually received the British response.

For the British, however, the matter did not end there. Six months later after learning of Captain Hart's démarche to Sayyid Sa'id, the India board in London, which also represented the British government, reacted strongly and negatively to this gratuitous naval intervention in a political matter. There could be but one "supreme authority" in India, it thundered. Interference by the British navy in political transactions within an area of the East India Company's former authority, the board insisted, was unconstitutional and impolitic. Hart had no knowledge of existing relations between the government of India and Sayyid Sa'id, nor could he be aware of how overall British interests might be injured or promoted by his actions.

In August 1834, the Secret Committee, the advisory staff of the India board, was asked to report on the circumstances under which a naval officer, Hart, had been deputed by the vice admiral to conduct communications with a foreign state. The Secret Committee first thought that Hart had simply imagined an American treaty. Americans, it observed, had never entered into such agreements in the eastern seas. But even if the treaty was authentic, however, there was no reason for concern: "Americans are not the object of political jealousy to us in India, and the trifling trade which they may carry on in their small vessels with the territory of the Imaum of Muscat is not likely to interfere with our own. We do not seek a monopoly of the trade with Muscat," it declared. The treaty was at most concerned with commercial, not with political, intercourse. All that Great Britain sought in Sayyid Sa'id's domains was most-favored-nation status.

Accepting the Secret Committee's observations, the India board "strongly recommended" to the admiralty that the commander-in-chief of British naval forces in the Indian Ocean and his officers be firmly instructed to abstain from future communications with the states of the East, except in concert with the government of India. The admiralty unanimously concurred in this judgment and instructed Gore and the naval officers in his command not to interfere in the political affairs of Asian nations. It was a serious and deserved rebuke to Gore and Hart. Gore took it in stride; Hart saw it as a personal rebuff. For years thereafter, Hart sought exoneration for the slur that he construed had been cast upon his conduct in Zanzibar. His efforts were unavailing. He had indeed been wrongly instructed, but he was also the victim of his own excessive zeal.

Americans may not have known it, but the die was cast. They could trade with the domains of Sayyid Sa'id without fear of British intervention. Roberts knew nothing of the intragovernmental controversy that his treaty with Muscat had stirred in British official circles. As he departed on his second mission, the issue had been resolved to the benefit of American citizens. The United States was free to pursue its own interests in the area. And Sayyid Sa'id could develop his relationship with the United States unhindered by British interference.

9

The Final Mission

On April 23, 1835, the refitted USS *Peacock* sailed from New York with Roberts aboard. This time there was no subterfuge about his status. All recognized him to be an accredited diplomatic representative of the United States on a special mission. It must have pleased Roberts's sense of dignity, even though he had not been accorded the ministerial rank that he believed his diplomatic mission merited. Neither he nor his family could know it, but he was embarking on a voyage from which he would not return.

The ship reached Rio de Janeiro on June 10. There, the US schooner *Enterprise* from the U.S. Navy's Brazil squadron was transferred to Commodore Kennedy's command. A month later, on July 12, the two warships sailed in company for Indian Ocean waters. Inevitably, on a voyage of that length and with differing sailing capabilities, the ships soon became separated. The *Peacock*, the swifter of the two vessels, arrived at Zanzibar on September 1 after a fifty-one-day passage.

To his disappointment, Roberts learned that Sayyid Sa'id was in Muscat, necessitating a trip to that Arabian port. Had the ruler been in Zanzibar and treaty ratifications exchanged there, the *Peacock* could have proceeded directly to Siam. Sayyid Khalid, the ruler's eldest son whom Roberts had met two years earlier in Muscat, acted as governor of the island. Sayyid Khalid hospitably entertained Roberts and the ship's officers before the *Peacock* departed a week later. The *Enterprise* arrived in Zanzibar on September 14 and, after four days in port with equally hospitable treatment, sailed directly for Bombay.[1] Both vessels were supplied with provisions at the governor's expense.

The Masirah Incident

En route to Muscat, the *Peacock* suffered what appeared to be a serious mishap. In the early morning hours of September 1 off the coast of the island of Masirah, the ship suddenly and unexpectedly ran aground on an extensive, submerged coral reef. Many vessels had previously been grounded in these uncharted and reef-strewn waters off the southeastern Arabian coast.

Unsuccessful in initial efforts to refloat the vessel, and fearing predatory intentions on the part of Arab tribesmen assembling on shore, Commodore Kennedy decided to send one of the ship's cutters to Muscat to seek help. It was believed that the seas were generally calm at that season of the year as the monsoon winds shifted, but the possible danger from piratical Arab dhows would have to be risked. Midshipman William Rogers Taylor and six crewmen were assigned to the mission. Roberts, believing he would be of more value in Muscat—where he had previously been—than aboard the crippled vessel, volunteered to accompany the party. He took the Muscat treaty documents with him.

Embarking on the cutter during the night, Roberts and his companions had by dawn made good their escape. Although followed for five hours by native boats, they outsailed their Arab pursuers. The seas were heavier than expected, and more than once the small boat threatened to capsize. On September 26, after almost three days at sea, the cutter with her sun-scorched and exhausted crew managed to reach Muscat harbor.[2]

On landing, fatigued though he was, Roberts at once went to the home of Sa'id bin Khalfan, who had acted as interpreter and translator during the treaty negotiations and, through him, obtained an immediate audience with the ruler. After explaining the *Peacock*'s predicament, Roberts sought Sayyid Sa'id's help in rescuing the stricken American warship. The sayyid at once agreed.

One of the sayyid's ships then in the Muscat harbor, the *Sultanah*, was placed under the navigational command of Midshipman

Taylor and, with the *Peacock*'s six crew members aboard, weighed anchor the following day for Masirah Island. Orders were also sent to the Omani governor of Zoar, near Ras al-Had, to provide assistance in the event the *Peacock*'s crew members had been forced to abandon ship and were attempting to make their way overland to Muscat. A party of bedouins was engaged by the ruler to proceed overland to the vicinity of Masirah Island to protect the Americans from hostile tribesmen. Roberts gave the Omani captain of the *Sultanah* a letter that could, if necessary, be used to explain the presence of two American warships in the area. He also sent the governor of Zoar an American flag to be used to reassure the *Peacock*'s crew, if stranded, of the bedouin rescue party's friendly intentions. Among European and American mariners, the tribesmen of the southern Arabian coast had long been reputed to be brutal and even murderous. For Americans in particular, the vicissitudes suffered by the crew of the Boston ship *Commerce* in 1792, when shipwrecked near Masirah Island, seemed to confirm that negative impression.

As it happened, the *Peacock*'s dilemma was not as serious as had been feared. Efforts had continued all day on September 22, after the cutter's escape, to extricate the vessel. By nightfall, after jettisoning all superfluous gear and eleven of the ship's guns, the vessel floated free of the reef and proceeded toward Muscat. En route, she encountered the East India Company's surveying brig *Palinurus*, captained by S. B. Haines. Captain Haines provided a certificate to the *Peacock*'s sailing master, John Weems, that the waters around Masirah Island were inadequately charted. This would help absolve the *Peacock*'s command of responsibility for the grounding. Five days later, after rounding Ras al-Had on September 28, the *Peacock* encountered the *Sultanah*. The next day the two vessels put into Muscat together. No lives had been lost aboard the *Peacock*. Roberts could once again breathe easily. Twice during the trying days of uncertainty about the *Peacock*'s fate, Sayyid Sa'id promised a deeply worried Roberts that, should the American warship be lost and the crew rescued, he would provide one of his own ships of war to repatriate the American ship's complement to the United States. Generously, he also offered to place another of his vessels at Roberts's disposal to enable the American emissary to accomplish the rest of his mission.

Treaty Ratification with Oman

With the *Peacock* safely in Muscat, and after princely congratulations over the fortuitous outcome of what could have been a fatal incident, Roberts could implement the first part of the diplomatic mission with which he had been charged. On September 30, he informed Sayyid Sa'id that he had the necessary U.S. instrument of ratification, to which was appended the original Omani treaty document that he had taken with him two years earlier, and he was now prepared to exchange treaty ratifications. He asked that Sa'id bin Khalfan translate into Arabic the American certificate of exchange, attesting that the requisite exchange of instruments of ratification had taken place. It was Roberts's understanding that in exchange for the American treaty package, he would receive the second signed original treaty document that Sayyid Sa'id had retained, together with a certificate of exchange signed by the ruler. He hoped the exchange could be accomplished quickly so he could pursue his other diplomatic assignments—the need to proceed to Muscat had already skewed his planning. So had the Masirah incident, although less so than might have been the case.

Now, however, a problem arose. To Roberts's surprise and disappointment, Sayyid Sa'id announced that he did not have the signed treaty document in Muscat. It had been left in Zanzibar, where the ruler had expected the exchange ceremony to take place months earlier. There was apparently no mention of having given the treaty to Captain Hart, or of the treaty's return by Captain Plumridge. Rather than wait for the treaty document to be sent from Zanzibar, which would have taken a minimum of three months, Roberts decided to prepare yet another treaty text for use in the exchange of ratifications ceremony.

By the following day, October 1, Roberts had prepared a new English original of the treaty. Not until two days later could Sa'id bin Khalfan complete the Arabic version. Inexplicably, formal signing and sealing of the new original by Sayyid Sa'id and Roberts was further delayed until October 10. Nevertheless, the sayyid's letter transmitting the treaty document to Roberts was dated September 30, which came to be regarded as the date of Omani ratification. In fact, no formal treaty ratification procedure existed in Sayyid Sa'id's realm. The ruler's signature and seal signified not only the conclusion of a treaty but also ratification. In this case, however, since no Omani instrument of ratification existed, a certification of exchange was handwritten at the bottom of the newly prepared treaty original.

With the exchange of ratifications, such as it was, completed, Roberts inquired when the treaty should become effective. He was obviously unaware that, according to American law, it could not go into effect in his own country until it was proclaimed in the U.S. *Official Gazette*. Ever the grand seigneur, Sayyid Sa'id left it to Roberts to designate the date. Roberts proposed June 30, 1834, the date on which Senate "advice and consent" had been accorded.[3] Although such a retroactive arrangement could cause some revenue loss, the sayyid readily acquiesced. The possibility now existed that American shipmasters who had paid higher duties in the ruler's domains after June 30, 1834, could demand rebates, but Sayyid Sa'id personally stood to lose nothing from such an arrangement. In the previous year he had again farmed out revenue collection to an expatriate Indian custom collector for a fixed fee, paid yearly and in advance. If rebates were necessary, it was the customs farmer's loss.

While still in Muscat, Roberts prepared a circular letter, dated October 10, 1835, to inform American shipmasters of this concession and to advise them of their right to claim refunds for any higher customs duties that they had paid. Roberts sent a similar letter to the ruler's agent in Zanzibar. There is no indication that any visiting American shipmaster saw a copy of Roberts's letter, or that American captains or supercargoes sought refunds.

At Sayyid Sa'id's request, Roberts also wrote a letter advising American shipmasters that Omani naval forces were still blockading Mombasa, where the Mazrui were in rebellion, and that all trade with that port was prohibited.[4]

Although Roberts had initially contended that no presents for the ruler were necessary at the ratification ceremony, he had acquiesced in Secretary Forsyth's view that custom demanded such gifts for the occasion. Hence, presents were again presented to Sayyid Sa'id. These consisted of two sets of richly mounted glass lamps with a new form of shade; three barrels of American manufactured nankeens; a map of the United States on richly gilt rollers; eight satin dresses, all richly trimmed; one embroidered lace dress with satin underdress; one satin-faced Tibet dress; three embossed pocket handkerchiefs; three pairs of silk hose; three pairs of gloves; three pairs of shoes; a corded shirt; a rich satin coat and vest; a blonde dress hat; a blue cloth uniform coat with major general's insignia; a military hat and plume of equivalent grade; a gold-mounted sword; an American flag; a patent rifle with gold inscription; a patent carbine; a set of American coins; and various smaller items.[5] Presents were also again given to Sa'id bin Khalfan and to his brother, Abdullah, who had hosted Roberts during his second Muscat sojourn.

During Roberts's stay in Muscat, he and senior members of his party met frequently with the Omani elite. Although Sayyid Sa'id had offered Roberts a house in town or residence facilities on board one of his ships in harbor immediately after he had arrived aboard the cutter, Roberts chose to accept the hospitality of his old friend Sa'id bin Khalfan, who reputedly had the most comfortably furnished house in Muscat. There, in a highly unusual gesture of esteem, the sayyid paid a call on the American emissary on the very day that the *Peacock* and *Sultanah* arrived. On the following day, Roberts presented Commodore Kennedy and the ship's officers to Sayyid Sa'id, who congratulated them on their safe arrival. It was Allah's wish, the pious Muslim ruler declared—Allah be praised. The ruler also informed Kennedy that he had given orders that the *Peacock*'s guns be retrieved by divers and asked where the guns should be sent. When jettisoned off Masirah Island, their location had been marked with a buoy. No one could be sure whether the sayyid was simply making idle talk, but his offer was nevertheless appreciated.

A few days later, on October 2, the ruler gave a dinner for Roberts and the ship's officers at his palace. Although the sayyid excused himself from participating, two of his sons, along with the governor of Zoar and the Khalfan brothers, attended. The ships' officers and crew members were also accorded opportunities to wander around Muscat and its environs. It is doubtful that many were impressed, although the ship's surgeon, Dr. W. S. W. Ruschenberger, perceptively recorded the sights and sounds of that Arab town. Roberts wrote one of his daughters that he had been made a chieftain of a bedouin tribe. Perhaps that was so, but more likely is that he and the ship's officers were presented with Arab headgear and clothing and treated to an outdoor, native Arab feast arranged by the ruler.

On October 5, while Roberts and the sayyid awaited the final exchange of treaty ratifications, Sayyid Sa'id, accompanied by one of his sons and by Sa'id bin Khalfan, visited the *Peacock*. A twenty-one-gun salute was rendered and the yardarms were manned. These honors were repeated when the Omani party left a half-hour later. During the vessel's stay in Muscat, the sayyid bountifully supplied her crew with food and water and otherwise demonstrated his warm feeling toward the American visitors in many other ways. At sunset, October 10, after firing a farewell salute, the *Peacock* set sail for Bombay, where refitting would be necessary before proceeding eastward.[6]

Refitting in Bombay

Twelve days later, on October 22, the *Peacock* docked in Bombay. A survey of the structural damage the vessel had incurred when she foundered on the Masirah Island reef revealed that repairs would be more extensive than had been expected. A new false keel would have to be installed, and the ship's bottom needed to be caulked and coppered. To Roberts's disappointment, it would take almost six weeks for these repairs to be completed. The voyage was proceeding more slowly than he had hoped. The day after he arrived, Roberts reported to the secretary of state, by dispatch from Bombay, that treaty ratifications had been exchanged with the ruler of Muscat.[7]

The English East India Company graciously made its dockyard facilities available for the refitting process. New guns to replace those thrown overboard at Masirah Island could be purchased from John Company stores. Roberts and his party made calls on appropriate British officials, who received them cordially and with no trace of rancor. In smaller matters such as provisioning, the Indian Parsi firm of Jehangeer and Monockjee Nowrojee assisted.[8] (The firm handled all American commercial transactions in Bombay, though trade between American ports and Bombay was in fact limited: No more than six to eight American vessels visited Bombay each year.[9])

Such British courtesies notwithstanding, an undercurrent of suspicion of U.S. purposes in the Indian Ocean area persisted. Thus, on October 24, after announcing the arrival of the *Peacock*, the *Bombay Gazette* recalled "rumors" of the previous year that two American warships had cruised the Indian Ocean and had sought from the imam of Muscat permission to establish a "factory" at that port. Their application to do so had been successful—through coercion, it was implied—until Sayyid Sa'id had sent a remonstrance to the British admiral, indicating that he had no wish to grant such privileges to the Americans. Noting American ("Brother Jonathan's") perseverance in such matters, the paper wondered whether the reappearance of a U.S. warship portended an intention to pursue such a design.

Reading the article, Roberts and his colleagues could chortle that the British-sponsored paper was uninformed. It showed no knowledge that treaty ratifications had in fact been exchanged in Muscat only a fortnight earlier. Relying on earlier hearsay either in Muscat or in Zanzibar, Ruschenberger observed that some British officers had presented such a remonstrance in an interview with Sayyid Sa'id, and had disparaged the United States as insignificant in the eyes of Europe. To this, the sayyid had allegedly responded, "How can that be? I see in my ports ten of their ships for one of yours, and I have read they flogged you in two wars."[10] How many of the statements that Hart and Ruschenberger attributed to Sayyid Sa'id were actually made is anyone's guess. But Americans and British alike found no difficulty in quoting him, each side to its advantage. At a minimum, the sayyid was skillful in dealing with foreign representatives. He seemed to empathize with all who were immediately at hand, yet avoided excessively close commitments to any foreign polity.

As if to emphasize Sayyid Sa'id's friendship for the United States, the American party received another tangible indication of his goodwill and reliability. In late November, the native vessel the *Lord Castlereigh* arrived in Bombay from Muscat. As part of her cargo, she carried the eleven guns that the *Peacock* had thrown overboard at Masirah Island; the sayyid had arranged their salvage and transport to Bombay. The guns were no longer needed, but the gesture was generous and appreciated.

In a letter addressed to Commodore Kennedy, dated November 6, 1835, the ruler indicated that the vessel he had sent to the spot where the grounding occurred had returned. After having salvaged the guns and ten broken spars, he was forwarding the recovered guns, the freight on which he had already paid. The broken spars were of no use, but the jettisoned anchors and cable chains would be sent as soon as these they could be recovered. Responding on December 1, a grateful Kennedy profusely thanked the ruler for his "untiring and indefatigable exertions" on behalf of the American navy.[11] In due course, President Martin Van Buren, in his annual message to the Congress, paid public tribute to the ruler for his generous action.[12]

For Roberts and those members of the *Peacock'*s complement not involved in the refitting process, the idle days were largely spent sightseeing and paying calls around Bombay. There was plenty of time to explore all parts of the city, and excursions were made to the ruins on nearby Elephanta and Salsette Islands. Roberts and ships' officers attended the British governor's official reception, observing how English and native Indian officers were separately received. By invitation, they also visited the American Baptist missionary school, which enjoyed a high reputation for its educational effectiveness in the face of sharp Indian caste distinctions. Pleasant though these outings were, Roberts chafed at the prolonged delay. He still had much to do before his diplomatic mission could be completed.

Eastward Bound

On December 4, with refitting finally completed, the *Peacock* sailed from Bombay. She was accompanied by the *Enterprise*, which had arrived in early November. By then, a large number of ships' officers and men were suffering from high fevers brought on by exposure to winds laden with "miasmata, exhaled from the marshy lands over which they blew."[13] The ships remained in Ceylon, at Colombo, from December 16 to 24, largely so the crew could rest. Colombo, the Americans concluded, was the "brightest spot in the colonial possessions of the British crown."[14] Roberts and Ruschenberger lauded an American Baptist missionary school for, like its

missionary school counterpart in Bombay, its educational effectiveness and the high reputation it enjoyed in local society.

From Colombo, the two vessels sailed for Batavia, where they
arrived on January 11, 1836. Hospitality was again extended to
Roberts and to the ships' officers by Mr. Forestice, the American
businessman resident in Batavia who had befriended Roberts on
his earlier visit to that Dutch-held settlement. Roberts was anxious
to proceed as quickly as possible to Siam, but he would have to remain in Batavia for over a month.

Family News

Despite Roberts's prolonged absence from his family, his touching
solicitude for his daughters and theirs for him continued. In Batavia, much to his pleasure, fourteen letters from his six daughters
in Portsmouth awaited him. Written between six and eight months
earlier, all informed him that they were well. To his annoyance,
however, there were no letters from his daughter Harriet or her
husband, Congressman Parker, or from his daughter Mary Ann,
who was living with the Parkers in Delhi, New York.

Acknowledging receipt of the letters, Roberts expressed his
pleasure and offered some paternal advice. Objecting that the fi-
ancé of one had no money and could not support her, he urged that
she marry a man of means. One wonders whether his own family
experience and continued straitened financial circumstances may
have influenced his advice. On another matter, he objected to two
other daughters going to the market in a packet; they should go, he
insisted, only in a horse carriage. He would not write to the Parkers in New York, he angrily added, until he had first heard from
them.[15] From Roberts's earlier correspondence with his children,
one gains the impression that Harriet was his favorite daughter,
hence his disappointment in not hearing from her. He was also
anxious to hear about the status of plans for the publication of his
journal from the Parkers.

Siam

Monsoonal weather conditions—incessant rain and heavy seas—
delayed departure for Siam and made for slow sailing.[16] Not until

the morning of March 25 did the two vessels find themselves near the mouth of the Menam River. To save time, the *Enterprise* was sent ahead carrying a letter from Roberts to the *phra khlang*, which Roberts had prepared the previous day. Announcing his arrival, Roberts wrote that he had brought with him the ratified Siamese treaty for the purpose of exchanging it for its counterpart in the possession of the government of Siam, once that document had been ratified by the king and the royal seal had been affixed to the articles of the treaty. The necessary certificates of ratification could then be prepared and exchanged.

Roberts advised that he had brought with him all the items that had been requested, except for the stone statuary desired by the king, which he had earlier warned might be unobtainable, and the *phra khlang*'s trees, plants, and seeds, which were jettisoned when the *Peacock* ran into the reef on the Arabian coast. A suitable vessel was requested to receive the gifts. The *phra khlang* was also asked to provide proper vessels, "capable of protecting from the inclemencies of the weather," to convey Roberts and a party of twenty-five persons to the capital. He was anxious, Roberts said, to conclude the exchange of ratifications as quickly as possible since he had still to visit "many kingdoms," which would take another year.[17]

Roberts's hopes of expediting the exchange of ratifications were soon dashed. As he should have learned on his previous visit, the Siamese had their own finely honed protocol and would not be hurried.

When the *Enterprise* crossed the Menam River bar and arrived at Paknam, her commander, Lieutenant Campbell, took Roberts's letter ashore and asked the prefect to forward it to the *phra khlang* at once. Predictably, the prefect would not agree to do so until considerable palaver and interpretation of the contents of the letter had transpired.

On March 28, as the *Peacock* lay off the Menam bar, she was visited by the heir apparent to the throne of Siam. The prince spoke English passably well, having been taught the language by the American missionaries in Bangkok, of whom he spoke favorably. Fearing seasickness, however, he soon returned to shore.

While awaiting a reply to Roberts's letter, Ruschenberger and a naval colleague decided to try to go to Bangkok, presumably to buy such provisions for the ship that were not available at Paknam. As their small boat sought to pass Paknam, they were hailed and ordered ashore. Taken to the prefect, that functionary insisted he did not have authority to allow them to proceed to Bangkok. Piedade, the Portuguese captain of the port, who asserted he had just come from the capital with a letter for Roberts, gave the same response. If provisions were required, he stated, a letter might be sent to Robert Hunter, a British merchant in Bangkok known to Roberts, who could supply whatever might be needed. To violate the rules of Siam, the prefect and Piedade cajoled, might break the friendship that obtained between the United States and Siam as a result of the treaty. Their remonstrations took place over a bottle of gin that an officer of the *Enterprise* had presented to the prefect. The gin produced high spirits, but no permission to proceed.

The prefect was finally prevailed upon to seek permission from the *phra khlang* for Ruschenberger and a companion to visit Bangkok. Although permission was eventually received, Ruschenberger had by then returned to the ship. Only his naval companion ascended the river to Bangkok.[18]

Meanwhile, Roberts and his party waited impatiently for the royal barges that Piedade, on the *phra khlang*'s instructions, had assured him would be provided. It was necessary for the Siamese authorities in Bangkok to make appropriate arrangements to receive Roberts and his companions, Piedade explained. They must travel in state. Roberts could hardly be pleased when the American brig *Maria Theresa*, which arrived four or five days after the *Peacock*, received almost immediate permission to proceed upriver to Bangkok. Official status had its disadvantages.

Finally, on April 5, the promised river conveyance arrived. A three-masted royal ceremonial barge, she was crewed largely by native Christians who had been educated by Portuguese missionaries. Piedade and an interpreter were aboard. The presents for the king and the *phra khlang* were placed on the barge, after which Roberts, Kennedy, and twenty-three members of the complements of the two ships boarded her. Included in the American party were Ruschenberger, a Dutchman named R. I. Jacobs who had been engaged in Batavia as an interpreter, nine musicians from the *Peacock*'s band, and five servants. This time Roberts clearly intended to produce an impression.

Arriving at Paknam, the American party visited the prefect, who gave the customary feast in their honor. In return, Roberts presented the prefect with a double-barreled gun and two cases of Dutch gin, bought in Batavia. Both gifts were gratefully received. Once the feast was completed, the prefect asked for a list of the presents intended for the king. Roberts declined to fulfill the request, and the prefect did not insist. The prefect recorded the names of all the officers in the American party, which would be forwarded to the capital by courier.

After overnighting at Paknam, Roberts and his party reembarked on the royal barge and proceeded upriver. Five boats accompanied the royal barge, carrying an honor guard of some 300 armed and uniformed soldiers. The riverbanks were lined with cheering Siamese citizens mobilized for the occasion. The event was something of a "jubilee," as Roberts later glowingly described it. That evening the party arrived at Bangkok, where it was ceremoniously escorted to the house that had been prepared to accommodate the Americans.[19]

On the morning after the American party's arrival at Bangkok, Ruschenberger called on the heir apparent, who had earlier visited the *Peacock*. A popular prince, and half brother of the ruling monarch, he was regarded by the king with some suspicion and played no role in governmental matters. For six months or more, he jocularly related, he had possessed an American newspaper containing a list of the officers of the *Peacock* and an announcement of the ship's projected voyage to Siam, but he had never seen fit to communicate the news to his royal sibling.[20] Such was the state of affairs in Siam. Later that day, Roberts, Kennedy, the naval officers in full dress uniform, and the ship's band called on the deputy *phra khlang* and, later, on the acting *phra khlang*, who acted as minister of foreign affairs in the absence of his brother in Chantibun. Toasts were drunk to the king of Siam and to the president of the United States.[21]

With protocol calls completed, Roberts now sought to arrange an expeditious exchange of treaty ratifications. This proved to be a more complicated and time-consuming procedure than anticipated. Siamese and American practices, not surprisingly, were again at variance. Roberts might fret, but his Siamese hosts would not be hurried.

On April 9, at the request of the king, Roberts formally delivered the treaty to the Siamese authorities. Accompanied by a contingent of ships' officers in full dress uniform, two of them bearing a box containing the treaty, the party marched in solemn procession from their Bangkok residence to the riverbank. The American flag and the *Peacock*'s band were in the van. Waiting to receive the box was a royal canoe, eighty-feet long with thirty-four rowers, a gold-embroidered canopy, and a crimson silk overhanging its center.

On reaching the river's edge, Roberts took the treaty box, held it above his head to show respect, and then ceremoniously handed it to the *phra khlang*'s secretary, who had been deputed to receive it. The secretary placed the box on a silver chalice, which was in turn set on a massive silver stand. The silver stand was placed on a raised seat under the gold-embroidered canopy. No servant was allowed to carry the treaty box or to touch it, even on the boat, lest it sully the document. As the ceremony was under way, the ship's band played "Hail Columbia," after which a Siamese band played a few microtonic notes.[22]

Soon after the treaty had been delivered, Roberts received a written notice that the king was anxious to have the pair of gold-mounted swords, with massive gold scabbards, delivered to him. The swords had been made especially for the occasion. The crest of each hilt was surmounted by a golden elephant, the royal symbol of Siam, while its termination showed the American eagle with spread wings looking down on the elegant blade. The blade was of chased steel with a Siamese elephant and pagoda embossed on one side and the American eagle and flag on the other. The king had heard of these elaborately decorated swords and could not restrain his impatience to see them. They were delivered through Siamese emissaries. The other presents, including a set of rare American coins, were also delivered.[23]

The acting *phra khlang,* unacquainted with protocol niceties involving foreign treaties, asked Roberts to meet with a visiting vassal, the rajah of Ligore. The Malay tributary prince, who spoke English and Siamese, happened to be in Bangkok to assist in a funeral ceremony and, as Roberts was informed, had been designated by the king to arrange the Siamese aspects of the treaty ratification exchange. Accordingly, on April 12, Roberts, accompanied by Midshipman Taylor and several other naval officers in full dress uniform, called on the rajah at the junk where he resided.

The rajah, as Roberts understood it, was supposed to write the necessary certificate of ratification for the Siamese treaty original. Since this type of document was unknown to the Siamese, a form for such a certificate had been sent to the rajah some days earlier, in English with a Portuguese translation, in order to allow enough time for it to be translated into Siamese before the meeting with Roberts. To Roberts's chagrin, the rajah's secretary had mistaken the time of the meeting, and the Siamese translation of the certificate was not ready. The rajah was profusely apologetic, and another meeting was scheduled for the following day. However, Midshipman Taylor's service sword fascinated the rajah, who examined it with great care and unstinted admiration. He would doubtless have liked to have been presented with it as a gift for his services, but this was not to be.

Early the following morning, Roberts returned to the rajah's junk. This time, to the rajah's disappointment, Roberts was not accompanied by his naval entourage of the previous day. The Malay potentate clearly enjoyed being called upon by uniformed American naval officers—it elevated his status in Siamese eyes. Roberts stressed to the rajah that he alone had responsibility for treaty matters, hence there was no need for the naval officers' presence. An all-day session ensued, interspersed by elaborate meals and two visits by Siamese princes, during which the outstanding protocol details of the Siamese ratification process were hammered out. The pace was leisurely, as Roberts should have expected.

The rajah first asserted that the king's seal could be placed only on the Siamese certificate of ratification, not on the treaty itself. This, he insisted, was traditional Siamese practice. Roberts said that would not suffice, inasmuch as it was inconsistent with the provisions of the treaty. In the preamble of the treaty, Roberts pointed out, the king had promised to affix his seal to the articles of the treaty. Surely the king would abide by his word. Otherwise, why had the *phra khlang* agreed to include this arrangement in the signed document? It would, of course, also be necessary to place the royal seal on the Siamese certificate of ratification. Without it, Siam could not be considered to have ratified the treaty.

Although the rajah strongly demurred, he eventually acqui-esced to Roberts's procedural demand. The treaty language sup-ported Roberts's contention. The American-prepared Siamese cer-tificate of ratification, written in English, Siamese, and Portuguese, was then appended to the Siamese-held copy of the treaty text. By nightfall, Roberts could be gratified that significant progress had been made. It was agreed that he and the rajah would meet again the following day, at which time Roberts would be shown the treaty text with all Siamese seals affixed.

On April 14, as Roberts was about to leave for the rajah's resi-dence, he received an apologetic message asking that his visit be delayed. An error in dating the certificate had occurred the pre-vious day, it was explained, and it would be necessary to correct this by rewriting the document in all three languages. That same afternoon, however, with the dating error corrected, Roberts was invited to attend the seal-fixing ceremony. In his presence, the royal seal and those of six senior Siamese ministers, including that of the absent *phra khlang*, were solemnly affixed to the Siamese-held treaty document. The ceremony was followed by an elaborate official ban-quet to mark the occasion.

While these protocol negotiations were under way, an incident occurred that suggested divergent American and Siamese inter-pretations of the treaty provision dealing with the measurement of visiting American merchant ships for purposes of assessing duties (article 3). The American brig *Maria Theresa*, which was in port dur-ing Roberts's sojourn in Bangkok, he learned, had been measured by Siamese customs officers on the outside of the vessel rather than on deck, as had been agreed when the treaty was signed. The Sia-mese method of measuring the ship, Roberts believed, would result in higher duties and would set a precedent that would be followed with future American ships that visited Bangkok.

A disturbed Roberts called on the acting *phra khlang* to protest the system of measurement used for the *Maria Theresa* as inconsis-tent with the treaty provisions. The Siamese official insisted that the procedure followed by the customs officers was regularly applied to Siamese and Chinese junks. In response to Roberts's comment that the treaty dealt only with American-built vessels, the acting *phra khlang* adamantly insisted the measurement system in use was an old custom that could not be altered. He clearly knew nothing, or professed to know nothing, of the extended discussions that had taken place two years earlier between his brother, the *phra khlang*, and Roberts on the controversial issues of ship measurement and duties.

Roberts warned that he would recommend to the master of the *Maria Theresa* that a protest be registered with the Siamese government against what he considered a violation of the treaty. The violation would also be reported to the U.S. government. Coming at the very moment that instruments of ratification were being exchanged, Roberts predicted that a protest would cause immediate controversy between the two governments. His warning had some effect.

In a second call on the acting *phra khlang* to discuss the matter, it developed that the *Maria Theresa* had been measured a second time. On the second occasion, the Siamese measurement officials had taken half the ship's length in order to ascertain her breadth of beam. At that point, the deck was measured from one waterway to the other, omitting the waterways entirely, and including only part of the gunwale. As Roberts continued to object, the acting *phra khlang* sent for the ship's master and supercargo and asked if they were satisfied with the method of measurement. To Roberts's embarrassment, they at once acquiesced, since the second mode of measurement had reduced the vessel's duty by 170 ticals. With this, the Siamese dignitary indicated that the subject was closed. The difficulty over measurement techniques had been surmounted and the measurement method used on the second occasion for the *Maria Theresa* would henceforth be used to measure all American vessels.[24] Although Roberts regarded the revised measurement procedure as inconsistent with the negotiating history of the treaty, the *phra khlang* remained absent and could not be asked to intervene. Roberts swallowed his doubts and dropped his protest.

With this controversy resolved, arrangements could be made for the delivery of the Siamese treaty ratification documents to Roberts. Before this could be done, however, the king had to receive Roberts and those of his party who remained in Bangkok. By then, Commodore Kennedy had become ill and, accompanied by Dr. Ruschenberger, had returned to the *Peacock*. Two crew members aboard the ship had already died of Asiatic cholera.[25] Thus, Roberts's party was depleted in numbers and he could not make quite the show that he had hoped to do.

The audience with the king was set for April 16. Three Siamese barges, each rowed by thirty oarsmen, were provided for the occasion. In addition to the remaining twenty naval officers, each in full dress uniform, the master and supercargo of the *Maria Theresa* joined the American party. But the royal court rejected Roberts's request that the three American Baptist missionaries in Bangkok also be allowed to attend the ceremony. As the barges proceeded to the landing site, the *Peacock*'s bandsmen once more played "Hail Columbia." Ashore, Roberts was borne in a palanquin, while the officers rode richly caparisoned ponies along the short road to the royal palace. Throngs of people lined the way, and the royal elephants were paraded for the occasion.

Entering the audience chamber, where some of the mission's presents had been placed before the elevated throne, Roberts and his party found themselves in the presence of King Rama III. Some three hundred nobles and retainers, and several Arabs and Persians, were prostrate in the audience chamber before "His Magnificent Majesty." For Roberts and his party, the procedure was much the same as the American emissary had experienced two years earlier. Siamese court protocol officials had insisted that the naval officers leave their swords outside the audience hall. After doffing their hats, the members of the American party made three bows and advanced to seat themselves on designated carpets some distance from the throne.

As with the first royal audience, Roberts refused to agree that the American party members would remove their shoes and leave them outside, but they sat with their feet tucked behind them, as Siamese protocol required. After being seated, they made three bows from the waist down. As before, the king, after expressing his satisfaction at the presence of the American diplomatic mission, asked a few perfunctory questions of Roberts. These, and the answers to them, again went through the four-tier transmittal and translation process, which was hardly conducive to effective dialogue.

At one point, the king observed that the treaty placed the Americans on the same footing in Siam as the British. Although Roberts responded that such was not the intent of the treaty, he was later informed that the translator-transmitter had indicated Roberts's agreement with that royal judgment. One did not disagree with Siamese royalty, and especially not during a royal audience. After forty-five minutes, the curtain was drawn, signaling the termination of the audience. After again making three bows to the assembled party, the Americans departed. During the audience, water and betel nut were served.[26]

The royal audience concluded, the following day Roberts visited the rajah of Ligore. Shown the Siamese treaty ratification documents in their final form, the rajah found everything to be as he had recommended. The royal seal was affixed to the treaty text and to the certificate of ratification, as were the seals of the six senior ministers.

But now, the rajah informed Roberts, the treaty documents could not be delivered to him right away. A ceremonial box, he explained, in which the treaty and ratification documents would be placed, was still being crafted and would not be ready until the following day. The rajah also insisted that, once completed, the ornate box and its treaty contents would have to be delivered to Roberts aboard the royal barge, which would convey him and the box directly to the *Peacock,* anchored off the bar of the Menam River.

Asked by Roberts why the treaty box and its contents, once they had been formally delivered to him aboard the royal barge, could not be taken to their home ashore until they were ready to leave, the rajah expressed dismay. Doing so, he explained, would offend Siamese metaphysical beliefs. Any state document, the Siamese believed, if placed in a private house, would bring bad luck to the occupants and misfortune to the owner. Frustrating though it was, Roberts had no choice but to concur in the proposed delivery procedure. He managed to obtain agreement, however, that the treaty box would remain aboard the barge until he was ready to leave Bangkok.

On April 18, the box containing the ratified treaty was formally delivered to Roberts. He was notified early that afternoon that the royal barges were in sight. Prominently displaying the American flag, Roberts and the naval officers in full dress uniform, as well as the band, embarked in the three royal barges. The deputy *phra khlang,* accompanied by a Siamese band and a hundred soldiers in red costumes, were already aboard the barges. The curtains of each boat were made of gold cloth with a scarlet background. On the deck of one boat were several sacred umbrellas (*chat,* in Thai) of five tiers each, diminishing in size to the top. The treaty documents were conveyed in this boat in a box covered with yellow cloth woven with golden materials of no particular value. Inside, the box was lined with crimson silk velvet. The box was again placed in a massive silver dish, which was in turn placed on a large silver salver. The salver was placed under the canopy overhung by the royal umbrella.

The deputy *phra khlang* performed the honors for the Siamese side. Since no servant or low-born individual was allowed to touch so sacred a state document, that dignitary physically moved the treaty box from the ceremonial barge to Roberts's barge, placing it on another silver stand sent expressly by the Siamese for this purpose. While he was doing that, the Siamese band played soft music on pipes. Since the document had the royal seal affixed to it, the deputy *phra khlang* performed one bow to it, before solemnly handing the box to Roberts. The American envoy, on receiving it, elevated the box to the level of his head as a token of respect for the king before placing it on the stand. The stand and box were then conveyed to his cabin. As Roberts received the treaty box, the American band struck up "Hail Columbia."[27] The treaty ratification ceremony completed, plans were made for final departure. To Roberts's distress, it had taken almost four weeks to finish what should have been a relatively simple and short process.

Although Roberts's official party and the master and supercargo of the American trading brig *Maria Theresa* were well received, Roberts found that the American Baptist missionaries in Bangkok were no longer as well regarded by Siamese officialdom as had been the case two years earlier. There were by then six such American missionaries: Reverend and Mrs. Charles Robinson; Dr. D. B. Bradley, who together with his wife conducted a small medical dispensary; Reverend T. R. Jones; and Mr. W. Dean, a part-time preacher and paramedic who worked particularly with the Chinese. Apart from Jones, who had arrived during Roberts's first mission, the missionaries were relatively new in the country.

In the intervening years, the Siamese authorities had insisted that the mission premises be moved farther away from the royal palace so that they would not be seen on the king's annual procession through parts of the city. Some Siamese officials also suspected that the American missionaries might be receiving more public acclaim than the monarch because they were providing medical care in a community that had no other trained medical practitioners. The king, according to tradition, was not allowed to "do good" for more than ten days at a time.[28] The Siamese elite regarded missionaries, whatever their personal merits or services, as assertive and in a position to summon unwanted intervention from foreign officials.

As mentioned above, the king refused Roberts's request that the male missionaries be allowed to join the American party at the royal audience. This was unsurprising: Their presence would have elevated the Christian missionaries' status in the Siamese public eye and caused problems for the king with his Buddhist monks.

Before leaving Bangkok, Roberts petitioned the still absent *phra khlang* on behalf of the missionaries; in a document prepared by the missionaries, Roberts asked that they be allotted a plot of ground sufficiently large to erect a church and suitable private dwellings. Similar permission, the petition observed, had been granted to the Portuguese Roman Catholics, the Muslims, Chinese, and others.[29] Nothing came of this request.

With the treaty ratification exchange completed, Roberts prepared to leave. Several Siamese officials called on him on his last day in Bangkok to bid farewell and to offer to be of service to visiting American shipmasters. They clearly hoped that visits of American merchantmen to Bangkok would now be more frequent. Roberts, in turn, paid farewell protocol calls on the acting *phra khlang* and the deputy *phra khlang*.

At midnight, April 18, the ceremonial barge, towed by three galleys, left Bangkok with Roberts and his party. They reached Paknam the next day at noon. After Roberts made a brief protocol visit with the Paknam prefect, the barge got under way again at midnight. The barge reached the *Peacock* about noon on April 20, and the treaty box and its contents were taken aboard the American warship.

It was hardly too soon for Roberts. Both he and various naval officers who had accompanied him to Bangkok were unwell, some of them seriously so, having contracted fever and acute dysentery in the unsanitary conditions in which they had lived. At sunset on April 20, the *Peacock* and the *Enterprise* sailed for Cochin China.[30] Few aboard the vessels regretted leaving Siam.

Cochin China

The two ships were soon separated, as the *Enterprise* lagged behind. For those aboard each vessel, the voyage to Cochin China was agonizing. Virtually all of the officers and crewmen had at one time or another been ill during their sojourn in Siam. Aboard the *Peacock*, a quarter of her 260-man complement was on the sick list. To make things worse, by the end of the first week in May, they were put on short rations when the ship's remaining bread supply was found to be in a state of decay. Much of it had to be thrown overboard. The crew, those sick and otherwise, had to subsist on a diet of salted meat and rice. In this wretched condition, the *Peacock* finally reached Turan Bay on May 13. The *Enterprise* appeared a little over a week later, on May 21, her crew in an equally sickly state.

Predictably, as on the previous occasion at Vung Lam, the *Peacock*'s unexpected appearance roused Annamese apprehensions. Shortly after the vessel anchored, three pennant-bedecked canoes appeared alongside, carrying three local officials and their retinues. Boarding the ship, they sought to ascertain her identity and intentions. As before, communication between the Americans and the Cochin Chinese was difficult, this time even more so because there was no one aboard who spoke Chinese.

Through the limited Annamese vocabulary that Roberts had acquired three years earlier at Vung Lam, he made an attempt to explain the purpose of the ships' visit. Roberts also gave them a letter addressed to the chief minister in nearby Hué, written in English and French, announcing his arrival and his purpose. The letter asked for a speedy reply because the vessels' crews were in a poor state of health and Roberts himself was seriously ill. Because of the large number of Frenchmen believed to reside in Hué, it was assumed that at least some Vietnamese officials there would be able to read the French translation of the note. The local dignitaries accepted the letter and seemed to indicate that an answer might be expected in three days.

The following day, Ruschenberger and another ship's officer went ashore to purchase badly needed provisions. They were directed to the local mandarin's home where, lacking an interpreter, they drew pictures of the desired food items. Local vendors were quickly invited, from whom urgently needed foodstuffs could be bought. With a little bargaining, prices could usually be reduced to half or even a quarter of that originally demanded.

Three days later, the local officials who had boarded the ship on the first day reappeared, accompanied by a person who spoke Malay. Since Jacobs, the Dutch interpreter Roberts had engaged in Batavia, also spoke some Malay, communication was better than it had been that first day. Taken to the ship's cabin, the officials first asked the respective ranks of the Americans present. Told that Roberts was the American emissary, they expressed disbelief since he wore no epaulettes, as the commodore and the captain did.

The emperor, they stated, was not at Hué, so Roberts couldn't expect a reply to his letter for another five days. To Roberts, already suffering acute discomfort and impatient to proceed, this news was discouraging. Recalling his visit to Vung Lam in 1833, he remarked that he believed several mandarins there had been punished by order of the emperor for not forwarding his letters promptly. Where Roberts obtained this information is puzzling. John Morrison's aforementioned letter from Canton reported no such thing, and there is nothing in Roberts's papers that suggests the origin of this notion.

If this implied threat was intended to spur on his local interlocutors, it failed. They simply responded that they had forwarded Roberts's letter the same evening it was received, and the matter was now out of their hands. In hopes of expediting matters, Roberts mentioned the presents he had brought for the emperor. Roberts, who had refused to talk of presents on his earlier visit, had changed his tactics. Nevertheless, his gambit had no effect. Mistakenly thinking that some samples of rice and sugar that had been placed on the table were the presents, the local visitors loftily observed that their sovereign had plenty of these commodities. They could not furnish the ship with any substantial provisions, they stated, until an answer had been received from Hué.

The wait continued. On May 20, the local mandarins informed him that no answer could be expected for another eleven days. That same evening, the mandarins stated there was no one in Hué who could read the English or French texts of Roberts's letter, and that the emperor had sent a high officer to Turan to ascertain the purpose of the vessel's visit. The high officer had arrived and would be pleased to meet with Roberts ashore. Roberts declined that invitation, still stoutly maintaining, as he had during his 1833 visit, that protocol required the emperor's officer to call first on the American emissary. The local mandarins returned to the ship later that evening, but Roberts was too ill to receive them. Not being permitted to go below to Roberts's cabin, they left, clearly displeased with what they regarded as discourteous treatment.

By then, the poor health of Roberts and large numbers of the crew made it imperative for the ship to sail without much further delay to a more salubrious port. Before leaving, however, Roberts wanted to determine, if at all possible, whether the Annamese government might in principle be interested in negotiating a treaty of friendship and commerce with the United States. If so, Roberts and the vessel would plan to return with interpreters; if not, there would be no need to return.

To this end, Roberts sent Dr. Ruschenberger, Midshipman Taylor, and Jacobs, the Dutch interpreter, ashore on May 22 to meet with the senior mandarin—the *lakak,* as he was called—sent from Hué by the emperor. They soon learned that the local mandarins, who had two days earlier been kept on deck while visiting the ship, had taken their treatment as a deliberate slight and had reported it to higher officials.

One of the local mandarins demanded to know why he and his colleagues had been treated so poorly. The issue arose again a short time later when a senior aide to the *lakak* arrived. That aide proposed he accompany Ruschenberger on board to seek a meeting with Roberts. Ruschenberger declined to do so, but said he would be pleased to accompany the *lakak* himself aboard to meet with Roberts. Dissatisfied with the reply, the dignitary remarked that Roberts had allegedly been ill that morning and had refused to see the Annamese visitors. Should the *lakak* now go aboard, the same might happen again. Ruschenberger assured his interlocutor that Roberts would receive the *lakak* if he went aboard ship.

Asked which of the three American officials with whom they were conversing was senior in rank, Jacobs identified Ruschenberger. In fact, on his own Jacobs informed the Annamese officials that Ruschenberger ranked next to the ship's captain. In the absence of Roberts, Jacobs asserted, the surgeon was authorized to transact business for the American emissary.

Ruschenberger curtly refused a second Annamese proposal to send an official aboard. If the *lakak* would not meet with the American party, the two vessels would sail that evening. Though Roberts would regret not seeing the *lakak* or even having heard directly from him, this was the way it would have to be. The Americans were again assured that the *lakak* would arrive shortly and a messenger was sent, probably to inform that official of what had transpired in these pourparlers.

While waiting for the *lakak* to arrive, the Annamese officials repeatedly complained about their recent treatment aboard the *Peacock*. Why had they not been permitted to go belowdecks to the cabin? Ruschenberger declined to answer. At their request, however, he provided a written statement setting forth the names and ranks of his party.

Shortly afterward, another senior Annamese official arrived. Asked if he were the *lakak*, he replied that he was not, but that he was equally authorized to deal with the American party. Claiming to have been unable to obtain a translation of Roberts's letter, the newly arrived dignitary stated that he and the *lakak* had both been sent by the court to determine the purpose of the American party's visit. He asked if Ruschenberger was empowered to represent Roberts in the meeting then under way. The ship's surgeon answered affirmatively and explained that the French translation of Roberts's letter had been sent in the belief that someone in the capital would understand French. The newly arrived mandarin declared that no one in the capital read or understood French. When the mandarin asked why Ruschenberger was taking notes, the ship's surgeon explained that he was doing so to ensure that Roberts, the sick American envoy aboard the *Peacock*, would be fully informed of their exchanges.

The *lakak* arrived during these discussions. After exchanging banalities with Ruschenberger, the *lakak* too asked why Roberts had refused to receive the Annamese officials who had boarded the ship earlier that day. After explaining Roberts's illness, Ruschenberger indicated that he had been deputed by the American emissary to inform the *lakak* of the American mission's purpose. Roberts carried a letter from the president of the United States to the emperor, along with presents, Ruschenberger explained, and was invested with full powers to negotiate a commercial treaty. If this was not desired, Roberts was to ascertain on what terms American merchantmen might be admitted into Annamese ports to trade. Unfortunately, Roberts's poor state of health, and the widespread illness among the ships' crews, required an early departure. Roberts regretted this, all the more so since he had been at Vung Lam three years earlier for the same purpose and had had to leave after a long delay without resolving the question. If the Annamese were interested in such a treaty, Roberts hoped to return at some future time, with interpreters, to conclude the arrangements.

The *lakak* next asked if Ruschenberger had the letter for the emperor. That letter, he was told, had to be delivered by Roberts in person. The *lakak* now wished to know to whom in Vung Lam Roberts had given the earlier letter. Ruschenberger explained that the earlier letter, written in Chinese, had been delivered to a mandarin in Vung Lam, who refused to forward it without first changing its contents. Robert had since heard that the emperor had punished the mandarin for his presumption. Was the person who had translated the first letter into Chinese still aboard, the *lakak* inquired? Told that he was not, the *lakak* mused that he didn't know how it was possible to negotiate a treaty without interpreters. It was an eminently sensible observation. Somewhat lamely, Ruschenberger explained that they had believed they could enlist the services of a French linguist at Hué, a mistaken assumption. Roberts would regret that he would be obliged to leave a second time.

Ruschenberger inquired whether the Vietnamese government would be prepared to conclude a commercial treaty with the United States now. American vessels, he observed, did not visit Annamese ports because of uncertainties about custom charges and other duties. Should a commercial treaty be concluded, a mutually advantageous commerce would ensue between the two countries. Americans had merchandise and dollars to offer. The *lakak* responded that both the French and the Dutch had been there the previous year to propose commercial agreements, but he professed no knowledge of what reply the emperor had given them. Nor could he say whether the emperor was disposed to negotiate a commercial treaty with the United States or to allow American ships into Annamese ports to trade. If this should be allowed, he confidently predicted, Cochin Chinese merchandise aplenty could be bought.

Ruschenberger stated that an American warship would visit Cochin China again at some future time. When the *lakak* asked again for the presidential letter to the emperor, Ruschenberger politely refused. Apologizing that sickness aboard the American vessels and a lack of interpreters required an immediate departure, Ruschenberger was about to leave.

At that point, to Ruschenberger's surprise, the *lakak* unexpectedly changed his tune. He suddenly announced that he and Ruschenberger could settle the matter then and there. Asked his rank and whether he had full powers to negotiate a treaty, the *lakak* grandly observed that he resided in the palace with the emperor and was senior in rank to any Annamese official Roberts might have met in Vung Lam. The issue, he repeated, could at least be verbally settled between them, and he yet again requested the presidential letter to the emperor. Ruschenberger agreed to inform Roberts of the *lakak*'s views.

Once more the *lakak* suggested that Roberts come ashore. If he did so, the two might talk the matter over. Ruschenberger responded that protocol required the *lakak* to pay the first call on Roberts, but he undertook to inform the American emissary of the *lakak*'s proposal. By now Ruschenberger was thoroughly fatigued. Communication had been slow going and frustrating. Apart from repetition, four languages had to be employed. Ruschenberger spoke in French to the Dutch interpreter, Jacobs, who then translated into Malay for a Cochin Chinese interpreter. Since the latter spoke a different dialect, there was frequent confusion and need for clarification.

As Ruschenberger and his party were leaving, the *lakak* proposed that they meet again the next day for another talk. Ruschenberger agreed to inform Roberts of the suggestion, but opined that the vessels might have to sail that evening. The *lakak* indicated that a reply from the emperor would probably be received in three to five days and, as an inducement that the vessels remain, offered to provide medicines and potable water for the sick crewmen. During the extended talk, Ruschenberger had come to suspect that the *lakak* simply feigned ignorance of French and could at least read the language.

Late that afternoon, Ruschenberger and his companions returned to the *Peacock* and reported to the sick Roberts. The *lakak's* inducements were insufficient to cause departure plans to be changed. There was no trust in Annamese officials' promises. Moreover, Roberts's health problem was indeed serious, as were those of the two ships' crews. Accordingly, on the evening of May 22, the two American warships put to sea. They were bound for Macao.[31]

Macao—Journey's End

At midafternoon on May 26, the *Peacock* and the *Enterprise* anchored off Macao with their sick and exhausted complements. The following day, William S. Wetmore, an American merchant resident in that tiny Portuguese-held colony, helped them find a large house ashore to serve as a temporary lazaretto. On May 28, the sick from both ships were taken there for treatment and recuperation. Among them was Lieutenant Campbell, commander of the *Enterprise*. For him, it was too late—he passed away six days later. He was buried in the Protestant cemetery, formerly the English East India Company cemetery, with full military honors. At his grave, his fellow naval officers erected an inscribed marker in his memory.[32]

In the hope of facilitating Roberts's recovery, Wetmore asked Roberts to stay with him. Roberts's condition was critical, but the ministrations of Ruschenberger and the attention of Wetmore and his staff appeared to have a salutary effect for a brief time. In early June, he wrote to his children telling them of his illness, but indicating he was much improved and hoped soon to be able to depart for Japan to conduct negotiations there.[33]

From Macao, while seemingly recovering, Roberts wrote two other letters to his children in Portsmouth. One reflected his annoy-

ance that his journal had not yet been published. If Secretary Woodbury asked why the journal was not yet in print, Roberts told his
daughters in Portsmouth to refer the secretary to "Mr. Parker," his
son-in-law in Delhi, New York. Roberts expressed his exasperation
that he had been unable to get an answer from Parker on the progress of publication. He remained anxious that the journal be published without delay, lest someone on the *Peacock*'s earlier cruise
preempt him.[34]

Ever concerned about his family's financial welfare, Roberts also
wrote that he expected to send from Canton in a few days' time a
remittance of $1,000, plus another smaller one. These, together with
his expense account, would total about $7,000. He had earlier sent
a box of pearls, which he estimated were worth $3,000, and some
cashmere shawls and scarves, which he valued at between $2,000
and $5,000. The sources of the pearls, shawls, and scarves were not
indicated, but they may have been unreported presents received
from Sayyid Sa'id in Muscat. They were to be sold for his account
by Grinnell, Minturn and Company, which in 1838 succeeded Fish
and Grinnell.

His aggregate holdings, once these items were sold, Roberts
estimated at about $12,000. The interest on this amount, he cheer-
fully predicted, would be more than enough to support his family and, he reiterated, would enable him to never have to leave
home again.[35] Roberts was engaging in wishful thinking. Grinnell
and Minturn sold the pearls in France for just over 2,250 francs, or
about $600. The cashmere shawls and scarves proved difficult to
sell. Once again, Roberts's business judgment proved to be flawed.
His family gained virtually nothing from his last speculation.

Death

The burdens of the long voyage and acute dysentery took their toll.
Soon suffering a relapse, Roberts died on June 12. His remains were
interred at the Protestant cemetery, close to those of Lieutenant Ar-
chibald Campbell. Buried in the same small cemetery was Roberts's
erstwhile mentor on Eastern matters, the Reverend Robert Morrison, who had died the previous year. A small number of Americans,
men and women who had at various times been associated with the

American factory at Canton and had died there or in Macao, also repose in the Macao burial ground.

To honor Roberts's memory, the small American merchant community in Canton placed a large stone over his grave. It bears this inscription:

The Remains
of
EDMUND ROBERTS, Esq.
Special Diplomatic Agent of the United States to
several Asiatic Courts,
Who Died at Macao,
June 12, 1836.
He devised, and executed to their end, under instructions from
his Government, Treaties of
Amity and Commerce between
the United States and the
Courts of Muscat and Siam.

On the opposite side of the stone the inscription reads:

Erected
To the Memory of
EDMUND ROBERTS, Esq.
of Portsmouth, N.H.,
by his fellow citizens resident in Canton.
1836.[36]

Three years later, a naval chaplain aboard the USS *John Adams*, Fitch W. Taylor, visited the cemetery and recorded the inscription. It was published in his account of the voyage and may have reminded his readers that an American merchant-diplomat was buried in distant Macao.[37]

Roberts's long journey into diplomacy had ended. At fatal cost to himself, he had traveled thousands of miles by sea to further his nation's commercial interests and those of his fellow countrymen. Sadly, his reward was to be buried in a remote corner of the world, far from family and friends. Some of his legacies, personal and official, were short-lived; others would endure in one form or another for many years.

10

The Roberts Legacies

With Roberts's untimely demise, it was left to Commodore Kennedy to wind up the mission. Probing putative Japanese interest in negotiations and renewal of talks with Cochin China, both of which Roberts had envisioned, were no longer feasible. The conditional authorization the State Department had given Kennedy to exchange treaty ratifications with Muscat and Siam did not extend to negotiating treaties with Japan, Cochin China, or any other state.

Kennedy informed the secretary of state that Roberts had died, and that he had taken possession of Roberts's personal papers, including the emissary's unfinished report on his second diplomatic mission and the ratified Muscat and Siamese treaty documents. Also among those personal items were several books that Roberts had acquired. The commodore undertook to forward these materials to the State Department.[1] The Dutch interpreter, Jacobs, was discharged at Lintin to make his way from Canton to his home in Batavia.

Kennedy also told the secretary that the *Peacock* would not sail to Japan, as initially contemplated. The two American warships remained in the roadstead for another eleven days while taking on provisions and allowing sick crewmen to recuperate in Macao. Chinese officialdom viewed them with suspicion, as on the *Peacock*'s previous visit; they clearly wanted the ships to depart as soon as possible. "[As] soon as the sick men have recovered, it is necessary that they be taken back to their ships, unfurl their sails and return home; they will not be permitted to delay and loiter about, and the day of their departure must be made known. Hasten, hasten!" reported one Chinese official on June 3, 1836.[2]

On June 23, with most of the crew again at least reasonably fit, the *Peacock* and the *Enterprise* weighed anchor to proceed on their homeward odyssey. The *Enterprise* sailed under a new acting commander, Lieutenant Richard L. Page, who had been second in command of the schooner. A leisurely sail, by way of the Bonin Islands, the Sandwich (Hawaiian) Islands, and Spanish-controlled Californian and Mexican coastal ports, brought the vessels to Callao, a Peruvian port, in January 1837. Kennedy, having received word that neither ship would be returning to the United States in the foreseeable future, sent one of his officers, Lieutenant William Green, to Washington on the first available naval conveyance to deliver Roberts's documents to the secretary of state.[3] Lieutenant Green delivered the papers to the State Department some two months later. With that, Kennedy's role in Roberts's mission ended.

By then, the Jackson administration had also received Roberts's earlier reports of the exchange of treaty ratifications with both Muscat and Siam. President Jackson, in his eighth and final annual message to Congress on December 5, 1836, lost no time in advising that body that commercial treaties had been concluded with these states, "promising great advantages to our enterprising merchants and navigators." The ratified treaty documents had not yet reached the State Department, he explained, but copies would be transmitted to the Congress as soon as they were received. Should receipt be delayed until after the current congressional session had adjourned, the documents would be published and would thus be available for public perusal.[4]

These two treaties, the first between the United States and Indian Ocean polities, enhanced the Jackson administration's considerable foreign policy accomplishments. During Jackson's eight years in office, treaties were concluded with the Ottoman Empire, Russia, Morocco, Great Britain, Mexico, Colombia, Chile, Venezuela, the Peru-Bolivia Federation, Siam, and Oman. French, Spanish, Danish, and Neapolitan spoliation claims were also settled. All in all, this record was commendable. Roberts's contribution to these achievements was modest, but he inaugurated American diplomacy in the broader Indian Ocean area. For the United States, it was the beginning of a learning process, one that would mature only later in the century.

Word of Roberts's death was received in Portsmouth five months after the event. Among his family, it caused profound grief but could hardly have been surprising. To New Englanders long associated with seafaring, the risk of mortality on protracted voyages to remote parts of the world was omnipresent. On November 19, 1836, the *Portsmouth Journal* carried a lengthy obituary eulogizing Roberts's character, courage, and devotion to his family.

Summarizing his treaty missions, the paper lauded the stellar role of New Hampshire's native son in enlarging opportunities for American commerce in the Indian Ocean area. He had performed nobly in a great cause and would be sorely missed. Except for the description of him as a "commercial agent" in the employ of the U.S. government, a rank that Roberts would have considered demeaning, the eulogy would have pleased him. The same issue of the paper carried a brief notice of the concurrent death in Macao of Lieutenant Campbell, commander of the *Enterprise*.[5]

Family Matters

When Roberts departed on his final voyage, his eight surviving daughters ranged in age from twenty-two to seven. Consistent with Roberts's petition, the Rockingham County Court had named his eldest daughter, Catherine Whipple Roberts, legal guardian of her five minor sisters.[6] The burden was a heavy one, but was shared by her two slightly younger adult sisters. Although Roberts had made arrangements with the State Department to allot a large portion of his salary to his daughters, they were required to live frugally, as before Roberts's death, and finances were a constant problem.

In Roberts's absence, Catherine was befriended by the Reverend Andrew Preston Peabody, who had in 1833 become assistant pastor of the South Parish Unitarian Church in Portsmouth; shortly thereafter he was named pastor there, a position he held for twenty-seven years before joining the faculty of Harvard University's School of Divinity.[7] Peabody and Catherine Roberts were married on September 12, 1836, before word of Roberts's death had reached

Portsmouth. Roberts had been away so long that his daughters had had to fend for themselves in their personal lives.

Two years earlier, in August 1834, shortly after Roberts's return from his first mission, his third daughter, Harriet Langdon Roberts, had married the Honorable Amasa J. Parker of Albany, New York, and gone with her husband to live in Delhi, New York. Parker had for a number of years been a regent of the State University of New York, and he later became vice chancellor of that institution. He subsequently became a federal circuit judge, then a member of Congress from New York State (1838–1839), and, finally, like Levi Woodbury, an associate justice of the Supreme Court of the United States.[8] Both Parker and Peabody assisted their wives and sisters-in-law in settling Roberts's estate.

Roberts's Estate

When Roberts died, his financial situation was grave. His tastes verged on the extravagant, his personal expenses had been relatively heavy, and he tended to speculate in uncertain ventures. His assets were limited and, as events were to prove, he not only was owed money but also had incurred some long-outstanding financial obligations of his own.

Anticipating that he might not return from his second diplomatic mission, Roberts had executed a will before leaving; during his terminal illness in Macao, he had reaffirmed arrangements for handling his affairs.[9] Roberts appointed as executors of his will his eldest daughter, Catherine; Reverend Peabody, Catherine's pastor (but not yet her husband); and his second eldest daughter, Sarah. Since the will would have to be probated before the New Hampshire court, the executors designated Edward Cutts, an attorney from Northampton, New Hampshire, as administrator of the deceased's estate. Cutts had previous knowledge of some of Roberts's financial affairs. For almost four years, Cutts would be engaged in litigation before final disposition could be made of the Roberts's estate.

An inventory Cutts drew up on June 1, 1837, showed a number of assets, real or anticipated. Some of these represented French spoliation claims compensation. As indicated earlier, Roberts had claimed $7,310.50 for the loss of his ship *Victory* in 1809, a claim that the U.S. Treasury had accepted as valid. On January 1, 1836, the bulk of four indemnity installments, amounting to $4,000, were disbursed to Fish and Grinnell for Roberts's account. Although Catherine could not draw directly on these funds in her father's absence, the money served as collateral against the sums she had to borrow occasionally to meet family living expenses.

On April 17, 1837, the administrator of the Roberts's estate received $817.74 from the Collector of Customs in Portsmouth, acting as U.S. Treasury agent. This represented the balance still due on the first four spoliation installments and a part of a fifth installment. These funds, which were immediately placed in escrow, and the balance of the expected fifth installment and an expected sixth and final installment, which were collectively estimated at 12.5 percent of the total claim—that is, $913.81—were listed as liquid assets, even though they had not yet been disbursed. A writing desk and a gold watch, valued at $5 and $50, respectively, were also listed as liquid assets.

The inventory included Roberts's library, which consisted of some 140 volumes. Many were of a religious or moral nature, but the collection also held an unusually large number of volumes on geography, travel, and diplomatic missions. His literary tastes were clearly eclectic, as evidenced by such works as Alexander Burns's *Travels into Bukhara*, Michael Russell's *Egypt*, Alexander von Humboldt's *Travels*, John Gilchrist's *East India Guide*, W. F. W. Owens's *Voyages* (two volumes), Karl Gützlaff's *China Opened* (two volumes), Basil Hall's *Account of the Great Loo-Choo Island*, John White's *Voyage to the China Sea*, Thomas Raffle's *History of Java* (two volumes), William Marsden's *History of Sumatra*, James Cordiner's *Ceylon* (two volumes), John Crawfurd's *Mission to Siam and Cochin China*, Jonathan Elliott's *American Diplomatic Code* (two volumes) and *History of the Indian Archipelago*, two volumes of the missionary publication *Chinese Repository*, and various other works. Among the latter were some on South America, which may have been acquired when Roberts resided in Buenos Aires.[10] The value of the library was not estimated. Roberts's library suggests that he read widely and had a particular interest in geohistorical studies.

In addition, Cutts cited as nominal assets nine notes signed between 1814 and 1821 and still largely unpaid. Seven of these notes, totaling $2,663.83, were owed by the late Robert Harris of Portsmouth, to whom Roberts had periodically extended financial loans. Although Harris had repaid some of his debts to Roberts, most of the sums he owed remained outstanding. On Harris's death, the New Hampshire court had awarded Roberts $1,300 of the Harris estate. Since the estate proved to be insolvent, this collection of unpaid notes was essentially worthless.[11] The total liquid assets of Roberts's estate amounted to $1,873.55.

Against these real or token assets were two claims against the Roberts estate. Charles W. Cutter of Portsmouth, who years earlier had taken possession of one of Roberts's ships, was appointed by the judge of the New Hampshire Probate Court, in March of 1838, to examine and dispose of such claims. One minor claim for $4 he readily allowed. A claim in the amount of $860, made on behalf of the estate of Caleb Hopkins, Roberts's former shipmaster, was disallowed.[12] The judge of the probate court upheld Cutter's decision.

But the matter did not rest there. The attorney for the Hopkins estate, acting on behalf of the deceased's widow, Margaret Hopkins, appealed the finding to a higher state court. The case would tediously make its way through the New Hampshire legal system. The attorney for the Hopkins estate claimed both unpaid wages and commissions on freight that Roberts allegedly had owed the shipmaster. Hopkins, according to his widow's attorney, had advanced personal funds to Roberts on two voyages in 1808, one to Guadeloupe and the other to Cherbourg. When both Hopkins and Roberts were still alive, Hopkin's widow contended, Roberts had acknowledged his obligation and had promised to pay, but had failed to do so.

Following Hopkins's death in December 1832, the appeal asserted, Roberts had reiterated his commitment. He had promised Hopkins's widow that he would pay the $860 when his French spoliation claim had been settled. Although he had received $4,000 in partial spoliation disbursements in January 1836, the appeal observed, the promised payment had not been made. Roberts was, of course, on his final voyage abroad when the initial indemnification disbursement was made. Predictably, the administrator of Roberts's estate insisted there was no evidence that any such promise had ever been given. The case was eventually sent to the Superior Court of Judicature at Exeter, New Hampshire, where a jury found for Hopkins's widow and assessed $910 (the principal plus interest) against the Roberts estate.[13]

With these claims settled and the sixth and final French spoliation claim installment finally paid, the New Hampshire probate court decreed in April 1841 that the balance of Roberts's estate might be released to his heirs. By then, several changes had taken place. The liquid assets of Roberts's estate had increased somewhat, following belated receipt of $5,820.06 from the U.S. Treasury. This represented the unpaid balance of Roberts's salary for diplomatic services, $62.79 that the U.S. Navy owed him, and $745.13, the sixth and final installment of his French spoliation claim.

The probate court was reminded that Roberts's eldest daughter, Catherine, had been named guardian of her five still minor sisters.[14] The inheritance, once creditors had been paid, was equally divided among the eight surviving sisters. Each received $681.55, hardly a munificent sum after Roberts's lifetime of arduous service.[15] Catherine and her husband, Dr. Peabody, took charge of the shares of the minor children.

Roberts had collected various memorabilia on his travels, which he brought home with him. Most of those items could properly be called souvenirs. A few, such as one of the three original versions of the Muscat treaty and the unsigned copy of the Siam treaty, should arguably have been the property of the U.S. government, but believing otherwise, Roberts had kept them. They appear to have been retained in the family after his death and were eventually passed to his grandchildren. In 1936, Mrs. William Gorham Rice, a great-granddaughter of Roberts, presented items of Roberts's memorabilia, including the treaty documents, to the Portsmouth Historical Society, where they are on display. The disposition of his library is unknown. The Peabodys probably retained most of the volumes.

Roberts's Literary Legacy

When Roberts departed on his second mission, the matter of his journal's publication was still pending. Although the State Department had given its approval in principle, it had declined to give formal sanction until it had received and reviewed all portions of the journal for information that might be deemed diplomatically sensitive. Moreover, the department had expressed concern that nothing be published that might jeopardize Roberts's second mission. Roberts gave the State Department the Muscat portion of the journal before he left the United States on his second mission and forwarded a redrafted version of the Cochin Chinese portion from Rio de Janeiro in January 1835.

Roberts was anxious to have the journal published as soon as possible. He clearly hoped that publication would bring in some additional, much needed income. By the time he left on his final voyage, he had been told that someone else might be considering writing an account of the *Peacock*'s first voyage to the East.

In May 1834, within days after his return, Roberts received a letter from Dr. B. Ticknor, who had been ship's surgeon aboard the *Peacock*, asking about Roberts's publication plans. Ticknor indicated that he was being urged to publish a book on the voyage. Harper and Brothers had allegedly expressed interest, and Ticknor asked if Roberts planned to use the "drawings" that a fellow officer had made during the voyage.[16] If Roberts did not intend to become an author, Ticknor wrote, he might decide to do so. Ticknor was a friend, but his letter lent an element of urgency to Roberts's own publication plans. Although Roberts informed Ticknor that he did plan to publish his journal, he still had to reckon with the possibility that Ticknor or someone else on the voyage might break into print before he was able to do so.

Immediately after Roberts's return, Secretary of the Treasury Woodbury had urged him to arrange publication without delay. It was perhaps a way for the secretary to avoid involvement in Roberts's efforts to obtain additional compensation. Woodbury seemed less concerned than his cabinet colleague, the secretary of state, about any diplomatic damage that publication might produce. Since the book was still being revised when the *Peacock* sailed, Roberts asked his son-in-law, Amasa Parker, to advise his eldest daughter, Catherine, and her sisters on the subject. Diverse views soon emerged among the Roberts sisters on how the matter should be handled.

Sarah, the second-eldest daughter, proposed sending the manuscript journal to Secretary Woodbury and asking him to arrange publication. Judge Parker, however, had doubts about that idea. A laconic letter from Woodbury, in answer to one Parker wrote, must have caused the judge to conclude that whatever Woodbury might say, he had at most a passing interest in the project. While in Albany, Parker had consulted with what he called some reputable New York publishers. They had suggested the manuscript be turned over to a Mr. J. Reynolds, a New York literary agent. When Parker asked Woodbury about Reynolds, Woodbury merely observed that the individual was "suitable." Rightly or wrongly, Parker gained the impression that Woodbury was essentially ambivalent on the project.

Uncertain how to proceed, Parker, after consulting with his wife and his sister-in-law Mary Ann, who was staying with the Parkers in Delhi, suggested that the publication of the journal await Roberts's return. Roberts, he had concluded, would best be able to arrange publication. Parker was doubtful that publication would prove "profitable" if entrusted to a stranger. If, despite his views, Sarah (or Catherine) still wanted the manuscript to be published immediately, he would forward the manuscript to Reynolds.[17]

Word of Roberts's death abroad ended the controversy. The family, with Woodbury's continuing tacit encouragement, entrusted the publication of the journal to Harper and Brothers. It appeared in print in late 1837 with the lengthy title, *Embassy to the Eastern Courts of Cochin-China, Siam, and Muscat; in the U.S. Sloop-of-War* Peacock, *David Geisinger, Commander, During the Years 1832–3-4.* Consistent with Roberts's express wish, the volume was dedicated to Levi Woodbury.

The published volume represents Roberts's literary bequest to the American people. At once a diplomatic narrative and a travelogue, the volume is replete with historical, geographical, and sociological lore on the places and peoples he visited. Parts of it, like the detailed recital of the abortive Cochin China negotiations, read like an apologia to explain failure. Inexplicably, except perhaps because the secretary of state had expressed concern, Roberts's successful talks in Siam are only sparsely covered, although the equally successful and not particularly difficult negotiations in Muscat are fully recounted.

Roberts was a perceptive observer. His descriptions embrace cities, temples, tombs, ritualistic ceremonies, governmental structures and leaders, and a host of other matters that interested him. His vignettes are vivid and graphic. They are suffused with carefully collected data on the commercial and trade patterns of the countries on his itinerary, even those where he had no mandate to negotiate, and on their military and naval capabilities. In recording these data, he was following the instructions the State Department had given him, but it was clear that such matters were also of intense personal interest.

American shipmasters and supercargoes had visited many of the places that Roberts described long before he undertook his first diplomatic mission. Whatever they may have recorded in logbooks or private journals, only a handful of them—like John White—had published their impressions. Thus, Roberts's published memoir is an invaluable literary period piece of Muscat and various Southeast Asian entities before the industrial age.

Roberts's death cut short any plans he may have had to publish the record he was keeping on his second diplomatic mission. Posterity is fortunate that his friend and shipboard colleague Dr. W. S. W. Ruschenberger, ship's surgeon aboard the *Peacock* during Roberts's second diplomatic voyage, was an equally inveterate diarist. Ruschenberger recorded in detail his sketches, as he called them, of the events of that journey. To supplement Ruschenberger's personal observations, Roberts shared with him the written record that Roberts kept of official meetings. Midshipman Taylor also lent Ruschenberger his notes. Moreover, in Cochin China, by which time Roberts was too ill to go ashore, Ruschenberger had been deputed to conduct talks for the emissary. Thus, Ruschenberger had firsthand, participatory knowledge of the diplomatic mission, as well as access to the diaries Roberts and Taylor kept.

Ruschenberger's account was published in Philadelphia in 1838, a year after the appearance of Roberts's posthumous memoir, under the title *A Voyage Round the World, Including an Embassy to Muscat and Siam in 1835, 1836, and 1837*. The two are companion pieces. Together they constitute a narrative of Roberts's diplomatic career. They deserve a contemporary audience; look for the works online at *books.google.com*.

Roberts's Diplomatic Legacy: Muscat and Zanzibar

Once the ratification documents were received in Washington, the final steps could be taken to validate the treaties with Muscat and Siam. After being officially proclaimed by Jackson's confidant and successor, President Martin Van Buren, on June 24, 1837, both treaties were ready for implementation.

Muscat

The Muscat treaty applied territorially to Oman on the eastern side of the Arabian Peninsula and to much of the East African coast, including Zanzibar.[18] Although it would be discovered a hundred years later that the English and Arabic texts of the Muscat treaty diverged significantly,[19] there was general agreement on what should be done to strengthen the commercial ties between the United States and Sayyid Sa'id's domains. Even before the treaty was formally proclaimed, an American consul, Richard Palmer Waters of Salem, Massachusetts, assumed his duties in Zanzibar in March 1837. A year and a half later, in October 1838, an independent American consul, Henry P. Marshall of New York City, arrived in Muscat. Fittingly, given the exclusively commercial nature of the U.S. interests in Sayyid Sa'id's realm, both were merchant consuls who retained their business associations with American firms. They spent as much of their time, if not more, promoting their own interests and those of their principals as they did on official consular duties. This was especially true of Waters in Zanzibar, where business was brisk. In contrast, Marshall found time on his hands in Muscat.

Initially, Sayyid Sa'id, who had no choice but to accept Waters, found the new American consul in Zanzibar trying. Unaware that Roberts had died, the sayyid wrote to him in the summer of 1839 lamenting the fact that the United States had not named a person of "more sense" to Zanzibar.[20] Fortunately, he subsequently came to appreciate Waters more. Waters seems also to have mellowed and to have developed a greater regard and respect for the ruler.

Despite Roberts's long connection with the New York firm of Fish and Grinnell (Grinnell, Minturn and Company after 1838), that enterprise showed no interest in establishing itself in either the Zanzibar or the Muscat markets. In the case of Oman, however, another New York firm, Scoville and Britton, arranged for one of its associates to obtain the Muscat consular post.

Robert Starr Parker, a member of Scoville and Britton's counting house, had obtained access to Roberts's papers, presumably through his brother, Amasa J. Parker, Roberts's son-in-law. As always, such family connections could prove useful. With the Zanzibar post preempted, the Scoville and Britton firm was sufficiently encouraged by what Roberts had written that it determined to vie for the Muscat appointment and succeeded in procuring it.[21] One wonders, however, whether Roberts's papers had been studied in depth. Compared with Zanzibar, Muscat offered far fewer trade prospects. Within a year, Scoville and Britton had gone bankrupt and its erstwhile employee, Marshall, had left Muscat. For a number of years thereafter, Sa'id bin Khalfan, the translator of the Muscat treaty, was the State Department's designated American consul in Muscat, but he was never recognized in that capacity by the Omani authorities.[22]

The consular post in Muscat was staffed only intermittently from 1838 to 1915, when it was closed. Nevertheless, one or two American ships put into Muscat each year until the 1880s, when such traffic ceased. The export of a particular type of Omani date, the fard date, to American buyers became the principal element in the miniscule trade between the two countries. Occasionally, too, a U.S. warship visited that Arabian port. American missionaries labored in Muscat from the 1890s onward. Although they contributed significantly to health and educational development in the country, their hopes for converts went unfulfilled. The United States concluded a new treaty with Oman on December 20, 1958, not long after oil was discovered in Oman.[23] This treaty superseded the Roberts treaty, which had remained in effect for over 120 years. An American embassy was established in Muscat in 1972.

A one-time, largely symbolic derivative of Roberts's dealings with Sayyid Sa'id warrants notice. Although the ruler regularly welcomed American merchantmen to his ports, he retained the idea of sending one of his ships to the United States to probe directly what trade opportunities might exist. Not until 1840 was he able to do so. In that year, he dispatched his vessel *Sultanah* to New York with a commercial cargo and a special Omani envoy aboard.

(Five years earlier, the *Sultanah* had been sent to succor the *Peacock* when the American warship had temporarily foundered off Masirah Island.) For several months, the vessel, her crew, and the Omani envoy lent further color to New York City's already kaleidoscopic social panorama.

In appreciation for the help Sayyid Sa'id offered to the stricken *Peacock*, the U.S. government extended the hospitality of the Brooklyn Navy Yard to the envoy and to the *Sultanah*. The *Sultanah* was refitted, at U.S. government expense, before she returned to Zanzibar under a Philadelphia ship captain and with official gifts for the ruler.[24] Sayyid Sa'id found the venture commercially unprofitable and did not repeat the experiment. Thereafter, he was content to allow American vessels to conduct the trade between the two countries.

Zanzibar

In contrast to Muscat, the American consulate in Zanzibar was more or less regularly staffed from 1837 until the revolution of early 1964, which eventually resulted in the incorporation of that island into Tanzania. American trade with Zanzibar, while always of modest proportions, was quantitatively greater than that with Muscat, especially since Zanzibar remained for years the entrepôt for East African commerce. Although the Roberts treaty continued to apply to Zanzibar even after its separation from Oman in 1861, a supplementary treaty was concluded between the United States and Zanzibar on July 3, 1886. This agreement raised the duty on alcoholic liquor imports and defined consular jurisdiction more clearly. In 1905, the United States formally relinquished extraterritorial rights in Zanzibar.[25] Duties had initially been fixed and extraterritorial rights acquired in Roberts's 1833 treaty with Muscat and Oman. These agreements, including the by now emasculated 1833 treaty as it applied to Zanzibar, remained in force until Zanzibar lost its independence.

Siam

Implementation of the treaty with Siam was excruciatingly slow. Despite the reputed advantages conferred by the treaty, the limited nature of the Bangkok import and export market meant that visits by American merchantmen continued to be sporadic and irregular. Moreover, despite treaty stipulations, Siamese bureaucratic vexations persisted and caused problems. In one form or another, the royal Thai monopoly on trade continued. Ship measurement charges, whatever the acting *phra khlang* had told Roberts, remained disputatious, and visiting American shipmasters and supercargoes complained, as before the treaty, of discriminatory treatment. As a result, American commerce with Siam failed to flourish. Roberts's initial expectations had been grossly inflated.

In 1850, Townsend Harris—who would eventually become the first American consul general to Japan—conducted new negotiations to correct existing treaty inequities, but these failed. Not until 1856 was a new U.S.-Siamese treaty signed that abolished the odious ship measurement duties, established fixed duties on exports and imports, and guaranteed to American merchants the same privileges accorded to Siamese and Chinese traders.[26] By then, there were reasons for the more accommodating Siamese attitude.

The enforced opening of China by Britain and France in 1840–1842 undoubtedly contributed to the Siamese change of heart. So did Commodore Matthew Perry's naval demonstration of 1854, which not only opened Japan but also reminded recalcitrant Asian rulers that the United States was prepared to resort to threats of force to assure unhindered trade and equality of treatment for its citizens trading abroad. The new American treaty with Siam was modeled on an Anglo-Siamese treaty concluded the previous year, but the new one had a peculiar twist. Whatever discrimination the American Baptist missionaries had suffered in Siam was to be redressed. The new treaty stipulated that the Reverend Stephen Mattoon, who had been a Baptist missionary in Bangkok for ten years, would be the American consul and accepted as such by the Siamese authorities. Mattoon opened the first American consulate in Bangkok on May 29, 1859.[27]

The 1856 treaty with Siam and the establishment of an American consulate in Bangkok had more symbolic than practical significance, however. Trade with Siam remained limited. True, opium could now be brought into the country, but only if it was sold to the Siamese opium "farmer" or his agent. Roberts would doubtless have been gratified that American merchants could finally participate in the opium trade with Siam. This was the trade he had sought to open and, had it not been for his Chinese consultant in Bangkok, he might even then have succeeded.

More important, the United States henceforth stood for the open-door policy in Siam, as it came gradually to do elsewhere in the Far East. Since the United States generally eschewed political or territorial ambitions, it was increasingly viewed by Siamese leaders as a disinterested power whose political help should be sought to prevent European encroachments on its sovereign prerogatives. To be sure, only rarely was the U.S. government willing to become involved in such controversies, and then only if the interests of its citizens threatened to be adversely affected. But active or not, the United States gradually earned Siamese respect and confidence for the values that it was deemed to represent.

Consequently, in the late 1890s and early 1900s the Siamese government began to engage private Americans as advisers to various government departments. Such advisers, it believed, could be trusted to give sound and impartial counsel, and they did so. In 1920, during the administration of President Woodrow Wilson, a new treaty was signed in which the United State renounced the extraterritoriality rights in Siam that it had acquired under the most-favored-nation provision of Roberts's treaty and in subsequent agreements. It was the first major power to do so.[28] Finally, on May 26, 1966, a new U.S.-Thai treaty of amity and economic relations was signed, which superseded all earlier agreements.[29] Although Roberts's hopes for more extensive American trade with Siam failed to materialize, he had laid the groundwork for an eventual close economic, political, and even military relationship with that country. In slightly frayed form, that relationship endures to this day. Indeed, the United States is Thailand's second largest trading partner (after Japan).

Japan: Repeated Failures, Final Success

Roberts's death halted his planned trip to Japan to attempt to negotiate a commercial treaty with the Japanese authorities. He had been optimistic about concluding a treaty: In Batavia he had learned that the Dutch frequently chartered American merchantmen to transport their annual shipment of goods and presents to their factory at Deshima, and that such vessels were well received by the Japanese authorities in Nagasaki. Only the United States, he had confidently written, could open Japan to foreign commerce.

Would he have succeeded? We cannot know, but it is likely that his information was distorted and therefore that his estimate of presumed Japanese receptivity to American overtures was overoptimistic. Most American ships chartered by the Dutch flew the Netherlands flag into Nagasaki harbor, not the Stars and Stripes, although Japanese authorities recognized the ships' masters and crews to be largely American. The Dutch at Deshima described Americans to the Japanese as "Englishmen of the second chop," implying inferiority and weakness.[30] If the Japanese disliked the English, as Roberts's informants in Batavia steadfastly insisted, and Americans were slyly described by the Dutch as a step below Englishmen, the United States unquestionably faced formidable obstacles in securing access to Japan.

In the Japanese cultural context, such a lower stature was hardly conducive to successful treaty negotiations, even if Roberts had arrived aboard an American warship. In fact, the *Peacock* was a small sloop of war, and the *Enterprise* was even less imposing. They would scarcely have impressed the Japanese with U.S. power. Moreover, the State Department's tightfistedness would in all probability have meant that presents Roberts would have brought for the Japanese emperor and the shogun (military governor) would have been seen as paltry. The Dutch, their reputed parsimony notwithstanding, recognized what Washington was loath to admit: Lavish presents were necessary to impress the Japanese leadership.

Events in the next two decades were to demonstrate that, contrary to Roberts's optimistic views, the Japanese had no special regard for Americans. Even occasional efforts by American shipmasters to repatriate shipwrecked Japanese sailors, for purely humanitarian reasons, were coldly received by the Japanese authorities. By imperial decree, Japanese who had sojourned abroad, even if involuntarily through shipwreck, were forbidden to return on pain of capital punishment. Still more disturbing, reports persisted of Japanese mistreatment and imprisonment of shipwrecked American (and other) sailors who had been cast ashore on one or another of the Japanese islands.

Despite these obstacles, the United States remained interested in opening Japan. American merchants envisioned promising Japanese markets. American missionaries were anxious to spread Christianity and save the souls of what they regarded as the benighted heathens of Japan. And the U.S. Navy envisioned a naval base in Japan for its East India squadron, a command formally established in 1840. In February 1845, Congress passed a joint resolution urging the administration of President John Tyler to press Japan (and Korea) to allow free American trade.

Cushing and Everett Designations

In 1844, the special American commissioner who negotiated the first American treaty with China, Caleb Cushing, sought presidential authority to try to conclude an agreement with Japan also. By the time the requisite full powers to do so were forwarded, however, Cushing had left the area.[31] A year later, Alexander H. Everett, who succeeded Cushing and was to be sent to exchange treaty ratifications with China, was also given full powers to negotiate a treaty with Japan. Taking a cue from the Roberts's experience, the credentials were made transferable to some other qualified agent in the event of Everett's incapacitation.

Biddle's Attempt

While at Rio de Janeiro, en route to the Far East, Everett became ill and could not proceed. Commodore James Biddle, who commanded the two American warships that were to accompany Everett, thus assumed charge of the diplomatic mission. Biddle arrived at Yedo Bay on July 20, 1846; his welcome there was not gracious. The shogun's reply to Biddle's request that Japan agree to a trade treaty similar to the one concluded with China was met with disdain. The response bore no address, date, or signature, and it stated that Biddle's ships should leave immediately. Biddle himself was physically manhandled by a Japanese soldier. The ships departed on July 27, 1846, Biddle's mission unachieved, and with American prestige lowered still more in Japanese eyes because of the commodore's seeming complacency in the face of studied insult.[32]

Glynn's Visit

Commodore David Geisinger, commander of the *Peacock* during Roberts's first mission, was in charge of the navy's East India squadron in 1849. In April, he dispatched Commander James Glynn to Japan to demand the release of the score or more of shipwrecked American mariners who were believed to be incarcerated there. His instructions were to be conciliatory but firm, and Glynn complied. When the Japanese tried to block Glynn's ship, the USS *Preble*, from entering the Nagasaki harbor, he forced his way through the cordon of Japanese boats and anchored in the middle of the bay, within cannon shot of the city. For several days, Japanese officials and interpreters boarded the *Preble* to negotiate with Glynn, but he remonstrated that he needed to speak to higher-ranking officials. Ultimately, he threatened direct action, saying he would open fire on the city. Faced with Glynn's obvious determination, the Japanese released the surviving Americans. To save face, however, the Japanese released them not directly to Glynn but to the Dutch at Deshima, who then turned them over to Glynn.[33] Having succeeded in his mission, Glynn departed.

Aulick's Designation

Glynn's success led him to hope that he would be appointed head of a diplomatic mission to negotiate a treaty with Japan. This was not to be. He was outranked by Commodore John Henry Aulick, who was well known to senior officials of the Navy Department. At the request of the secretary of the navy, Aulick met with Secretary of State Daniel Webster in early May 1851. Shortly thereafter he received letters of credence from the State Department, authorizing him to negotiate a treaty with Japan and to obtain coaling facilities in that country for American naval vessels.

Traveling aboard the USS *Susquehanna*, the first steamship in the U.S. Navy, and accompanied by two sloops of war, Aulick left for Japan in June 1851. To his chagrin, however, reports were sent to Washington about his disputes with the *Susquehanna*'s captain about command responsibilities and his misunderstandings with a foreign diplomatic passenger, and Aulick was relieved of his command in November 1851. Commodore Matthew G. Perry, he was curtly informed, would succeed him and would undertake the Japan mission.[34]

Perry Opens Japan

Perry, one of the most senior officers in the U.S. Navy, was officially appointed commander in chief of the East Indies squadron on March 24, 1852. Because of his senior rank, he was initially reluctant to accept that command, but he was persuaded to do so when he was assured that a new diplomatic mission to open Japan would concurrently be entrusted to him. For this purpose, the Navy Department promised him eleven ships, the largest American naval flotilla ever sent to eastern waters. This impressive show of force, Washington believed, would so awe the Japanese that they would accede to American demands.

Perry was not ready to leave the United States until late 1852, and he transferred his command pennant to the USS *Susquehanna* in April 1853. Before he left for Japan, he was briefed in Washington about Asian customs and the need for pomp and circumstance in dealing with the Japanese. Perry relished the information—such displays were congenial to his flamboyant character.

Landing first at Napa in May 1853, where an American naval party was without ceremony sent ashore to look for a suitable coaling station, Perry ostentatiously demanded all honors and cowed the disconcerted Japanese local officialdom. He peremptorily refused all Japanese requests for information on the flotilla's armaments and ships' complements. Thereafter, entering Urago Bay, near Edo (Tokyo), on July 8, 1853, with two steam vessels and two sailing vessels in tow, Perry ordered the ships stripped for action and demanded that a high-ranking Japanese dignitary come aboard to welcome the American visitors. If no official deemed of sufficiently high rank to receive President Millard Fillmore's letter came aboard, Perry ominously warned, he would himself go ashore with an armed party and carry the letter to the emperor in Edo.

By July 14, after protracted Japanese efforts to negotiate, which Perry took as evasion, agreement was finally reached. Perry might come ashore to deliver the letter, along with Dutch and Chinese translations, to a high court official. On that day, the commodore, with an impressive naval escort in full-dress uniform, landed and solemnly presented a scarlet-wrapped, gold-inscribed rosewood box containing the presidential message.

While promising nonintervention in Japanese internal affairs, President Fillmore's communication insisted that American sailors stranded in Japan must be protected and repatriated. It also stipulated the desire of the United States for a coaling station in Japan. Perry had developed ideas of his own of forcibly annexing the Japanese Liu Chiu Islands for this purpose, but these did not have specific presidential endorsement. The court dignitaries who received the presidential letter undertook to convey it to the emperor. The letter delivered to the Japanese grandees, Perry departed, ominously announcing that he would return the following year—probably with more ships—to receive a reply.

True to his word, Perry, with a still larger naval squadron, returned to Edo on February 11, 1854, after again touching at Napa. This time Perry demanded that five Japanese ports be opened to American ships, although for the moment three would suffice—Matsumai, Napa, and either Uraga or Kagoshima. After considerable procrastination and internal debate, the Japanese leadership grudgingly bowed to the inevitable. A treaty of peace and amity, known as the Convention of Kanagawa, was signed on March 31, 1854, according the United States and its citizens commercial and most-favored-nation privileges in the heretofore closed Japanese empire. But only two ports were opened to American shipping, Hakodate and Shimoda. Some three months later, in June 1854, two supplementary agreements were signed, clarifying provisions of the earlier treaty and regulating pilotage and provisioning of American ships entering the port of Shimoda.[35]

Perry labored under a misapprehension in signing the treaty. He believed his treaty had been signed in the name of the emperor. In fact, it was signed on the authority of the shogun, which for a time caused some Japanese hard-line isolationists to consider the agreement illegal. Although such opposition may have made the life of Townsend Harris, the first U.S. consul general to Japan, a little more difficult, it ultimately made little difference. Four years later, in still another treaty, this one signed aboard the visiting USS *Powhatan*, Japan reluctantly agreed to open the ports of Kanagawa,

Kobe, Nagasaki, and Niigata. The United States also acquired rights in the Liu Chiu Islands.³⁶ There was no turning back for Japan. It would soon embrace Western technology with astonishing vigor.

Roberts's vision, and that of so many other Americans, had finally been realized, even though Roberts did not live to see it. He would have approved of Perry's high-handed conduct. It vindicated his conviction that a demonstration of naval might was necessary to deal successfully with Eastern societies. By a curious quirk of history, Roberts has been remembered by the public media less for his achievement of treaties with Siam and Muscat than for his designation as the American who was to have opened Japan but was prevented from doing so by illness and death.³⁷

Cochin China

Roberts's two attempts to negotiate a commercial treaty with Cochin China had come to naught. The second was hardly a full-fledged effort, considering Roberts's illness and inability to participate in talks. It represented at most a probe to determine future prospects for such an agreement. The results, as we have seen, were unpromising.

USS *Constitution* Visit

Official U.S. interest in Cochin China lapsed with Roberts's death. There is no record of any American merchantman having visited a Vietnamese port for many years. Nine years after Roberts's second appearance, however, a visiting American naval captain comported himself in a manner that the Annamese could only consider hostile. In 1844, the Navy Department dispatched Captain John ("Mad Jack") Percival, aboard the USS *Constitution*, on a round-the-world cruise with general orders to explore trade prospects for Americans in East Africa and the Indian Ocean area. Borneo, where coal deposits were believed to be plentiful, was of special interest. The *Constitution* put into Turan Bay in May 1845 to load supplies.

Receiving a covert message from an imprisoned French bishop (Monsignor Lefebvre) that he and other Europeans in Hué were being persecuted and faced death at the hands of the Cochin Chinese authorities because of their Christian missionary activities, Percival decided to intervene. Although the bishop's appeal was addressed to the senior French naval officer in the area, Percival led an American landing party ashore and abducted five local mandarins as hostages for the bishop's safety. Three armed junks, believed to belong to the emperor, were also seized, and an ultimatum was sent to Hué warning that if the bishop was not released in four days, the American warship would fire on Turan. To demonstrate his resolve, Percival had a few shots fired over the captured junks as they unsuccessfully tried to escape under cover of a squall. Percival acted entirely on his own; he had no instructions from the U.S. government to undertake such bellicose action.

His bluff was effectively called, by default, by the Cochin Chinese. The ultimatum expired without any Cochin Chinese response. Gradually realizing his untenable situation, Percival released his hostages three days later and shortly thereafter sailed away, ostensibly because of lack of provisions. His performance at Turan hardly enhanced local impressions of American intent. At Macao, Percival informed resident French officials of the bishop's predicament. He was gratified to learn some time thereafter that the imprisoned cleric had been released to a French naval corvette and was safe.

The secretary of the navy, when later apprised of Percival's high-handed intervention, expressed sharp disapproval and acknowledged that it may have been a violation of international law. However, no reprimand was issued to the errant naval officer.[38]

USS *Saginaw* Visit

In June 1861, as the French were in the early stages of seeking militarily to subdue Cochin China, the commodore of the U.S. East India squadron received word that the American barque *Myrtle* had been lost on the Annamese coast the previous year and that her American crew might be prisoners. The USS *Saginaw* was sent to Qui Nhon harbor, where the vessel's commander displayed a white flag to indicate peaceful intentions and a desire to parlay.

Before any communication could be arranged with shore authorities, a nearby fort, perhaps thinking the warship was French, fired three artillery rounds at the *Saginaw*. The ship's thirty-two-pounder gun immediately returned fire, causing an explosion at the fort and silencing the shore batteries. Lacking sufficient men to attempt a landing, however, the *Saginaw*'s commander returned to Hong Kong, and the French admiral at Saigon was asked to make inquiries about the *Myrtle*'s crew.[39] There is no evidence that they were ever found.

From the 1850s onward, Cochin China came increasingly under the political influence of the French, despite the determined efforts of successive Vietnamese emperors to maintain their independence. Contributing to a growing French focus on establishing political primacy in Cochin China were the continued presence in that country of assertive French missionaries, especially after papal recognition of French missionary hegemony in the Far East in 1839; sporadic Annamese persecution of Catholic Christian converts and missionaries; and the quest for a countervailing French territorial foothold in Annam after the British seized Hong Kong in 1841. The French objective gained impetus after the establishment in 1851 of the Second French Empire under Louis Napoleon.

French influence in Cochin China was slow and progressed in fits and starts. It is beyond the scope of this study to present that story in detail. Suffice it to say, however, that a French naval squadron was deployed to the China Sea as early as 1842, ostensibly to protect missionaries in Cochin China; the harbor forts at Turan were shelled in 1851; and a commission was established in Paris in that same year to consider whether a base on the Annamese coast should be sought. Some years later, in 1858, as a result of the committee's positive recommendations, Turan was temporarily occupied. In the ensuing decades, other geographical areas in Cochin China were seized and garrisoned. Not until 1883, however, after numerous abortive talks with Cochin Chinese officials, was a Franco-Vietnamese treaty concluded, imposing a vague form of French protectorate over the country. A year later, in a Franco-Chinese convention, the Chinese emperor reluctantly recognized the French protectorate over what had been his suzerain territory.[40] French control gradually expanded thereafter, although not without persistent indigenous resistance and hostility.

Vietnam remained outside the purview of U.S. interests in Southeast Asia for many years. Not until a century later, when

France withdrew from Indochina after the loss of the Dien Bien Phu stronghold in 1954, did the United States again become involved in Vietnam. Then began the slow and inexorable sanguinary internal and East-West conflict from which the United States, too, was ultimately forced to withdraw. American dialogue with Vietnam, from its beginnings with Roberts to more recent times, has been contentious. Only since the normalization of diplomatic relations between the United States and the Socialist Republic of Vietnam in 1995 have the two countries begun to broaden their political exchanges. In July 2000, they signed a bilateral trade agreement, and in January 2007, the U.S. Congress approved permanent normal trade relations for Vietnam. Roberts would have been pleased.

Requiem

Officers of the American consulate general in Hong Kong periodically visit Roberts's grave in Macao and lay a wreath in memory of this early American merchant-diplomat. His grave, like those of others interred in the English Protestant cemetery, is tended by the chapel authorities.

On August 21, 1884, Mrs. John V. L. Pruyn of Albany, New York, a granddaughter of Roberts, presented St. John's Episcopal Church in Portsmouth, New Hampshire, where Roberts and his family had initially worshipped, with a stained-glass memorial window in memory of her grandparents. She did so on the occasion of the golden wedding anniversary of her parents, Amasa J. Parker and Harriet Langdon Roberts Parker. The inscription reads in part:

> To [the] loving memory of Edmund Roberts and
> Catherine Whipple Langdon, his wife.
> Married at Portsmouth, September 10, 1808.
> Both Glorified God in their lives,
> The one as a faithful wife and mother,
> The other died in the service of his country
> On his second mission to Eastern courts
> as Envoy Extraordinary and Minister Plenipotentiary
> of the United States.[41]

The inscription is slightly in error. Roberts indeed coveted the title of minister and used its generic synonym, "envoy," to describe himself in communications to foreign governments, but he was never accorded that senior diplomatic rank. Instead, he was "commissioner" and, later, "special agent."

No slur against Roberts was intended. It simply reflected the prevailing policy of the United States to stay out of foreign political affairs and, as part of this design, to give its diplomatic representatives abroad, especially its itinerant emissaries, the lowest feasible diplomatic rank. Whatever the rationale, this practice often made the representatives' work more difficult, as Roberts's experiences in Cochin China and Siam attest. Washington did not understand the minimal requirements of effective global diplomacy. Roberts's family may be forgiven for this inflation of his personal diplomatic status. He deserved to have it.

A marker in memory of Edmund Roberts was later placed in the South Cemetery of Portsmouth, where his parents, his wife, and other members of his family are interred. The Reverend Peabody, Roberts's son-in-law, was instrumental in arranging this recognition.

Roberts was a product of his times. He embraced all of the graces and was imbued with all of the prejudices that characterized the New England mercantile community in the early nineteenth century. His official saga was part of the epic of early U.S. diplomacy at a time when national objectives focused primarily on promoting American commerce. Whatever errors of judgment he may occasionally have made, he performed his responsibilities to the nation with flair, distinction, and verve. Sadly, he often had to neglect his family, some might say shamefully so. Yet his concern for his wife and children was constant, and his protracted absences were prompted, at least in part, by a desire to improve his family's economic well-being.

He was doubtless genuine in that purpose, but other possible reasons for his seeming compulsion to be away from home suggest themselves. Without trying to psychoanalyze Roberts, the absence of a son at home must have deeply pained him. Conversely, to a man of his background and temperament, he must at times have felt overwhelmed as the only man in a household of numerous women. Regardless of one's ultimate judgment of Roberts as paterfamilias, he retained the affection of his family. From a domestic point of view, that must surely be the litmus test. Finally, for his services to his country, in whose cause he ultimately gave his life, he deserves the nation's unalloyed gratitude.

Fama semper vivat.

Endnotes

CHAPTER 1: ANTECEDENTS AND EARLY YEARS

1. For conditions of commerce in the Indian Ocean, see C. Northcote Parkinson, *Trade in the Eastern Seas, 1793–1813* (Cambridge: University Press, 1937), 304–316; and Holden Furber, *Rival Empires of Trade in the Orient, 1600–1800* (Minneapolis: University of Minnesota Press, 1976), 31–210. Naval protection for East India Company vessels, when available, largely took the form of convoying.

2. The literature on the Barbary Wars is copious. Among the better studies are Stephen Cleveland Blyth, *History of the War between the United States and Tripoli, and Other Barbary Powers* (Salem, MA: Salem Gazette Office, 1806), 4–144; Ray W. Irwin, *The Diplomatic Relations of the United States and the Barbary Powers, 1776–1816* (Chapel Hill: University of North Carolina Press, 1931), 20–204 (available online at *books.google.com*); Samuel Edwards, *Barbary General; The Life of William H. Eaton* (Englewood Cliffs, NJ: Prentice-Hall, 1968), 92–223; and William Armstrong Fairburn, *Merchant Sail, 1876–1947* (Center Lovell, ME: Fairburn Marine Educational Foundation, 1945), 1:625–751. For texts of treaties with the Barbary states, see Hunter Miller, comp, *Treaties and Other International Acts of the United States of America* (Washington, DC: Government Printing Office, 1931), 2:184–219 [Morocco]; 2:276–312, 2:617–640 [Algiers]; 2:350–367, 2:530–545 [Tripoli]; 2:387–414, 3:141–143 [Tunis].

3. For background on the protracted negotiations with the Ottoman Empire, see James A. Field Jr., *America and the Mediterranean World, 1776–1882* (Princeton, NJ: Princeton University Press, 1969), 104–152. For the text of the treaty with Turkey, see Miller, *Treaties*, 3:541–547.

4. For a biographical sketch of Roberts, see E. Wilder Spaulding, "Edmund Roberts," in Dumas Malone, ed., *Dictionary of American*

Biography, Published under the Auspices of the American Council of Learned Societies (New York: C. Scribner's Sons, 1928–58), 16:4–5. An extensive, though sometimes overstated, account of his mission is set forth in John M. Belohlavek, *Let the Eagle Soar! The Foreign Policy of Andrew Jackson* (Lincoln: University of Nebraska Press, 1985), 162–170. Brief general accounts of Roberts's mission may be found in Henry M. Wriston, *Executive Agents in American Foreign Relations* (Baltimore: Johns Hopkins University Press, 1929), 335–339, 806–807; Tyler Dennett, *Americans in Eastern Asia: A Critical Study of the Policy of the United States with Reference to China, Japan, and Korea in the 19th Century* (New York: Macmillan, 1922), 128–134 (available online at *books. google.com*); Charles Oscar Paullin, *Diplomatic Negotiations of American Naval Officers, 1778–1883* (Gloucester, MA: P. Smith, 1912), 352–355 (available online at *books.google.com*); John H. Latané and David W. Wainhouse, *A History of American Foreign Policy*, 2nd rev. ed. (New York: Odyssey Press, 1940), 325–326; Thomas H. Bailey, *A Diplomatic History of the American People* (New York: F. S. Crofts, 1940), 321–322; Robert Erwin Johnson, *Far China Station: The U.S. Navy in Asian Waters, 1800–1898* (Annapolis: Naval Institute Press, 1979), 6–8, 11–15; and John W. Foster, *American Diplomacy in the Orient* (Boston: Houghton, Mifflin, 1903), 47–55 (available online at *books.google.com*). Somewhat distorted summaries are in Harry Emerson Wildes, *Aliens in the East: A New History of Japan's Foreign Intercourse* (Philadelphia: University of Pennsylvania Press, 1937), 195–196 (available online at *books.google. com*); and Samuel Flagg Bemis, *A Diplomatic History of the United States*, 5th ed. (New York: Holt, Rinehart, and Winston, 1965), 344.

5. J. Henry Bowles to "My cousin, Miss Mary Peabody," Brooklyn, NY, June 14, 1871, in Edmund Roberts Papers, folder 1, New Hampshire Historical Society (NHHS); and Frank Farnsworth Starr to "Mr. Pruym," Middletown, CT, July 9, 1884, Edmund Roberts Papers, folder 1, NHHS. Starr, a professional genealogist, was engaged by Roberts's descendants to trace the origins of the family. The results were limited. For a time, various of Roberts's descendants confused Captain Moses Woodward with a contemporary Portsmouth namesake, Colonel Moses Woodward.

6. Statement on "Captain" Edmund Roberts, n.p., n.d. [1871?], Edmund Roberts Papers, folder 1, NHHS. This information was probably gathered by Farnsworth Starr, the genealogist.

7. New Hampshire Naval Commission of Edmund Roberts, Sr., Exeter, July 8, 1779, MSS779408, Frederick Chase Manuscript Collection, Dartmouth College, Hanover, NH, Baker Library (hereafter cited as

Dartmouth, FCMC). See also A. P. Peabody to Mr. Pruym, Cambridge, MA, March 12, 1884, Edmund Roberts Papers, folder 1, NHHS.

8. For the Penobscot fiasco, see *The American Rebellion: Sir Henry Clinton's Narrative of His Campaigns, 1775–1782* (New Haven: Yale University Press, 1954), 134–135; Carl Leopold Bauermeister, *Revolution in America: Confidential Letters and Journals 1776–1784 of Adjutant General Major Bauermeister of the Hessian Forces*, trans. Bernhard A. Uhlendorf (New Brunswick: Rutgers University Press, 1957), 295, 302–303; *Proceedings of the Massachusetts Historical Society*, 2nd series, 12:200–202 (available online at *archive.org/details/indexproceedings00massuoft*); and William G. Saltonstall, *Ports of Piscataqua: Soundings in the Maritime History of the Portsmouth, N.S., Customs District from the Days of Queen Elizabeth and the Planting of Strawberry Banke to the Times of Abraham Lincoln and the Waning of the American Clipper* (New York: Russell and Russell, 1968, c1941), 112–113.

9. Appointment of Sarah Roberts as Administratrix of Edmund Roberts, Sr., Estate, January 16, 1788, Probate Records 5322 D.S., Register of Probate, Rockingham County, NH (hereafter cited as Register, RCNH).

10. Inventory of Edmund Roberts, Sr., Estate, May 1788, Probate Records 5322 D.S., Register, RCNH.

11. Statement of Claims against Edmund Roberts, Sr., Estate, September 3, 1790, Probate Records 5322 D.S., Register, RCNH; Statement of Demands against Edmund Roberts, Sr., Estate, February 16, 1791, Probate Records 5322 D.S., Register, RCNH.

12. Probate Court Determination for Sarah (Roberts) Woodward, November 13, 1790, Probate Records 5322 D.S., Register, RCNH.

13. Account of Moses Woodward and Sarah (Roberts) Woodward for Administration of Edmund Roberts, Sr., Estate, February 20, 1793, Probate Records 5322 D.S., Register, RCNH.

14. [Mrs. William Graham Rice, a great granddaughter of Edmund Roberts], "Edmund Roberts" (typescript), n.d. [1903?], Portsmouth Historical Society (hereafter cited as PHS). After her mother's death in 1801, Sarah boarded with the Parrys for a number of years, until her marriage to Captain John Bowles.

15. *United States Trade and Portsmouth Advertiser* (Portsmouth, NH), January 15, 1803, 1–3; see also Ray Brighton, *Port of Portsmouth Ships and the Cotton Trade 1783–1829* (Portsmouth, NH: P. E. Randall Publisher, 1986), 54.

16. W. S. W. Ruschenberger, *A Voyage Round the World: Including an Embassy to Muscat and Siam in 1835, 1836, and 1837* (Philadelphia: Carey, Lea and Blanchard, 1838), 10 (available online at *archive.org/details/voyageroundworld00rusc*).

17. Bowles to Peabody, Brooklyn, N.Y. June 14, 1871, Edmund Roberts Papers, folder 1, NHHS. Bowles's letter summarizes various letters that Roberts sent to Sarah from London.

18. Ibid.

19. The Portsmouth Historical Society has the marriage certificate bound in a red leather binder. The wax bas-relief of Roberts, made in Paris, is also on display in the John Paul Jones home of the society.

20. Deed of Sale, George and Rebecca Wentworth to Edmund Roberts, Sr., Portsmouth, July 10, 1787, Dartmouth FCMC. The newly bought Roberts property adjoined that of the Langdons.

21. John Wentworth, *The Wentworth Genealogy: English and American* (Boston: Little, Brown, 1878), 1:331 (available online at *archive.org/details/wentworthgeneal03wentgoog*); see also List of Edmund Roberts Family Members, n.d., Edmund Roberts Papers, folder 1, NHHS.

22. George A. Nelson, comp., *Early U.S. Customs Records and History, Portsmouth, New Hampshire, 3: Builders, Makers, Owners, Importers* (Portsmouth Athenaeum: 1979), 259, 370. See also Anonymous, "Vessels Built and Registered in Portsmouth, 1800–1860," Peabody Museum of Salem (typescript, [1937?]), 55, 133.

23. See Bailey, *Diplomatic History*, 118–123.

24. Bailey B. Baggett to Roberts, New York, March 21, 1808, Edmund Roberts Papers, folder 2, NHHS. This reference includes a copy of a letter of abandonment, Baggett to John P. Mumford, New York, January 22, 1808.

25. Nelson, *Early U.S. Customs, 3.* See also W. M. Shackford to Roberts, New Orleans, June 11, 1815, Edmund Roberts Papers, folder 2, NHHS.

26. Nelson, *Early U.S. Customs, 3.* See also the handwritten fragment of a letter, unsigned and undated [1830?], in Edmund Roberts Papers, folder 2, NHHS.

27. Nelson, *Early U.S. Customs, 2: Commerce, Shipbuilding, Immigration,* 31. For Portsmouth merchants' preoccupation with privateering ventures in the War of 1812, see Saltonstall, *Ports of Piscataqua,* 149–169. Conceivably, the privateer *Mars,* in which Roberts held shares, was the vessel of that name mentioned in Edgar Stanton Maclay, *A History*

of *American Privateers* (Freeport, NY: Books for Libraries Press, 1970), 441. The evidence is inconclusive.

28. "Edmund Roberts," PHS.

29. Baggett to Roberts, New York, March 21, 1808, Edmund Roberts Papers, folder 2, NHHS.

30. March Benson to Roberts, New York, October 11, 1814, Edmund Roberts Papers, folder 2, NHHS.

31. *New Hampshire Gazette* (Portsmouth) 63:49, November 3, 1818.

32. Roberts to Mrs. Langdon Elwyn, Portsmouth, NH, December 21, 1821, and Roberts to Mrs. Elwyn, Portsmouth, NH, January 2, 1822, Edmund Roberts Papers, folder 2, NHHS.

33. U.S. House of Representatives, Report of the Committee of the House of Representatives of the United States to Which Were Referred the Memorials of Certain Merchants Praying Relief for Losses Sustained by the French Spoliations (Washington, DC: Government Printing Office, 1826). For the protracted spoliation claims negotiations with France, see Elizabeth Brett White, *American Opinion of France from Lafayette to Poincaré* (New York: Knopf, 1927), 67–68, 107–109; Samuel Flagg Bemis, ed., *The American Secretaries of State and Their Diplomacy* (New York: Knopf, 1928), 4:281–289, 305–316; and Belohlavek, *Let the Eagle Soar!*, 91–126.

34. Charles Stuart Osgood, *Historical Sketch of Salem, 1626–1879* (Salem, MA: Essex Institute, 1879), 162–165 (available online at *books.google.com*). See also Norman R. Bennett, "Americans in Zanzibar: 1825–1845," Essex Institute Historical Collections, 95:1 (January 1959), 240–243; and John Gray, *History of Zanzibar, from the Middle Ages to 1856* (London: Oxford University Press, 1962), 194.

35. Contract for "Sundry Ports on the Eastern Coast of Africa," Portsmouth, NH, March 1827, Edmund Roberts Papers, folder 3, NHHS. Subscriptions for the venture had begun as early as December 1826; Edmund Roberts Papers, folder 3, NHHS. For a brief background on the firm of Fish and Grinnell, see Walter Barrett, *The Old Merchants of New York City* (New York: Greenwood Press, 1968, c1863), 2:261–262 and 4:215.

36. Edmund Roberts to "His Highness Said Saide Ben Sultan Ben Imaum" [*sic*; properly, Sayyid Sa'id), Zanzibar, January 27, 1828, bound in Edmund Roberts Papers, 1: 1808–1832, Library of Congress (hereafter LOC). In that letter, Roberts outlined the obligations he had allegedly undertaken in connection with the voyage, obviously hoping to arouse the ruler's sympathy.

37. Copies of various contracts between Roberts and vendors, all dated May or June, 1827, Edmund Roberts Papers, folder 3, NHHS.

38. E. D. Gunilac to Sayyid Sa'id, Zanzibar, undated (but probably January 1828) Edmund Roberts Papers, folder 4, NHHS.

39. Roberts to Sayyid Sa'id, Zanzibar, January 23, 1828, Edmund Roberts Papers, 1:1808–1832, LOC. Bemis mistakenly suggests that Roberts had actually been a member of the U.S. consular service. Bemis, *Diplomatic History*, 344.

40. For a biography of Sayyid Sa'id, see Rudolph Said-Ruete, *Said bin Sultan (1791–1856) Ruler of Oman and Zanzibar: His Place in the History of Arabia and East Africa* (London: Alexander-Ouseley, 1929), especially 150–350. Said-Ruete's mother was a daughter of Sayyid Sa'id, who married a German Christian. Because of this, the ruler's family disavowed Said-Ruete's mother. Her son, who hyphenated his surname to include the family names of both of his parents, retained a lifelong interest in Zanzibar and in his grandfather.

41. For Sayyid Sa'id's relations with the British, see Reginald Coupland, *East Africa and Its Invaders* (Oxford: Clarendon Press, 1938), 186–216; and Gray, *History of Zanzibar*, 227–239.

42. Roberts to the Honorable Levi Woodbury, New York, December 19, 1828, Edmund Roberts Papers, 1:1808–1832, LOC. A somewhat contentious account of Roberts's talks with Sayyid Sa'id, which is not always consistent with Roberts's subsequent letters on the subject, may be found in Gray, *History of Zanzibar*, 194–195.

43. Ibid. Also see the materials on Edmund Roberts at the Portsmouth Historical Society: The anonymously written typescript on Roberts asserts that Sayyid Sa'id offered him $20,000 to escort an Omani "fleet" to the United States, but that the fleet did not appear before Roberts's scheduled departure. The story sounds exaggerated, but had apparently become family lore.

44. Fish and Grinnell Co.; Sales of Sundries Received from *Mary Ann* from Zanzibar o/a of Edmund Roberts, November 30, 1828, Edmund Roberts Papers, folder 3, NHHS.

CHAPTER 2: PREPARATION FOR ROBERTS'S FIRST MISSION

1. For a biographic sketch of Levi Woodbury, who played such a prominent part in promoting Roberts's career, see William E. Smith, "Levi Woodbury," in Malone, *Dictionary*, 19:488–489.

2. Roberts to Woodbury, New York, December 29, 1828, Edmund Roberts Papers, 1:1808–1832, LOC.

3. Woodbury to Roberts, Washington, D.C., December 22, 1828, Edmund Roberts Papers, 1:1808–1832, LOC.

4. Roberts to Woodbury, New York, December 26, 1828, Edmund Roberts Papers, 1:1808–1832, LOC.

5. Owen's account of the incident is recorded in W. F. W. Owen, *Narrative of Voyages to Explore the Shores of Africa, Arabia, and Madagascar; Performed in H.M. Ships* Leven *and* Barracouta, *under the Direction of Captain W. F. W. Owen* (New York: J and J Harper, 1833), 1:367–369 (available online at *books.google.com*). See also Coupland, *East Africa,* 168–169; and Gray, *History of Zanzibar,* 117, 138–139.

6. Woodbury to Roberts, Washington, D.C., January 1, 1829, Edmund Roberts Papers, 1:1808–1832, LOC.

7. Roberts to Woodbury, New York, January 5, 1829, Edmund Roberts Papers, 1:1808–1832, LOC.

8. Ephraim G. Ware to Roberts, New Orleans, April 14, 1830, Edmund Roberts Papers, folder 5, NHHS.

9. Ware to Roberts, New Orleans, April 30, 1830, Edmund Roberts Papers, folder 5, NHHS.

10. Ware to Roberts, Durham Jail (Louisiana), July 19, 1830, Edmund Roberts Papers, folder 5, NHHS.

11. Charles Dilly to Roberts, Near Troy (Ohio), June 30, 1830, Edmund Roberts Papers, folder 5, NHHS.

12. Roberts to Kilgour, Taylor and Co., Cincinnati, December 32, 1830, Edmund Roberts Papers, folder 5, NHHS.

13. Fish and Grinnell to Roberts, New York, November 17, 1831, Edmund Roberts Papers, folder 5, NHHS.

14. Catherine Roberts to "my dear Husband," Portsmouth, NH, March 12, 1830, Edmund Roberts Papers, folder 5, NHHS.

15. Catherine Roberts to "my dear Husband," Portsmouth, NH, May 16, 1830, Edmund Roberts Papers, folder 5, NHHS.

16. Roberts's four daughters to Roberts, Portsmouth, NH, November 14–16, 1830, Edmund Roberts Papers, folder 5, NHHS.

17. Roberts to "my dear children," New York, December 8, 1830, Edmund Roberts Papers, folder 5, NHHS.

18. John Shillaber to Secretary of State, Batavia, April 6, 1824, DS–1, Reports from the Consulate in Batavia, National Archives, Foreign Affairs Section (hereafter NAFAS).

19. Shillaber to Secretary of State, Batavia, December 10, 1830, DS–1, Reports from Consulate at Batavia, NAFAS.

20. Shillaber to Secretary of State, "At Sea," July 14, 1831, DS–1, Reports from the Consulate at Batavia, NAFAS.

21. For an account of various foreign efforts to open Japan, see Wildes, *Aliens,* 165–173 (Dutch), 133–155 (Russian), and 174–186 (British).

22. Shillaber to the Honorable Martin Van Buren, Secretary of State, December 10, 1831, DS–1, Reports from the Consulate at Batavia, NAFAS.

23. D. J. M. Tate, *The Making of Modern South-East Asia* (New York: Oxford University Press, 1971), 1:235n23.

24. A contemporary account of the Malay seizure of *Friendship* is in J. N. Reynolds, *Voyage of the United States Frigate Potomac ... during the Circumnavigation of the Globe, in the Years 1831, 1832, 1833, and 1834* (New York: Harper and Brothers, 1835), 88–94, 530–533 (available online at *books.google.com*). Commodore John Downes, who commanded the *Potomac,* a frigate that had been selected to deliver "chastisement" for the incident, was subsequently reprimanded in the United States for excessive chastisement of the Sumatran village Quallah Battoo. See also George Granville Putman, *Salem Vessels and Their Voyages; a History of the "George," "Glide," "Taria Topan" and "St. Paul," in Trade with Calcutta, East Coast of Africa, Madagascar, and the Philippine Islands* (Salem, MA: Essex Institute, 1924), 71–91; James Duncan Phillips, *Pepper and Pirates: Adventures in the Sumatra Pepper Trade of Salem* (Boston: Houghton Mifflin, 1949), 80–102; Fairburn, *Merchant Sail,* 1:567; and Belohlavek, *Let the Eagle Soar!,* 152–162.

25. Reynolds, *Voyage,* 11. See also President Jackson's third annual message to the Senate and House of Representatives, December 6, 1831, in which he refers to the dispatch of a naval frigate to Sumatra to demand satisfaction, failing which chastisement would be inflicted. James D. Richardson, comp., *A Compilation of the Messages and Papers of the Presidents* (New York: Bureau of National Literature, 1897), 3:111 (available online at *www.presidency.ucsb.edu/ws/index. php?pid=29473#axzz1x2vsqEie*).

26. Reynolds, *Voyage,* 11; and Edmund Roberts, *Embassy to the Eastern Courts of Cochin-China, Siam, and Muscat; in the U.S. Sloop-of-war* Pea-

cock … *during the Years 1832-3-4* (New York: Harper and Brothers, 1836), 5–6 (available online at *books.google.com*).

27. Woodbury to Livingston, Washington, D.C., "Wednesday evening" [December 7, 1831?], in Levi Woodbury Papers, no. 11, LOC. Bemis implies, wrongly, that the three naval vessels sailed together; Bemis, *Diplomatic History*, 344.

28. Livingston to Roberts, Washington, D.C., January 27, 1832, DS–1, Special Missions, December 15, 1823 to November 13, 1852, NAFAS.

29. Livingston to Roberts, Washington, D.C., February 14, 1832, DS–1, Special Missions, NAFAS. Copies of Roberts's presidential commission, "passports," and "full powers" documents are in DS–2, Credences, March 10, 1825, to September 21, 1841, NAFAS. The blank passport, signed by President Jackson, is at the Portsmouth Historical Society.

30. Livingston to Woodbury, Washington, D.C., January 3, 1832, DS–1, Special Missions, NAFAS.

31. Woodbury to Geisinger, Washington, D.C., January 6, 1832, in Levi Woodbury Papers, no. 11, LOC.

32. Roberts to "my dear children," Washington, D.C., January 27, 1832, and Roberts to Harriet Roberts (third daughter), Washington, D.C., February 4, 1832, Edmund Roberts Papers, 1:1808–1832, LOC.

33. Livingston to Roberts, Washington, D.C., January 27, 1832, DS–1, Special Missions, NAFAS.

34. Roberts to Livingston, New York, February 1, 1832, bound in DS–1, Special Missions, NAFAS.

35. Roberts to Fish and Grinnell, New York, N,Y., March 3, 1832, Edmund Roberts Papers, 1:1808–1832, LOC.

36. Roberts to Geisinger, Portsmouth, April 16, 1835, David Geisinger Papers, MS 1283, box 2, Maryland Historical Society (hereafter MHS).

37. Livingston to Roberts, Washington, D.C., July 23, 1832, DS–1, Special Missions, NAFAS. Sayyid Sa'id's letter, which has since disappeared, was forwarded by the New York firm of N. L. Rogers and Brothers under cover of a letter dated June 27, 1832. Rogers's letter is in DS Miscellaneous Letters, April–June 1832, NAFAS.

38. Livingston to Roberts, Washington, D.C., July 23, 1838, DS–1, Special Missions, NAFAS.

39. Roberts to Livingston, Anger Roads, Java, September 10, 1832, Edmund Roberts Papers, 1:1808–1832, LOC. For the *Potomac*'s punitive action, see Reynolds, *Voyage*, 104–124, 221.

40. Roberts to Livingston, Manila, October 6, 1832, Edmund Roberts Papers, 1:1808–1832, LOC.

41. Account Current of Edmund Roberts to the State Department for the Period January, 1832, to January, 1833, "On board U.S.S. *Peacock, Vaunglam Roads, Fu–yen [sic] Province, Coast Cochin China,"* January 9, 1833, Edmund Roberts Papers, oversize vault folder, NHHS.

42. Roberts to Livingston, Canton, December 20, 1832, Edmund Roberts Papers, 1:1808–1832, LOC. See also Roberts to Secretary of State John Forsyth, Portsmouth, N.H., January 22, 1835, Edmund Roberts Papers, 2:1833–1835, LOC.

43. Roberts to Livingston, Canton, December 20, 1832, Edmund Roberts Papers, 1:1808–1892, LOC.

44. For Robert Morrison, see Kenneth Scott Latourette, *A History of Christian Missions in China* (New York: Macmillan, 1929), 190, 210–215; and Suzanne Wilson Barnett and John King Fairbank, *Christianity in China: Early Protestant Missionary Writings* (Cambridge: Harvard University Press, 1985), 7.

45. Robert Morrison to Roberts, Canton, November 20, 1832 (private and confidential), Edmund Roberts Papers, folder 6, NHHS.

46. Morrison to Roberts, Canton, November 24, 1832, Edmund Roberts Papers, folder 6, NHHS.

47. Roberts to Morrison, "American Kong," Canton, November 24, 1832, Edmund Roberts Papers, folder 6, NHHS.

48. Edmund Roberts, Account Current with the State Department for January, 1832, to January, 1833, "On board U.S.S. *Peacock,* Vaunglam Roads, Fu-yen [sic] Province, Coast Cochin China," January 9, 1833, Edmund Roberts Papers, oversize vault folder, NHHS.

49. For early American missionaries in China, see Latourette, *Christian Missions,* 217–218.

50. Roberts to Livingston, Canton, December 19, 1832, Edmund Roberts Papers, Folder 6, NHHS.

51. Roberts to Livingston, Canton, November 4, 1832, Edmund Roberts Papers, 1:1808–1832, LOC.

52. D. Geisinger, "Notes of a Cruise Aboard U.S. Ship *Peacock,* Boston," David Geisinger Papers, MS 283, Box II, MHS.

CHAPTER 3: EARLIER COCHIN CHINESE AND SIAMESE CONTACTS

1. "Journal of a Voyage to Cochin China in 1803–1804 aboard the ship *Fame*," Jeremiah Briggs, PM–M656–3, no. 27, Peabody Museum of Salem, MA (hereafter Briggs journal, Peabody).

2. Alexander Barton Woodside, *Vietnam and the Chinese Model: A Comparative Study of Nguyen and Ch'ing Civil Government in the First Half of the Nineteenth Century* (Cambridge: Harvard University Press, 1971), 16–17. Woodside stresses the limited role of the French advisers. See also Virginia Thompson, *French Indo-China* (New York: Macmillan, 1937), 22–23; Donald Lancaster, *The Emancipation of French Indochina* (New York: Oxford University Press, 1961), 27–31; and Joseph Buttinger, *The Smaller Dragon: A Political History of Vietnam* (New York: Praeger, 1958), 198–243. A French naval adviser in Hué gave Captain Briggs a detailed account of the somewhat wavering nature of French assistance to Nguyen Anh in recovering his domains. See Briggs journal, Peabody.

3. Alastair Lamb, *The Mandarin Road to Old Hué: Narratives of Anglo–Vietnamese Diplomacy from the Seventeenth Century to the Eve of the French Conquest* (Hamden, CT: Archon, 1970), 229–234; and Denis Étienne, *Bordeaux et la Cochinchine sous la Restauration et le Second Empire* (Bordeaux: Delmas, 1965).

4. John Crawfurd, *Journal of an Embassy from the Governor-General of India to the Courts of Siam and Cochin China; Exhibiting a View of the Actual State of Those Kingdoms* (London: Colburn, 1828; 1st ed. repr. 1967), 255. A copy of the original journal is available online at *http://books.google.com*.

5. Pierre de Joinville, ed., *La Mission de la* Cybèle *en Extrême-Orient, 1817– 1818; Journal de Voyage du Capitaine A. Kergariou* (Paris: Champion, 1914) (available online at *books.google.com*). Also see Lamb, *Mandarin Road*, 246.

6. Lamb, *Mandarin Road*, 230–234.

7. Ibid., 205–226. Cochin Chinese officials later claimed that John Roberts had not been received by the emperor, but they were on at least one occasion corrected by the French mandarin Philippe Vannier; Crawfurd, *Journal*, 249.

8. Lamb, *Mandarin Road*, 229.

9. Crawfurd, *Journal*, 237–238, 247–249.

10. John White, *History of a Voyage to the China Sea* (Boston: Wells and Lilly, 1823), 31 (available online at *books.google.com*).

11. Crawfurd, *Journal*, 249n, 272–276.

12. Briggs journal, Peabody.

13. White, *History of a Voyage*, 185–186.

14. Ibid., 240–247. In these pages, White details his frustrations in dealing with local Cochin Chinese officials and merchants.

15. Ibid., 355. Before he arrived in Siam or Cochin China , the English envoy John Crawfurd was later wrongly informed in Singapore that two American vessels had loaded full cargoes at Saigon; Crawfurd, *Journal*, 44.

16. White, *History of a Voyage*, iv.

17. Ibid., 36.

18. For historical background on the Thai empire of Bangkok and its antecedents, see David K. Wyatt, *Thailand: A Short History* (New Haven: Yale University Press, 1984), 90–160; and Gilbert Khoo and Dorothy Lo, *Asian Transformation: A History of South-East, South and East Asia* (Kuala Lumpur: Heinemann, 1977), 336–340. See also Tate, *Modern South-East Asia*, 497–500.

19. Wyatt, *Thailand*, 112–118; and Tate, *Modern South-East Asia*, 501–503. Wyatt states that 500 French troops accompanied the French mission; Tate raises this number to 1,600 troops.

20. Wyatt, *Thailand*, 109–112; Tate, *Modern South-East Asia*, 501, 520n3.

21. Tate, *Modern South-East Asia*, 104–108.

22. Crawfurd, *Journal*, 76–77.

23. Ibid., 80–81.

24. Ibid., 91–100.

25. Ibid., 101–102.

26. Ibid., 121–122.

27. Ibid., 133–134.

28. Ibid., 141.

29. Ibid., 143–144.

30. Ibid., 144–145.

31. Ibid., 163–164.

32. Ibid., 167–169.

33. Ibid., 170–174.

34. Ibid., 159–160, 164–166.

35. D. G. E. Hall, *Henry Burney: A Political Biography* (New York: Oxford University Press, 1974), 38.

36. Ibid., 25.

37. Ibid., 43–46, 121–122.

38. Ibid., 77–79.

39. Ibid., 85–86.

40. Ibid., 111–115.

41. Ibid., 116–119.

42. Crawfurd, *Journal*, 154.

43. Ibid., 89–90.

44. Ibid., 133.

45. Ibid., 158–159.

46. Ibid., 175.

47. Hall, *Henry Burney*, 100.

48. Roberts to McLane, Washington, D.C., May 14, 1834, DS–10, Reports of Special Agents, Edmund Roberts, NAFAS.

49. Hall, *Henry Burney*, 273–290.

50. Abeel left Bangkok in 1829; he was engaged by the American Seamen's Friend Society to become chaplain to American seamen in Chinese waters. He moved to Canton/Macao. See Latourette, *Christian Missions*, 217.

51. Roberts, *Eastern Courts*, 268–269.

CHAPTER 4: ABORTIVE TALKS IN COCHIN CHINA

1. Roberts, *Eastern Courts*, 171–174. The Cochin China portion of Roberts's posthumously published memoir is virtually identical to his detailed manuscript report of these negotiations. That comprehensive report, entitled "Records of a Mission," was not sent to the State Department until January 1834, as Roberts was returning to the United States from Rio de Janeiro. Roberts to McLane, Rio de Janeiro, January 8, 1834, DS–10, Reports of Special Agents, Edmund Roberts, NAFAS. Some six months earlier, he had sent from Batavia a shorter account of the failed mission.

2. See Roberts, *Eastern Courts,* 174–175, for the text of the memorandum.

3. See ibid., 176, for the text of Roberts's letter.

4. See ibid.,178, for the dialogue with the priest.

5. Ibid., 181–182.

6. Tate, *Modern South-East Asia,* 439; and Woodside, *Vietnam and the Chinese Model,* 120–121.

7. Roberts, *Eastern Courts,* 183–184; and Crawfurd, *Journal,* 243.

8. See Roberts, *Eastern Courts,* 184–185, for the text of the revised letter.

9. Ibid., 186.

10. Ibid., 187–188.

11. Ibid., 191–192.

12. See ibid., 192–194, for John Morrison's talks with the Hué officials.

13. See ibid., 197–200, for Roberts's talks with the Hué officials.

14. Ibid., 217.

15. See ibid., 203–204, for the text of Roberts's letter to the minister.

16. Ibid., 108–211.

17. Ibid., 214–216.

18. Ibid., 219–220.

19. Roberts to Livingston, Singapore, May 10, 1833, DS–10, Reports of Special Agents, Edmund Roberts, NAFAS.

20. Roberts to Livingston, Batavia, June 22, 1833, DS–10, Reports of Special Agents, Edmund Roberts, NAFAS.

CHAPTER 5: NEGOTIATING A TREATY WITH SIAM

1. Geisinger's formal rank was still only master commandant, below that of captain.

2. Roberts's "Records of a Mission," his official report, contains the text of the letter. Unlike the detailed Cochin Chinese portions of his posthumously published account, Roberts's chapter on the Siamese negotiations is curiously devoid of details on the negotiations in Siam. Roberts's report is bound in DS–10, Reports of Special Agents, Edmund Roberts, NAFAS.

3. Roberts, *Eastern Courts,* 230–231. Roberts's published account pro-

vides extensive detail on all ceremonial aspects of the mission's reception.

4. See ibid., 234–238, in which Roberts vividly describes the prostrations rendered to the prah khlang by inferiors and by male members of his family.

5. Crawfurd, *Journal*, 80.

6. Roberts's report recounts these proceedings at length in DS–10, Reports of Special Agents, Edmund Roberts, NAFAS.

7. The English envoy, Crawfurd, received the munificent sum of 240 *ticals* (Crawfurd, *Journal*, 102). His accompanying party was more impressive.

8. Roberts's report contains the text of his initial draft treaty in DS–10, Reports of Special Agents, Edmund Roberts, NAFAS.

9. See ibid. for his lengthy exchange with the prah khlanq on the draft treaty.

10. See ibid. for the text of the prah khlanq's counterdraft.

11. Ibid., 253–259. The first English envoy, Crawfurd, had also made such obeisance (Crawfurd, *Journal*, 88, 95). So did Burney, the later British emissary (Hall, *Henry Burney*, 44).

12. For the text of the treaty as finally concluded, see Miller, *Treaties*, 3:742–769.

13. Roberts, *Eastern Courts*, 319.

14. Roberts to Livingston, Singapore, May 10, 1833, DS–10, Reports of Special Agents, Edmund Roberts, NAFAS.

15. Roberts to Livingston, Batavia, June 22, 1833, DS–10, Reports of Special Agents, Edmund Roberts, NAFAS.

CHAPTER 6: ON TO ARABIA AND HOME

1. Roberts, Eastern Courts, 320.

2. Roberts to Livingston, Batavia, June 22, 1833, DS–10, Reports of Special Agents, Edmund Roberts, NAFAS.

3. For the Phaeton incident, see Wildes, Aliens, 152–155; and C. Northcote Parkinson, War in the Eastern Seas, 1793–1815 (London: Allen and Unwin, 1954), 443–446.

4. Livingston to Roberts, Washington, D.C., July 23, 1832, DS–1, Special

Missions, NAFAS. The Russian naval vessel was the Nadezhda with Ambassador N. P. de Rezanov aboard. See Wildes, Aliens, 136–143.

5. Roberts to Livingstron, Batavia, June 22, 1833, DS–10, Reports of Special Agents, Edmund Roberts, NAFAS.

6. Livingston to Roberts, Washington, D.C., July 23, 1832, DS–1, Special Missions, NAFAS.

7. Roberts, Eastern Courts, 340.

8. Geisinger to Shields, U.S.S. Peacock, Indian Ocean, August 9, 1833, David Geisinger Papers, MS 1283, box 2, MHS.

9. Ibid.; and Geisinger, "Notes of a Cruise," entry of August 27, 1833, David Geisinger Papers, MS 1283, box I, MHS.

10. Ibid., and entry of August 31, 1833. See also "Journal of the United States Sloop-of-War Peacock, 18 guns, Captain David Geisinger, no. 8, February 19, 1833, to March 2, 1834," entries of August 31 and September 1, 1833, National Archives Naval Records (hereafter NANR); and "Journal of the United States Schooner Boxer, 10 guns, Captain (Lt. Commander) Wm. F. Shields, Commander, December 14, 1832, to July 26, 1844," entry of September 1, 1833, NANR.

11. For the most comprehensive accounts of the short–lived rule of Turkchi Bilmas in Mokha and the Yemeni Tihamah, see J. R. Wellsted, *Travels to the City of the Caliphs, along the Shores of the Persian Gulf and the Mediterranean, Including a Voyage to the Coast of Arabia, and a Tour on the Island of Socotra* (London: Colburn, 1840), 1:384–395; Felix Mengin, *Histoire de l'Éqypte* (Paris: Hachette, 1839), 2:34–38, 63–65; and R. Lambert Playfair, *A History of Arabia Felix or Yemen, from the Commencement of the Christian Era to the Present Time, Including an Account of the British Settlement of Aden* (Bombay: Education Society's Press, 1859), 141–144. For a dramatic, but somewhat garbled, account of Turkchi Bilmas by an American supercargo (officer in charge of the cargo) who visited Mokha in the early 1840s, see Joseph Barlow Felt Osgood, *Notes of Travel: or, Recollections of Majunqa, Zanzibar, Muscat, Aden, Mocha and Other Eastern Ports* (Salem, MA: George Creamer, 1854), 169; available online at books.google.com).

12. Roberts, Eastern Courts, 344–345.

13. Roberts, Eastern Courts, 343–350. Roberts's initial account of the Mokha visit is a draft letter; Edmund Roberts Papers, 5, n.p., n.d., LOC. He subsequently included much of this material in his journal; "Journal of Edmund Roberts on board the United States Ships of War Peacock and Lexington, during the years 1832, 1833, 1834," entries of

August 31 and September 1, 1833, DS–10, Reports of Special Agents, Edmund Roberts. NAFAS.

14. Roberts, Eastern Courts, 352–353. See also Geisinger, "Notes on a Cruise," David Geisinger Papers, MS 1283, box 2, MHS.

15. Roberts, Eastern Courts, 360–361. See also "Journal of Edmund Roberts," entry of October 7, 1833, DS–10, Reports of Special Agents, Edmund Roberts, NAFAS. After his return to the United States, Roberts submitted a supplementary report to the State Department on Muscat and on the newly concluded treaty with that country. See Roberts to McLane, Washington, D.C., May 14, 1834, Edmund Roberts Papers, 3:1834–1835, LOC.

16. Roberts to Secretary of State Louis McLane, Rio de Janeiro, January 13, 1834, Edmund Roberts Papers, 3:1834–1835, LOC. For the text of the treaty, see Miller, Treaties, 3:789–810. Curiously, no original is in the pertinent treaty files of the National Archives—it seems somehow to have disappeared. The Portsmouth Historical Society has a signed copy, which is probably the third original. It was given to the society in 1936 by Mrs. William Gorham Rice, a great-granddaughter of Roberts, and apparently was for many years among the Roberts memorabilia retained by his family.

17. Geisinger, "Notes of a Cruise," David Geisinger Papers, MS 1283, box 1, MHA; and "Journal of...Peacock," no. 8, entry of October 4, 1833, NANR; and "Journal of...Boxer," entry of October 4, 1833, NANR.

18. Roberts to Hon. J. Forsyth, Portsmouth, N.H., July 23, 1834, DS–10, Reports of Special Agents, Edmund Roberts, NAFAS. For the text of Sayyid Sa'id's grandiloquent letter to President Jackson, see Roberts, Eastern Courts, 430.

19. Geisinger, "Notes of a Cruise," David Geisinger Papers, MS 1283, box 2, MHS.

20. Roberts to McLane, Boston Harbour, April 24, 1834, DS–10, Reports of Special Agents, Edmund Roberts, NAFAS.

CHAPTER 7: INTERLUDE AT HOME

1. Roberts to Harriet Roberts, Washington, D.C., June 14, 1834, Edmund Roberts Papers, folder 7, NHHS.

2. Roberts to Livingston, Batavia, June 22, 1833, DS–10, Reports of Special Agents, Edmund Roberts, NAFAS.

3. Roberts to McLane, Washington, D.C., May 14, 1834, DS–10, Reports of Special Agents, Edmund Roberts, NAFAS.

4. *Daily National Intelligencer* (Washington, D.C.), October 31, 1833. The *Singapore Chronicle* originally published the account on June 6, 1833.

5. Roberts to McLane, Rio de Janeiro, January 17, 1834, bound in DS–10, Reports of Special Agents, Edmund Roberts, NAFAS.

6. Roberts to McLane, Washington, D.C., May 14, 1834, DS–10, Reports of Special Agents, Edmund Roberts, NAFAS.

7. Roberts to the Hon. John Forsyth, Portsmouth, N.H., August 12, 1834, DS–10, Reports of Special Agents, Edmund Roberts, NAFAS.

8. R. Latimer to Roberts, Washington, D.C., June 29, 1834, Edmund Roberts Papers, Folder 7, NHHS.

9. Roberts to McLane, Washington, D.C., May 14, 1834, DS–10, Reports of Special Agents, Edmund Roberts, NAFAS. He also included this detailed defense of the Siamese treaty in his posthumously published memoir (Roberts, *Eastern Courts*, 314–316).

10. *Essex Register* (Salem, MA), March 20, 1834, printed the text of Captain John Webster's letter to "Captains of American vessels at Zanzibar," Lamu, November 24, 1833.

11. Roberts to McLane, Rio de Janeiro, January 17, 1834, DS–10, Reports of Special Agents, Edmund Roberts, NAFAS.

12. Miller, *Treaties*, 3:742, 790.

13. John Morrison to Roberts, Canton, July 13, 1834, Edmund Roberts Papers, folder 7, NHHS.

14. Roberts to McLane, Washington, D.C., May 14, 1834, DS–10, Reports of Special Agents, Edmund Roberts, NAFAS. See also Roberts, *Eastern Courts*, 310–313.

15. Roberts to McLane, Washington, D.C., May 14, 1834, DS–10, Reports of Special Agents, Edmund Roberts, NAFAS. Although the letter has the same date as the one cited in note 14, this was a separate letter. See also Roberts, *Eastern Courts*, 361–363. Geisinger separately observed that Sayyid Sa'id's navy consisted of eight ships with between twenty-two and seventy-four guns, and sixty-seven "sail of vessels," variously rigged and carrying between four and eighteen guns. Geisinger, "Notes of a Cruise on Board U.S. Ship *Peacock*," David Geisinger Papers, MS 1283, box 2, MHS.

16. Roberts erred when he reported Ainslie had been sent on a special

mission. Rather, Ainslie had been sent as a member of a Dutch team from Java, where the Dutch were now nominally British subjects, to audit the accounts of the Deshima factory. Ainslee, who was an English-born physician, was initially instructed to remain at Deshima as resident medical officer. The mission was abortive and Ainslee did not remain in Japan. See Wildes, *Aliens*, 168–169.

17. William Milburn, *Oriental Commerce* (London: Kingsbury, Parbury and Allen, 1825), 515 (available online at *books.google.com*).

18. Allan B. Cole, "Plans of Edmund Roberts for Negotiations in Nippon," *Monumenta Nipponica* 4, no. 2 (1941), 497–513.

19. Roberts to McLane, Washington, D.C., (n.d., wrongly inscribed 1832 [May 14, 1834?]), DS–10, Reports of Special Agents, Edmund Roberts, NAFAS.

20. Roberts to McLane, Boston Harbour, April 24, 1834, DS–10, Reports of Special Agents, Edmund Roberts, NAFAS.

21. Roberts to McLane, Boston, April 25, 1834, DS–10, Reports of Special Agents, Edmund Roberts, NAFAS.

22. Treasury Department, Auditor's Office, to Geisinger, Washington, D.C., July 19, 1834, Edmund Roberts Papers, 3:1834–1835, LOC.

23. Forsyth to Roberts, Washington, D.C., August 5, 1834, DS–1, Special Missions, NAFAS.

24. Roberts to Forsyth, Portsmouth, N.H., August 12, 1834, DS–10, Reports of Special Agents, Edmund Roberts, NAFAS.

25. Forsyth to Roberts, Washington, D.C., January 30, 1835, DS–1, Special Missions, NAFAS.

26. Treasury Department (Fifth Auditor's Office) to Roberts, Washington, D.C., October 31, 1834, Edmund Roberts Papers, 3:1834–1835, LOC.

27. Roberts to the Hon. Samuel Bell, Portsmouth, November 8, 1834, Edmund Roberts Papers, 3:1834–1835, LOC.

28. Geisinger to Hon. Mahlon Dickerson, Secretary of the Navy, Washington, D.C., April 21, 1835, David Geisinger Papers, MS 1283, box 2, MHS.

29. Roberts to Geisinger, Portsmouth, April 16, 1835, David Geisinger Papers, MS 1283, box 2, MHS.

30. Dickerson to Geisinger, Navy Department, Washington, D.C., April 22, 1837, David Geisinger Papers MS 1285, box 2, MHS.

31. Forsyth to Roberts, Washington, D.C., August 5, 1834, DS–1, Special Missions, NAFAS.

32. Roberts to Forsyth, Portsmouth, N.H., August 12, 1834, DS–10, Reports of Special Agents, Edmund Roberts, NAFAS. Dickins served as chief clerk in the State Department from 1833 to 1836. On Dickins, see Graham H. Stuart, *The Department of State: A History of Its Organization, Procedure, and Personnel* (New York: Macmillan, 1949), 83–85; and John A. Munroe, *Louis McLane: Federalist and Jacksonian* (New Brunswick: Rutgers University Press, 1973), 403, 408–409.

33. Forsyth to Roberts, Washington, D.C., August 21, 1834, DS–1, Special Missions, NAFAS.

34. Roberts to Forsyth, Portsmouth, N.H., September 21, 1834, DS–10, Reports of Special Agents, Edmund Roberts, NAFAS.

35. Forsyth to Roberts, Washington, D.C., March 16, 1835, DS–1, Special Missions, NAFAS.

36. Forsyth to Roberts, Washington, D.C., March 20, 1835, and April 10, 1835, DS–1, Special Missions, NAFAS.

37. Ibid.

38. Forsyth to Roberts, Washington, D.C., March 26, 1835, DS–1, Special Missions, NAFAS.

39. Forsyth to Roberts, Washington, D.C., March 16, 1835, DS–1, Special Missions, NAFAS.

40. Forsyth to Roberts, Washington, D.C., March 17, 1835, DS–1, Special Missions, NAFAS.

41. Roberts to Forsyth, Portsmouth, March 24, 1835, Edmund Roberts Papers, folder 10, NHHS.

42. Forsyth to Roberts, Washington, D.C., April 16, 1835, DS–1, Special Missions, NAFAS. Copies of the letters of credence and full-powers documents are in DS–1, Special Missions, and DS–10, Reports of Special Agents, Edmund Roberts, NAFAS.

43. Forsyth to Roberts, Washington, D.C., April 16, 1834, DS–1, Special Missions, NAFAS.

44. Forsyth to Roberts, Washington, D.C., April 17, 1834, DS–1, Special Missions, NAFAS.

45. Forsyth to Captain Edmund P. Kennedy, U.S.N., Washington, D.C., April 17, 1834, and Forsyth to Roberts, Washington, D.C., April 18, 1834, DS–1, Special Missions, NAFAS.

46. Kennedy to the Hon. Mahlon Dickerson, Secretary of the Navy, New York, April 20, 1835, Letters Received from Officers Commanding Ships of War, RG45, NANR.

CHAPTER 8: BRITISH AND EUROPEAN CONCERNS

1. Among the many works on the English East India Company that show the evolution of its politico-economic role and the geographic span of its activities, the best are Marguerite Eyer Wilbur, *The East India Company and the British Empire in the Far East* (Stanford: Stanford University Press, 1945), 316–346; Holden Furber, *John Company at Work: A Study of European Expansion in India in the Late Eighteenth Century* (Cambridge: Harvard University Press, 1948), 32–259; and C. H. Philips, *The East India Company, 1784–1834* (Manchester: Manchester University Press, 1961), 276–298.

2. Roberts to Forsyth, Washington, D.C., May 14, 1834, DS–10, Reports of Special Agents, Edmund Roberts, NAFAS.

3. For the texts of these agreements and the Moresby treaty, see C. U. Aitchison, comp., *A Collection of Treaties, Engagements and Sanads Relating to India and Neighbouring Countries* (Calcutta: Office of the Superintendent of Government Printing, 1933, c1892), 11:287–292.

4. Gerald Sandford Graham, *Great Britain in the Indian Ocean: A Study of Maritime Enterprise, 1810–1850* (Oxford: Clarendon Press, 1967), 206–207.

5. Ibid. An English consul was not sent to Zanzibar until 1840, two years after an American consul had arrived there.

6. Ibid., 207. For a more generalized account of Hart's visit to Zanzibar, see Captain H. Hart, "Extracts from Brief Notes of a Visit to Zanzibar (belonging to H. H. the Imaum of Muskat), in H. M.'s ship *Imogene*, in the months of January and February 1834," *Selections from the Records of the Bombay Government*, new series (Bombay, 1854), 24:273–283 (available online at *books.google.com*).

CHAPTER 9: THE FINAL MISSION

1. Ruschenberger, *Voyage*, 12–15, 19, 52–53.

2. From Muscat, Roberts drafted a letter to his children giving a vivid account of the *Peacock*'s grounding and of his harrowing sail in the ship's cutter to Muscat; Roberts to "my dear children," Muscat, September

28, 1835, Edmund Roberts Papers, 4:1835–1842, LOC. His official report is in Roberts to Forsyth, Bombay, October 23, 1835, DS–10, Reports of Special Agents, Edmund Roberts, NAFAS. Commodore Kennedy's official report of the Masirah incident, including high praise for Roberts's bravery, is in Kennedy to Mahlon Dickerson, Secretary of the Navy, Bombay, December 1, 1835, Navy Department, Captains' Letters, December, 1835, NANR. Another account by a naval officer aboard the *Peacock* is in S. W. Gordon to Lieutenant G. Pendergast, Bombay, October 29, 1835, Naval Records Collection, Area 10, file RG 45, NANR. For a published account of the Masirah incident by the ship's surgeon, see Ruschenberger, *Voyage,* 54–64.

3. Roberts's official report is in "Records of a Mission, and Occurrences Connected with the Mission to the Courts of Muscat, Siam, Cochin China and Japan, by the Undersigned by Instructions from the Department of State of the United States of America, on board the United States Ship of War *Peacock*, E. K. Stribling, Acting Commander, under E. P. Kennedy, Commodore, April 20, 1836," DS–10, Reports of Special Agents, Edmund Roberts, NAFAS. See also Miller, *Treaties,* 3:807–810.

4. For the texts of Roberts's letters, see Ruschenberger, *Voyage,* 89–90.

5. DS–10, Reports of Special Agents, Edmund Roberts, NAFAS. The Portsmouth Historical Society has a typed list of the gifts presented to Sayyid Sa'id, taken from the aforementioned report.

6. Ruschenberger, *Voyage,* 65–66, 78–94, 97.

7. Roberts to McLane, Bombay, October 23, 1835, DS–1O, Reports of Special Agents, Edmund Roberts, NAFAS.

8. Ruschenberger, *Voyage,* 134.

9. Ibid., 106.

10. Ibid., 102–103.

11. For the texts of the letter, see ibid., 65–66.

12. Richardson, *Compilation,* 4:1593.

13. Ruschenberger, *Voyage,* 153.

14. Ibid., 210.

15. Roberts to "my dear children," Batavia, January 17, 1836, Edmund Roberts Papers, folder 11, NHHS.

16. Ruschenberger, *Voyage,* 251.

17. For the text, see DS–10, Reports of Special Agents, Edmund Roberts, NAFAS; and Ruschenberger, *Voyage,* 258.

18. Ruschenberger, *Voyage*, 263–269.

19. DS–10, Reports of Special Agents, Edmund Roberts, NAFAS. See also Ruschenberger, *Voyage*, 271–276.

20. Ruschenberger, *Voyage*, 296–297.

21. Ibid., 306–309.

22. DS–10, Reports of Special Agents, Edmund Roberts, NAFAS; and Ruschenberger, *Voyage*, 319–320.

23. However much the sword and other larger presents were appreciated, the American coins were not. The set, with two coins missing, reappeared in the United States in 1962 and was auctioned to an American coin company in September 1989; *New York Times,* September 10, 1989, p. 70.

24. Ruschenberger, *Voyage*, 329–330.

25. Ibid., 324–325.

26. DS–10, Reports of Special Agents, Edmund Roberts, NAFAS. Also see Ruschenberger, *Voyage*, 330–334. Although Ruschenberger did not attend the royal audience, having been required to return to the ship because of the large number of sick crewmen, he received full accounts of the audience from Roberts and from Midshipman Taylor, which he carefully recorded.

27. Ibid. See also Ruschenberger, *Voyage*, 335–336; and Miller, *Treaties,* 780–785.

28. Ruschenberger, *Voyage,* 311–324.

29. Ibid., 336.

30. Ibid., 347.

31. DS–10, Special Agents, Edmund Roberts, NAFAS. See also Ruschenberger, *Voyage,* 350–369.

32. Ruschenberger, *Voyage,* 369–372.

33. Roberts to "my dear children," Macao, June 4, 1836, Edmund Roberts Papers, folder 10, NHHS.

34. Roberts to "my blessed children," Macao, June 4, 1836, Edmund Roberts Papers, folder 11, NHHS.

35. Roberts to "my dear children," Macao, June 4, 1836, Edmund Roberts Papers, folder 11, NHHS.

36. [Commodore] Kennedy to the Hon. the Secretary of State, "off

Canton," June 21, 1836, DS–10, Reports of Special Agents, Edmund Roberts, NAFAS; and Benjamin Homans, ed., *Army and Navy Chronicle* 3 (July 1 to December 31, 1836): 409. Also see Ruschenberger, *Voyage*, 372–373. When I visited the gravesites of Roberts and Campbell in Macao in June 1982, I found that, apart from some cracking (probably the result of a fallen tree), Roberts's gravestone was still as described by Ruschenberger. The Portsmouth Historical Society has a small watercolor painting, by an unknown artist and of unknown date, of Roberts's gravesite; it was probably done shortly after his death and sent to his family by American merchants in Canton. Ruschenberger, *Voyage*, 350–369.

37. Fitch W. Taylor, *A Voyage Round the World, and Visits to Various Foreign Countries, in the United States Frigate,* Columbia; *Attended by Her Consort, the Sloop of War,* John Adams (New Haven: H. Mansfield; New York: D. Appleton and Co., 1845), 2:99. Taylor wrongly recorded Roberts's Christian name as "Edmond."

CHAPTER 10: THE ROBERTS LEGACIES

1. Kennedy to the Honorable, the Secretary of State, U.S. Flagship *Peacock,* "off Canton," June 21, 1836, DS–10, Reports of Special Agents, Edmund Roberts, NAFAS.

2. See Ruschenberger, *Voyage*, 374–377, for the Chinese communications on the presence of the two American warships.

3. Kennedy to the Hon., the Secretary of State, U.S. Flagship *Peacock,* "Harbour of Callas," March 4, 1837, DS–10, Reports of Special Agents, Edmund Roberts, NAFAS.

4. Richardson, *Compilation*, 4:1458.

5. *Portsmouth Journal,* November 19, 1836. The obituary wrongly gives June 11 (rather than June 12) as the date of Robert's death.

6. Decree, Rockingham County Court, Exeter, N.H., March 17, 1834, Probate Records, 13281 0.5, Register, RCNH.

7. For a biographic sketch, see Charles Graves, "Andrew Preston Peabody," in Malone, *Dictionary*, 14:334–335. Peabody would become one of Harvard's most beloved professors.

8. For a biographic sketch, see Edward Conrad Smith, "Amasa Junius Parker," in Malone, *Dictionary*, 14:214–215. See also Marion Harland, *More Colonial Homesteads and Their Stories* (New York: G. P. Putnam's Sons, 1899), 435.

9. P. Peabody to Hon. Amasa J. Parker, Cambridge, Mass., December 29, 1836, in Edmund Roberts Papers, folder 1, NHHS.

10. List of Books in Roberts Library, June 1837, Edmund Roberts Papers, folder 1, NHHS.

11. Inventory of Edmund Roberts Estate, Portsmouth, N.H., June 1, 1837, Probate Records, 13281 0.S., Register, RCNH.

12. Finding of Charles C. Cutter on Claims against the Estate of Edmund Roberts, September 20, 1838, Probate Records, 13281 0.S., Register, RCNH.

13. Award of the Superior Court of Judicature of New Hampshire in the case of Hopkins' estate vs. Roberts' estate, December, 1840, Probate Records, 13281 0.S., Register, RCNH. This series contains the various judgments rendered by the claims commissioner and the New Hampshire courts in the case.

14. Statement of Edward Cutts to the Probate Court, Portsmouth, N.H., March 28, 1838, Probate Records, 13281 O.S., Register, RCNH.

15. Account of Edmund Roberts (deceased), Portsmouth, N.H. April 1, 1841, Probate Records, 13281 0.S., Register, RCNH.

16. B. Ticknor to Roberts, New York, May 31, 1834, Edmund Roberts Papers, folder 7, NHHS.

17. Amasa J. Parker to "My dear Sister," Delhi, N.Y., May 7, 1836, Edmund Roberts Papers, folder 11, NHHS. Woodbury's letter to Parker, dated March 30, 1836, is copied on page 3 of Parker's note.

18. These areas remained a single political entity until five years after the death at sea of Sayyid Sa'id, when it appeared that a civil war was likely to break out between two of the sayyid's sons who governed the Arabian and African segments of the Al Bu Sa'id empire. To prevent that war, in 1861 the British governor general of India, Lord Charles John Canning, intervened and effectively severed the Muscat-Zanzibar tie. Henceforth, Oman and Zanzibar existed as separate states. For the so-called Canning Award, see R. Coupland, *The Exploitation of East Africa, 1856–1890: The Slave Trade and the Scramble* (London: Faber and Faber, 1939), 14–378.

19. For a comparison by Professor C. Snouck Hurgronje of Leiden of the divergent English and Arabic language texts, see Miller, *Treaties*, 3:798–801.

20. See the letter from Sayyid Sa'id to Roberts, undated but received by Roberts's family in August 1839. The letter is in Arabic, but an English translation exists; see Edmund Roberts Papers, 2:1834–1835, LOC.

21. For the origins of Scoville and Britton's interest in Muscat, see Barrett, *Old Merchants*, 2:102–103.

22. See Osgood, *Notes of Travel*, 79–80.

23. The text of the Treaty of Amity, Economic Relations, and Consular Rights is at *tcc.export.gov/Trade_Agreements/All_Trade_Agreements/exp_005876.asp*.

24. See Hermann Frederick Eilts, *Ahmad Bin Na'Aman's Mission to the United States in 1840: The Voyage of al-Sultanah to New York City* (Muscat, Oman: Petroleum Development Limited, 1962).

25. For the texts of the treaties, see Charles I. Bevans, comp., *Treaties and Other International Agreements of the United States of America, 1776–1949* (Washington, DC: Department of State, 1968–76); the 1886 agreement is at 12:1290–1297, and the 1905 agreement is at 12:1298–1301.

26. Eldon Griffin, *Clippers and Consuls: American Consular and Commercial Relations in Eastern Asia, 1845–1860* (Ann Arbor, MI: Edwards Brothers, 1938), 14. For the text of the treaty, see Miller, *Treaties*, 7:329–358.

27. Miller, *Treaties*, 7:466.

28. See David A. Wilson, *The United States and the Future of Thailand* (New York: Praeger, 1970), 24–25. For the text of the treaty, see Bevans, *Treaties*, 11:997–1007.

29. The text of the Thailand Amity and Economic Relations Treaty is at *tcc.export.gov/Trade_Agreements/All_Trade_Agreements/exp_005404.asp*.

30. Wildes, *Aliens*, 127.

31. Ibid., 226.

32. Ibid., 29–233; and Johnson, *Far China Station*, 41–43.

33. Wildes, *Aliens*, 237–239; and Johnson, *Far China Station*, 45–46.

34. Wildes, *Aliens*, 243–246; and Johnson, *Far China Station*, 57 –58.

35. Wildes, *Aliens*, 257–282; and Johnson, *Far China Station*, 63–65, 78–71. See also Paullin, *Diplomatic Negotiations*, 244–281. For the texts of these agreements, see Miller, *Treaties*, 6:440–467, 471–489, 490–493.

36. Miller, *Treaties*, 7:947–1170.

37. See, for example, the *New York Times* magazine section, August 6, 1905.

38. Johnson, *Far China Station*, 36–37; and Lamb, *Mandarin Road*, 288.

39. Johnson, *Far China Station*, 109–112.

40. Lancaster, *Emancipation*, 23–50; and Buttinger, *Smaller Dragon*, 325–385.

41. Harland, *More Colonial Homesteads*, 433, contains a black and white picture of the window. I visited St. John's Church in 1980 and recorded the inscription.

.

www.ingramcontent.com/pod-product-compliance
Lightning Source LLC
Chambersburg PA
CBHW030410100426
42812CB00028B/2904/J